As The

Timeclock Turned

By

Rick Lampkin

As The Timeclock Turned

Published by Rick Lampkin

First Edition

Printed by CMYK Graphix, Inc.

ISBN: 978-0-692-89796-6

The Author...

Rick Lampkin is a retired Store Director for Hy-Vee, Inc. of West Des Moines, IA. He was employed by Hy-Vee for over 34 years beginning in 1966 at Hy-Vee in his hometown of Washington, IA.

During his long career, Rick worked at eight different stores for the Grocery Company. He was a successful Store Manager/Director for Hy-Vee at three locations in Ottumwa, IA, Pleasant Hill, IA and Moline, IL.

While serving as the Store Manager/Director at Pleasant Hill, IA. Rick served a coveted one-year elected position on the Hy-Vee's Board of Directors.

A 1973 Graduate of now Truman State University at Kirksville, MO, Rick holds a Bachelor of Science Degree in Business Administration from the University.

Rick and his wife, Jane, reside in Fort Myers, FL and also spend time with family in Moline, IL. The couple are parents to three married children with spouses and four grandchildren.

In Memory Of

JAMES HARRIS

This book is dedicated to the memory of James Harris of Washington, IA. Jim was the Store Manager at Hy-Vee in Washington, IA from 1955 until 1970.

Jim hired me in the Summer of 1966 at Hy-Vee on West Madison Street in Washington. He was a rather large man with a wide grin, a dark-complexion, heavy black-rimmed glasses, a cropped-close haircut and a heart as big as a bushel basket. Jim was a wonderful guy and a loyal friend.

This successful man was a perfect example of 'The Cream Comes to The Top' belief Hy-Vee has built its Heritage on in the Midwest of America. He was truly 'self-made'. Born in Mystic, IA in 1921, Jim began his career at Hy-Vee in nearby Centerville, IA around 1940. He was a WWII veteran serving four years in the South Pacific as a member of the United States Coast Guard. Upon returning from Military Service, Jim worked his way 'through the ranks' in the Centerville Store and in 1949, he moved up to successfully manage the Unionville, MO Store until 1955.

In 1955, Jim was selected by Hy-Vee to be the Store Manager at a new Hy-Vee being built in Washington. He was a 'perfect fit' for that store and town and Jim

has been universally 'Loved and Respected' by everyone there who ever knew him... Everyone.

Jim was a great teacher of the Philosophies of the Hy-Vee Founders. He believed in the things that you will read about in this book and everyone who ever worked for Jim knew the Washington Store would be a place you could find the Hy-Vee Fundamentals that have built the Company.

I will always remember the fun we had working for Jim at the Washington Store. We worked hard and we played hard. Those memories will live in my heart forever. Mostly, though, I will remember him fondly as 'Jim The Man'. I will always respect him and look up to him. So many others will too.

We owe him GREATLY...

Jim passed away in late March of 1970. We all still miss him. He would be proud of all the people whose Hy-Vee careers he started and influenced. He was a great Hy-Vee mentor.

Rest in Peace, Jim...

'This One's For You'...

Hy-Vee, Inc.

Hy-Vee, Inc. is a Midwest Grocery Store Chain that operates in 8 States of The Heartland of America. Its Stores in Iowa, Missouri, Nebraska, Kansas, Illinois, Minnesota, South Dakota and Wisconsin are well-known in those States.

The Company started in 1930 as a partnership between Charles Hyde and David Vredenburg at Beaconsfield in Southern Iowa's Ringold County. It was known then as 'The Hyde and Vredenburg Supply Stores' or simply 'The Supply Stores'. The year 1938 brought the incorporation of the Company with 15 original stockholders. It remained known as 'The Supply Stores' throughout the 1930's and 1940's. In early 1952, a Company Contest produced the name 'Hy-Vee'. The name was born from a contraction of the Founders' names. 'Hy-Vee Food Stores' operated as such until the mid-1990's when it became known as 'Hy-Vee, Inc.'.

Hy-Vee, Inc. now operates over 240 Stores in 8-States and it is also the Parent Company of several large warehouses and many successful subsidiary companies that serve the Retail Stores of Hy-Vee.

This book will give insight as to the very early years of Hy-Vee and the Operating Philosophies that grew

from the small fledgling company founded so long ago by two men who had a vision of 'What Could Be'.

Headquartered in West Des Moines, Iowa since 1994, Hy-Vee is a substantial factor in the Grocery Business of The Upper Midwest of America.

Hy-Vee's very famous slogan

'A Helpful Smile in Every Aisle'

lives strong today in every Market Area they serve.

"And Who Are You ??" ...

In 1930, at their tiny little store in Beaconsfield, IA, Hy-Vee's Co-Founders, Charles Leverett Hyde (Hy) and David Milton Vredenburg (Vee) realized that they could set their stores apart from other competitors by offering the 'Best Service' to their Customers that they could. Charles and David knew early on that people liked shopping where they felt comfortable and felt welcome. The crews that these two men hired for their stores in those early years were 'Friendly' and had a 'Down-Home' attitude while working around the Customers coming in.

The Founders worked hard at searching out and procuring the best possible merchandise at low prices for their Customers in 'The Hyde and Vredenburg Supply Stores' as they were known in the 1930's. Quality and Price played large roles in their 'formula' for success, but The Founders also knew that those two items combined with 'Great People' to serve the Customers would be a very strong 'glue' to 'Keep the Customers Coming Back'.

They were 100% right.

The decades of the 1930's, 1940's and 1950's were rather 'relaxed' in the areas of 'Regulation' for Employee Relations in America. All sorts of businesses would 'spring-up' over the next 30 years and there would be many things to 'Regulate'.

Charles and David, however, were already 'on the road' to knowing that treating people with respect was the way to long-term Loyalty, both in their Employees and their Customers. They didn't need laws to set them on course for great Employee Relations.

As the years rolled along, Employment Laws in The United States evolved through 'trial and error' in businesses. It's safe to say that for every law on the books, 'something' or 'lots of somethings' happened to cause that law.

In mid-1955, the Washington, IA Hy-Vee Store had opened new with the Store Manager being a great man named Jim Harris. Jim started his Hy-Vee career in the Centerville, IA Store and he had managed the Unionville, MO Store before coming to Washington. Jim's time with Hy-Vee of working in a store and then managing a store had been entirely in small farm communities where everyone knew everyone else and those acquaintances produced a continual source of young kids to work in the stores.

Jim had developed some policies in his store at Washington that were not unique at the time, but would certainly not be allowed today within the laws and practices of 'Modern Day Business'. One of those policies of Jim's was allowing the use of 'Substitutes' in the Store. 'Substitutes' or 'Subs' as they were called were a 'substitute' for the Part-timers scheduled to work. I became part of it all as a 'Sub'

in 1966. I was 15 years-old...just a kid with so many things to learn.

It worked like this at the Washington Hy-Vee.

There were no 'time-off requests' needed by the Part-timers who worked at the Washington Store. An existing Part-timer needing a day off or several days in a row off would merely find a 'Sub' for himself and make the arrangements with the 'Sub'. No request at the store was necessary. The 'Sub' was pretty much working for the Part-timer, even though he worked at Hy-Vee. He was told what to wear, when to show up at Hy-Vee and he would even be paid by the Part-timer for the hours worked. Most times, he would even wear the name badge of the Part-timer he was 'Subbing' for. I actually wore several different name tags while I was a 'Sub'. How the Customers ever knew who they were talking to was a question for anyone's guess.

So, what were the store's requirements to be a 'Sub'...?? The requirements were simple. Pretty much, it was 'be a guy, be 15 years-old and have a pulse'.

Yes, that was it.

It was mind-boggling to say the least. The Full-timers in charge of the store during the evenings were responsible for a whole list of things to get done. Those things were not Rocket Science, but they did require some knowledge, intelligence and

motivation. Sometimes, a 'Sub' had 'none of the above' to bring with them to work. Bottle sorting, stocking shelves, cleaning the Restrooms, filling the weekly ad items on the shelves, bagging groceries, filling sacks, hanging window banners, sweeping up and mopping up after broken items in the aisles were all parts of the job. Most of all, the part called 'Customer Service' and the 'Politeness' of all of that was never in the equation. The 'Subs' had received no Orientation or formal training whatsoever.

It was a 'Nightmare' in almost every sense of the word.

Perhaps the only really good part of it was that the 'Substitute Policy' at the Washington Store allowed the Full-timers the opportunity to see who would emerge out of the whole group as 'worthy enough to hire' when they actually turned 16 years-old. By then, Jim and the Full-timers had seen enough to guide them to the best ones for the jobs that would open.

It was almost a 'Rite of Passage' to be a 'Sub' at the Washington Hy-Vee. A kid sort of 'earned his stripes' that way and it was fun. I became a Hy-Vee employee by way of the 'Substitute Policy' at the Washington Hy-Vee as did many others. I have been thankful for the opportunity all of my life.

I will always remember the night that out of the 12 Part-timers that were scheduled to work, there were 10 'Subs' that showed up for work. You can only imagine the 'Chinese Fire Drill' that went on that

night. I am glad I wasn't the Full-timer in charge of the store that night. It was a late night when we got finished.

When I think back on all the different 'Subs' there were, I can't help thinking of Abbot and Costello and the 'Who's on First' story...

Because we didn't always know

'Who' Was At Hy-Vee !

“Your employees will be the biggest asset you ever have.”

David M. Vredenburg

Hy-Vee Co-Founder

(Deceased)

"ANY TAKERS ??"

The Hy-Vee Stores of the 1950's and 1960's were just as busy and active as today's stores are. There were trucks to be unloaded, shelves to be stocked, groceries to be checked-out by the cashiers and groceries that needed bagged and then carried to the Customers' cars.

Every Hy-Vee Store had a designated area for the crew to sit down and take a break for a cup of coffee, a snack, a smoke or even for lunch. The 'Break Area' was just simply an area in the Backroom with a picnic type table and a sink with a cabinet that held the coffee pot and supplies for the coffee pot. The coffee was offered free to anyone and the rest of the items consumed were purchased by the crew members. It was a really fun place because the lighter side of the Grocery Business got discussed and we got to know each other pretty well while sitting around the Break-table.

I was a Crew Member of the Washington, IA Hy-Vee for over 4 years. The store was 16,500 square feet in size and it had a large Backroom. The Break Area sat in an area just behind the Meat Department and it had a table about 6' long with benches on both sides. It would seat about 10-12 people and usually, the others would pull a full carton of cereal or bath tissue over to sit on. There was the usual cabinet for supplies and a sink with running water. Lots of stories were told there. I looked forward to my 'Breaks' and I know the others did too.

One Saturday in 1968, I arrived about an hour early for work and I pretty much just sat at the Break Table waiting for my scheduled time so I could punch the Time-clock and go to work. As the time passed, I noticed that the 'leftovers' from everyone else's breaks were accumulating on the table. Wrappers, crumbs, juices, coffee and pieces of anything that didn't get consumed started to build up on the table and soon, one of the Full-timers started putting it all in a 16oz. pop bottle. Pouring liquids in and shoving stuff down in. Then, they'd shake the bottle and mix it all up. There was really nothing in the bottle that would hurt anyone. It was just a 'God-Awful' mixture of stuff.

And then it came...'The Challenge'...

'Who would drink it for money'...??

The whole 'Mixing and Shaking' and 'Challenging' thing went on for about an hour and everyone that came by the table would throw in a nickel or dime and the 'Challenge' to drink it grew larger and became a more valuable venture. So, I sat and watched and I laughed along with everyone else about 'The Mixture' and 'The Challenge'. It was getting interesting. How much money would it be worth to someone...??

At the time, I was making $1.60 per hour and I would usually have 'take home pay' of about $20 per week. That was pretty good as it did buy gas and left spending money for the week. There was usually enough money for about one nice date with a girl and I sure liked those dates.

So, I sat there and watched. I had fun watching the junk going into the 16oz. pop bottle. The time was getting closer to me having to go to work, so I quickly assessed how much money was in the offer and I came up with the total of just under $5 in the 'Pot'...Actually, a pretty fair amount of money.

Well, "Should I?" or "Shouldn't I?" became the thought on my mind. I really wanted the nearly $5, so I made a 'big production' out of it to everyone sitting there at the table and with that, lots of others who had been there just a short time before were summoned...and the whole 'show' began.

I first made sure I had the money close enough to me that I wouldn't lose control of it...You know, just in case I barfed after I drank it. That would have been embarrassing. So, I just kept telling myself that it wouldn't hurt me and I picked up the nearly full bottle of 'Mixed Stuff' and I shook it for about 30 seconds. As I shook it, I bragged about "Not Being A Sissy" ... and then I 'chugged it down' just as fast as I could so I wouldn't lose my nerve.

When I finished, I set the bottle down to the utter amazement of the nearly 20 people now gathered

there, I picked up the money and put it in my pocket and then I proudly announced "Well, I better go to work." And I walked away ...not 100% sure of the mixture now rolling around in my gut.

I had done what I said I could do and I soon became the 'Hero of The Day' with the tale of the 'Junk in The Bottle'. I had the $5 in my pocket for the whole ordeal and life went on...

Enough money for another date.

And The Best Part ?...

It All Stayed Down ! ...

The Broom...

One image that we all have of the 'Old Country Store' is one where a Clerk is 'Sweeping' with a Broom. Oh, there were other things that are images in our minds, but that one is 'Pretty Universally' used to denote 'The Old Days'.

There may be a reason for that.

In 1930, The 'Hyde and Vredenburg Supply Stores' were just beginning their operations in those small and very primitive Stores of about 1200 Square Feet in size. They were engulfed in the early parts of 'The Dust Bowl' of the 1930's, just like the entire 'center section' of our Country was. It's a fact that during those 10 years, America nearly 'Dried Up and Blew Away' with the hot winds that never seemed to stop. It was necessary to 'keep sweeping' to make sure The Supply Stores were presentable to the Customers coming in to do their grocery shopping.

So, it's really fitting this story deals with 'A Broom'. It is one of my personal favorites in the entire group of stories in this book.

Here's the scoop...Or 'dust pan' if you prefer...

It was in the late Summer of 1967. I had hired on the year before at Hy-Vee by being a 'substitute' Part-timer in June for $1.26 per hour and I was starting to feel comfortable in my job. My 'official' employment training had included all of the 'Basic Functions' of the 'Bagger/Carryout' job. Several of us new employees had gone through the simple 'training' on 'bagging' and we had learned a little about 'stocking shelves' too...Just in case we had to go and get something.

Mostly, however, we had received a 'very rigorous browbeating' about 'being friendly' and also 'talking to the Customers'. Both were important because in those days, we carried the groceries out to the Customer's car and the trip out to the car was to be 'As pleasant for the Customer as possible'. That meant lots of conversation and hopefully, the display of 'personality' so the Customers would leave us with 'good thoughts' on their minds...

The 'last impression' so to speak.

We'd all been told the idea that 'The Customer is always right' and it was to be our '#1 Rule' with which we based our conversations on. If they weren't right...We were to 'remember our #1 Rule'. It worked and we never lost our focus on that.

Well...we never lost it, but it got 'borderline' a few times. Yes, 'borderline'...and that's what this story is all about...

Now, with 'The Customer is always right' driven into us that this would be 'Rule #1', we went about our jobs as 'Carryouts' trying to live up to that 'cornerstone' of Hy-Vee's Philosophy and also

remembering to 'Always talk to the Customers!' Just like we'd been told to do.

As the weeks rolled along, I found myself working away at my 'Carryout' job and I was trying hard to 'talk to everyone' when we were at the Checkout Lanes and on the way out to the cars. I knew lots of people in town and it was easy for me to find things to say to them. Things like "So, did you take a vacation this Summer?" and "It's a really nice day." And "How do the crops look out your way?". These were all topics that were 'pretty safe' and I knew they'd keep me out of trouble.

I had become pretty proud of my skills at the conversation part of my job and I thought I was now at a point of adding a little humor here and there as I talked to people. It was on that late Summer day in 1966 that I got a little 'over-confident' and my 'Creativity and Humor' were about to catch up to me. Little did I know that I would nearly take 'the beating of my life' because of my new ability to talk to the Customers.

Late on that Summer afternoon, I was bagging some groceries for a Customer I did not know. This lady had a rather small order and it was a pretty sure guess that no 'Carryout' would be needed and that she'd just carry it all out herself. The largest item she had purchased was a broom...Just a plain old wooden handled broom. Yes, just one small paper bag of items and a broom.

The only thing I needed to add to her order was some 'conversation' and the transaction would be complete and she'd be headed home.

So, being the 'quick thinker' I thought I was, I waited until she had paid the Cashier for her things and then I handed her the small paper bag and the broom. As she took hold of the broom, I looked at her and said "Would you like to ride this or carry it?" and then, I sort of smiled.

By the 'immediate' change in the look on her face, I could tell that my 'Creativity and Humor' had placed me squarely in 'Harm's Way'. As she took the broom, she very boldly said "Young man, I don't think that's one bit funny and I might just knock that smirk off your face."

Now, I could quickly tell that she was serious as she kind of stepped toward me. I took a step backwards and I said "Gee, I'm sorry. I was just trying to make conversation and be funny. I'm really sorry."

At this point, she realized I was just trying to be funny and she said "I'd joke a little differently if I were you. You may not be so lucky next time." And then she was off to her car and she drove away. I was left standing there to face the laughter of my fellow-workers who had witnessed it all.

From that day forward, I measured my comments a little more and I tried to stay with the more

traditional 'Startup Lines'. I had learned my lesson and a valuable lesson it was.

It was the day a Customer just about

'Swept' The Smile

Right Off My Face !...

“Watch the pennies and nickels and the dollars will fall into place.”

Charles L. Hyde

Hy-Vee Co-Founder

(Deceased)

The 'No Brainer'...

When Charles Hyde and David Vredenburg formed their Partnership in 1930, little did they know that their efforts and planning would produce a Company that would be 'going strong' nearly 90 years later in the 21st Century. Their Company would go on to be one of the Greatest Stories ever told. It is 'The Story of Hy-Vee'.

Those early 1200 Square Foot Stores of Southern Iowa and Northern Missouri were 'primitive' to say the very least. They were pretty 'barebones' for sure. The original Store of The Partnership still stands at Beaconsfield in Southern Iowa in Ringold County. You can find it on the internet when you 'Google' "Hy-Vee Beaconsfield, IA". The town has preserved it with help from Hy-Vee over the years to let it stand as a permanent reminder of the formation of 'Hy-Vee' all those years ago.

Soon after the forming of the partnership, The Great Depression came on in America. It hit the Midwest very hard and survival of everything was a 'struggle'. Charles and David endured the hardships with those 'barebones' stores they had and as the 1930's moved into the 1940's, some 'new innovations' were beginning to show up in the stores of America. Some of those innovations were added to The Supply Stores. Since the stores were larger than ever before, 'loudspeaker systems' were installed in the ceilings and at various locations in the stores.

Microphones were also put in for those loudspeakers. Usually, the microphones hung on a hook in prominent locations around the store or on a small pole at the Cash Registers. These became the way the crew would communicate with each other for the next 40 years.

It was not uncommon for the microphones to be used for the purposes of calling more help to the Front End, calling someone to a phone call, asking an employee to come to a certain spot in the store and then, there were those 'comments' made over the loudspeakers that were just sort of 'blurted-out' with little forethought of what was going to be 'said…and answered'. These were the fun parts of the microphone system because you really never knew what was coming. The 'answers' were what made the stories complete.

It was an 'answer' that came in response to a question asked over the loudspeaker that this story is about…

It was 'broadcasted' like this.

I was a Part-timer at the Washington, IA store from 1966-1971. I loved my job there and I learned lots and lots of things while I worked there. I learned as many things 'not' to do as I did the other direction.

I was always amused and entertained by the questions 'asked and answered' over the loudspeaker. It had a pattern as to the way these

were done. Some of the employees seemed to have some 'charisma' while on the microphones. Their voices were smooth and their delivery was thought out and clear. On the other end, there were some employees whose voices were loud, high pitched and 'anything but' thought out in their delivery. They were the ones who became 'The Entertainers' for the rest of us.

One of our 'Entertainers' on the microphone was a Cashier named Eloise. Now, 'Ellie', as we all called her, was in her mid-60's and was known by everyone in Washington and in the county too. She wore her hair in a 'Beehive' style on top of her head and she seemed to have lots of perfume and makeup on most days. It was common for her to 'always be talking'...nearly non-stop.

Since Ellie was just 'absolutely loved by everyone', she would have several people waiting in her line at most times of the day to check-out their groceries. Other lanes would be quicker, but those folks waiting 'wanted Ellie'. As you can imagine, Ellie had several 'conversations' going on at most given times of the day. She was the one 'Entertainer' that gave us all the most laughs over the years because at a very unexpected time, she'd lean over her microphone and 'blurt out' something that would 'bring the house down' with everyone laughing.

So, one hot Summer afternoon in 1967, Ellie's Customer was busy telling Ellie that she'd looked for

some 'Beef Brains' and couldn't find any in the Meat Department. With that comment, Ellie did 'what she usually did' to appease her Customers, she asked 'The Question of The Day' over the loudspeaker. It is 'Classic Ellie' in my memories of the 'airwaves of the store'.

Ellie simply leaned over the microphone and sort of blurted out to our Meat Manager "Daryl, do you have any brains?" and then she turned back to her Customer and talked a little while waiting for Daryl's reply...

And boy, what a reply it was.

About five seconds went by and then Daryl jumped on her comment like a 'fly on honey'...The microphone crackled a little as he took it off the hook and he simply said "No, Ellie, we're all stupid back here today."

Instantly, the employees and Customers 'erupted' in laughter. It must have taken a good 5 minutes to bring everything back to a normal level in the store. It took several weeks for the story to come down to just an occasional mention of 'The Brains'. It went all over town and everyone knew about it.

Ellie took it all very well and laughed about it right along with everyone else. Daryl got teased too and it became known as the day

Daryl Became A 'Brainiac' ! ...

“Pssst... Hey, Would You ??” ...

The Prohibition Era of 1920-1933 in America had lasted just long enough to see the first three years of the ‘young partnership’ between Charles Hyde and David Vredenburg. That early partnership was known as ‘The Hyde and Vredenburg Supply Stores’ or just ‘The Supply Stores’ for short. Those early ‘Supply Stores’ of the 1930’s came along that in time of American History when the sale and consumption of alcohol was very much a controversial and illegal thing.

That very first store was in Iowa’s Ringold County at Beaconsfield was ‘nestled’ into a very conservative area of America. The other stores that were soon added to ‘The Supply Store’ era were also in small towns in Southern Iowa and Northern Missouri and those towns were very much the same in their values and ‘anti-alcohol’ beliefs. They were all in a very serious ‘Bible Belt’ of America and even though alcohol sales and consumption would eventually become an everyday way of life there, that wouldn’t come in the Midwest for many years after 1933 when alcohol became legal again all over America.

It was a ‘slow walk back’ in the Midwest for public acceptance of alcohol and it would take Iowa ‘many decades’ to do that ‘walking’.

After 1933, the decade of the 1930’s got into ‘full-swing’ in America regarding alcohol and each State

had to decide just 'how' they would make alcohol fit in to their laws and also into its acceptance by the citizens of their State. Missouri, chose a more 'open' approach and let private stores and sales by those stores proliferate on an 'as voted basis'...mainly, by county vote of 'Wet or Dry' counties.

Iowa, on the other hand, was so conservative that the legislators enacted laws to keep complete and full control over the consumption of alcohol. That legislation put the State of Iowa 'in the liquor business' and since people in Iowa still believed alcohol to be 'the root of evil' in families and in social settings, it would take a long time to convince a majority to think otherwise.

It took nearly 50 years.

In the 1930's, with those laws newly enacted, the Iowa Liquor Commission was created, a large warehouse was built and the producers and suppliers of alcohol were forced to sell directly to The State of Iowa. In turn, Iowa sold to their own Iowa State Liquor Stores creating a complete monopoly on Wine and Liquor. Iowa depended on the revenues and incomes from these stores more and more as the years went along. Liquor was a real 'moneymaker' for Iowa. By the early 1940's, packaged beer was allowed to be sold by license in Iowa, but still not Wine and Spirits.

The State's decisions of where they would put those Iowa State Liquor Stores became a matter of 'ease'

and 'location'. In other words, 'an easy location to find'.

One major thing Iowa did to control the Consumption on an 'individual basis' was to put an 'annual limit' on how much Wine and Spirits one person could buy in a calendar year. That was done by each store having a Master Card File and there was a card in that file for each person above legal age in that County. A resident's 'card' was where their residence was. No exceptions. Non-residents of Iowa could not buy alcohol in the Liquor Stores of Iowa.

When a resident of a county wanted a bottle of Wine or Spirits, they would drive to their designated Liquor Store and go to the counter to ask the clerk for their choice of bottle. The clerk at the counter would go to the back shelves and retrieve the Customer's requested alcohol and then the 'card' for that person was recorded with the information of their purchase. When a resident in a county had reached their annual limit, they were 'shut-off' until January 1st of the next year.

No more purchases that calendar year.

Now, we all know that everyone's alcohol consumption varies. Some 'never use it', some 'use a little' and some 'use lots'. The last category being what this story is about...We found those people.

This is all 'How It Went Down'...literally.

I started in The Washington, IA Hy-Vee in the Summer of 1966. I was 15 years-old. I had been around alcohol to the extent that my father and his father too, drank alcohol once in a while and I witnessed that. Neither were what would be considered to be 'big drinkers'. Moderate perhaps, but not 'big'.

I had been to the Iowa State Liquor Store with my father several times and its location happened to be immediately next door to the Washington Hy-Vee on West Madison Street in Washington. There was a space of about 2 feet between the walls of the buildings. Its location, next to Hy-Vee, was not the first location for the Iowa Liquor Store in Washington, but it had been moved there because of its location next to Hy-Vee and the high volume of traffic it would have there. It was a good location for the residents and for the Iowa State Liquor Store.

The first week I started at Hy-Vee, I kept noticing men standing out by the corner of Hy-Vee's building. They would park on Hy-Vee's parking lot and then just stand there at the corner of the building. It went on almost every day and with me starting at Hy-Vee in the Summer, about half of the year was already gone for 1966. That timing played into the numbers of men we saw there and it seemed to increase as the year rolled along. It was an 'everyday occurrence'.

These men would stand there on the corner of Hy-Vee's building until someone they knew was leaving

Hy-Vee to go next door to the Liquor Store to get something. In those days, many people preferred to park at Hy-Vee so as not to have their car on the parking lot of the Liquor Store...You know, because of the 'image' of not wanting to be seen in the Liquor Store. Prohibition had ended 33 years before, but the 'image' was still strong.

So, as those Customers who were on foot and headed to the Liquor Store from Hy-Vee started to go around the corner to the Liquor Store, you could see the men who'd been standing there ask them something. Sometimes money would change hands and sometimes not. If it did change hands, it wasn't long until the person who'd been given the money would return with a sack for the man who'd been standing there.

Then I figured it out.

Mid-way through each year, one man had used his 'annual allotment' and the other man was 'helping out' by procuring some liquor for him. It went on like that each day in the late part of the year and it got to the point where we knew exactly 'who' was standing out there. It was lucky for them, that January 1st was coming and it would begin the calendar all over again for their Liquor Purchases. It was really cold standing there in the snow and ice of November and December, but they were there, just the same.

This went on for many years and it only stopped when the State of Iowa changed the laws in the mid 1980's

and the State of Iowa 'got out' of the Liquor business. All of it went to private sales through Distributors and licensed retailers like Hy-Vee. After 50 plus years, Iowans had finally become 'liberal enough' to make that turn. It is still that way some 30 years after the change.

These days, it's hard to imagine those long lines at the Iowa State Liquor Stores of a now 'by-gone era', but they were there...For Sure.

Yes, all those guys were standing patiently out there on Hy-Vee's Corner saying

"Hey Buddy, Would You Do

Me A Favor?" ...

“Put ‘Em Where ??” ...

The ‘Carryout’ position in the Hy-Vee Stores of the 1940’s, 1950’s, 1960’s and the 1970’s was really an interesting position. The Carryouts bagged the groceries and then walked along with the Customer taking the groceries to the Customer’s car. Carryouts either carried a few sacks of groceries in their arms or pushed the larger orders in a grocery cart. When they arrived at the Customer’s car, the groceries were then put into the trunk or on the seats of the car. In the ‘Farm Towns’ of Iowa, Missouri and the Midwest, groceries were also loaded into the back end of many ‘dusty’ pickup trucks too.

The ‘small army’ of Carryouts at every Hy-Vee Store was made up of pretty well-known young people in the community. Many of the kids were involved in school activities like Football, Basketball, Band, Swimming or Chorus and the Customers recognized that Hy-Vee hired the good kids and then worked around their school activities to provide jobs for them. It was a ‘Public-Relations Thing’ on both sides of the equation.

Now, I hired on in the Summer of 1966 at the Washington Store and I was paid $1.26 per hour in the beginning... We all felt like lucky to have the work. It paid as much as the farm work available and it was less physical. It was also a way for kids to work around lots of other young people while ‘making a buck’.

This story deals with something that happened to me when I was a Carryout at the Washington Hy-Vee... It's a great story...

And here's how it got 'Carried-out'...

It was in mid-Summer of 1967. I was working one evening when two women came in and shopped for a 'long-long time'. These two women bought several carts of groceries and it was obvious it was going to add up to be a great order for Hy-Vee. So, we all helped these two women as they gathered their groceries and when it came time to go through the Check-out Line, several of us got involved in the bagging of the groceries. 'bag after bag' were filled and it took about 5 or 6 grocery carts to load it all up and prepare them to go to the car for loading it to go home.

As it was being bagged in all those big paper sacks, I kept thinking about how much it might add up to be and when the 'Total' button on the cash register was punched, it was pretty close to the number I had in my mind. It was just under $300.

It was a 'HUGE ORDER' for 1967.

So, with the groceries bagged and the bill paid, it was time to go out and get the bags loaded into their car. It took 3 of us to push the 5 or 6 carts of groceries out and I happened to be the first one out the door, so that meant I'd be the one to stay at the car and 'load it up' for the trip home.

As we went outside and headed to their car, it became obvious 'which car' these two ladies were walking to...And it wasn't going to be easy.

It was the 'shock of the week' for me!

We walked up to a 1960's Volkswagen Bug with four children in it and one of the ladies said "We'll put some in the front and the rest inside." Whaaaat ???... I thought.

Now, I am always an optimist, but I quickly said "I don't think all of this will fit in this car with the kids in there." and my previous experience of loading groceries in cars told me I was pretty correct... They may not fit.

So, I loaded one of the carts and part of another one all in the small front-trunk area of the Volkswagen and then I looked inside the car for any hope of having room for the other 3 or 4 carts of groceries that remained. It was really adding up in my brain that the Basic Law of Physics was going to be true in this case that 'No Two Objects Can Occupy the Same Space at the Same Time'.

I had to do something so I said to the woman who had told me to put some in the front-trunk "Okay, where next?" And then I pointed to the inside of the car. With that question, she leaned over and looked at the kids in the back seat of the Volkswagen (all four of them) and she said "Okay kids, make room back

there." The kids had the same look on their faces that I probably had on my face...

'Okay, JUST WHERE?'

So, I started handing bags of groceries to the kids in the back seat and one by one, I emptied a couple of grocery carts, but there was still a cart and a half of groceries to load and short of tying them on top of the car, the only other place to put them was the passenger's seat on top of the other lady who had gotten in and taken her place in the VW Bug.

So, I started loading groceries in at her feet and around her knees and then on her lap and I even closed the door and put a couple of bags in through the window and leaned them against the door'...

Completely covering the lady passenger.

Finally, it fit! I might have been better off to have a 'shoe horn' to squeeze it in, but I had put it in where the 'Customer wanted it' as we'd been instructed to do.

The six of them drove off in the Volkswagen Bug with almost $300 worth of groceries in it and I pushed the nested-together grocery carts back into the Store. Everyone inside wanted to know "Just where on Earth did you put them?" and it was a fun story for several days.

To this day, when I look at a Volkswagen Bug, I can't help thinking of everything those little cars will hold...

And then I remember putting all those groceries everywhere inside that tiny little car...

You Know...As 'Snug As A Bug' !

“If you have a Customer and a fire at the same time, take care of the Customer and then put out the fire.”

David M. Vredenburg

Hy-Vee Co-Founder

(Deceased)

"Over Here ! ---I Found Some" ...

As far back as those early 'Supply Stores' of Charles Hyde and David Vredenburg's, one major goal of the Stores was to 'Keep the Customers Coming Back'. The stores weren't fancy in those decades and 'Friendly Service' along with 'Product Selection' were pretty much the mainstays in those early Stores. Now, coming out of the 1930's and 1940's, America was changing and lifestyles were more 'on the go' than ever before. The 'Supermarkets' of the day had to create some new ways to 'Keep the Customers Coming Back'.

Part of the new services offered in the communities the Hy-Vee Stores and other Supermarkets served in the 1950's, 1960's and the 1970's was to cash the weekly (or bi-weekly) paychecks of the Customers who shopped with them. We believed that 'If' we could get those Customers in our doors and cash those checks for them, a large portion of the money would be spent at our store in return. It really did work well. It had some flaws later on, but it also had the 'huge advantage' of getting the Customer to shop at Hy-Vee in the first place.

One night, while working at the Washington store in the Summer of 1968, something happened that proved Hy-Vee would go 'above and beyond the call of duty' to help our Customers. We must have had our 'Guardian Angel' on our shoulders to pull it off.

Here's how it all went down…The sewer that is….

One evening, a man came into the store to cash his check of about $280 and change. He was a 'regular' and we always knew that we'd get lots of the money back the next day when his wife came to do the weekly shopping for their family. They were great Customers. So, we cashed his check and like always, he went out the door to go home.

Within a couple of minutes, our Customer came running back into the store and he was nearly frantic. The wind had caught his fistful of money and blown it all over the parking lot. He said that he "Saw lots of it going across the street flying in the wind".

We went into high gear and into 'Response Mode'. Lynn was in charge of our store that night and he quickly sprang into action and told about 5 of us to get the flashlights used in Power Outages from the drawers in each checkout counter and to follow him. We did as he asked and before we knew it, we were all out on busy West Madison Street in Washington shining our lights on the ground and looking for money. Across the street was a 'Do-it-Yourself Carwash' and pretty quickly, we all ended up there. The wind was blowing that direction, so it seemed logical some of it might be there.

As we combed the parking lot of the carwash, money started showing up in the gravel against the building that housed the carwash. Bit by bit, we found several of the $20 bills. There were 14 bills that were

missing and we didn't have it all, but we were closing in on finding a large portion of it, so we continued to search in the darkness.

Then, one of our guys took his flashlight and shined it down into the storm drain in the parking lot and there it was... 'The Jackpot'! Several of the $20 bills were right there in that storm drain. The only problem was that they were about 6 or 7 feet down in the drain-hole. It looked way too hard to get in and out of. All of a sudden, Lynn said... "Rick, take everything out of your pockets, you're going down into the hole."

Now, at 5' 5" and 120 pounds, I had no idea on Earth how I was going to get down into that hole and still get back out. That didn't seem to bother Lynn though. He looked the two biggest kids with us and said "Each one of you grab a leg. He's going in upside down and he can snatch the money and then you can pull him back out."

GREAT PLAN! ... Unless you're the guy going down into the hole... 'A dark, smelly, cold, wet and scary hole'.

So, I emptied my pockets, tucked my tie into my shirt and laid down flat on the gravel, the cover was lifted from the top of the Storm Drain and the guys grabbed my legs. 'Upside Down' I went and before I knew it, I was being lowered down into the Storm Drain to fetch the money. All the flashlights were fixed on the bottom of the drain and I started gathering the $20

bills as quickly as I could. I quickly retrieved every one of the $20 bills in the drain and with that, I hollered to get me out of there and the 'Big Guys' started pulling me out. By this time, the blood had all rushed to my head and I felt dizzy coming out and trying to stand up. That feeling soon passed though.

We were 'elated' and our Customer thought we were 'Heroes'. Every bit of the $280 had been recovered and a real tragedy had been averted. It was all by the quick thinking of Lynn and the good work by us. We went back into the store feeling like we had just scaled Mt. Everest or something...And in a way, we had. We had taken on a nearly impossible situation and we had come home completely 'Victorious'.

We were proud.

Word soon spread around town about the 'Adventure of the Lost Money' and many of the Customers from Washington would comment on our "Good Deed". We were sort of local 'Folk Heroes' for a short time and we soaked up all the attention as it came our way.

Now, almost 50 years later, I cannot drive by that spot where the old car wash was without thinking about dangling upside down in that storm drain retrieving $20 bills...

Like We Were Mining For Gold !

"Go Ahead...Toss It To Me" ...

Pranks and Practical Jokes in grocery stores are an everyday occurrence and it has been so in Hy-Vee since its inception in the those primitive 'Supply Stores' of Southern Iowa and Northern Missouri in the 1930's. All the way from those days and forward now for nearly 90 years, whenever Hy-Vee people who truly love what they are doing get together, you will see expressions of that 'Love' come out in happy ways and that means 'Fun for Everyone'....

Well, mostly everyone.

The 'Pranks and Horseplay' parts of Hy-Vee have become large parts of the 'History' in many Hy-Vee Stores and the people who were part of those 'incidents' will remember them always. Usually, as they look back on those times, it's with a smile or a smirk on their face as they 're-live' the fun moments of it all. Anyone from any decade in Hy-Vee's History will be able to tell you of at least one 'Good One' that got pulled on someone or even themselves...

In most cases, it's 'A Bunch of Good Ones' they talk about.

Over my years with Hy-Vee, I was involved in 'lots and lots' of pranks and practical jokes and many seem to come to mind when I look back on each of the stores I worked in. One such prank and practical joke I was involved with was at the Washington store. It happened in 1968.

The story goes like this...

I was a Part-timer in the Washington, IA Hy-Vee from 1966 -1971. It was about 4 ½ years all together. We had a great Store Crew there and just like every store in Hy-Vee, we had people in the Washington Hy-Vee that ranged all over within the definitions of 'Different Personalities'.

One of our crew's 'Personalities' was a great friend of mine named Don. He worked in the Produce Department as a Part-timer stocking the Produce Rack and taking care of the evening duties that are necessary in every store to take care of the Fresh Produce and the Customers that came in to buy it.

Don was the kind of young man that was always in a good mood and he had a personality that made him very popular in the store, both with the Customers and with the others in store's crew. I don't know that I ever heard any disparaging words about Don...Ever. He was liked by all and I am sure it was his great rapport with others that originally landed him working in the Produce Department in an 'unsupervised' atmosphere in the evenings.

Now, having said that, Don also had a 'gullible side' to him and it was something that enhanced his personality in a group setting. He would occasionally get 'caught-up' in a prank or practical joke because of his 'gullible side'. It was rather fun to watch his innocence develop into laughter around him.

So, rather late one Summer evening in 1968, I was working and doing my usual duties of bagging groceries, carrying out groceries, sorting pop bottles and running stock from the Backroom to the shelves on the sales floor.

In the evenings, there was always a Full-Timer in total charge of the store and of course, every Part-timer knew exactly where that Full-timer was at every moment so they could stay clear of 'the wrath' should something go wrong at 'Just the Right Time'.

On this particular evening, we'd just received a fresh load of watermelons and they were all in Grocery Carts in our Backroom waiting to be taken to the sales floor to be lined up in rows under the Produce Display Racks for our Customers to buy. At this point in the story, however, they were still in the Backroom. A 'prank' was just around the corner and Don would be the target.

Here's the Story...

As I walked through the Backroom, I spotted Don coming across the pathway between the stacks of merchandise in full cases that were all waiting to be stocked to the shelves on the sales floor. He was trying to organize the carts of watermelons so they'd take less space and be in fewer carts. He was 'ripe' for what was about to happen.

I said to Don "Great looking watermelons that came in today." And with that, Don returned my comment

with one of his own. He said "Sure are. They will sell fast." We both knew they really were going to be popular with the Customers.

So, as I walked across the Backroom pathway to where Don was, I teasingly said "Hey, I have an idea. Bob's up front and he won't catch us...Toss me one of those melons and we'll play catch." In return and 'very sheepishly', Don said "Oh, I don't think we better. Besides, you probably won't catch it if I do throw it."

With that, I struck a serious look on my face and I returned his comment by saying "Aw, come on... You know me better than that. Sure, I'll catch it." And just as soon as I finished that statement, I picked up a watermelon of medium size and I motioned to him that I was going to toss it to him. He caught-on quickly and when I could see he was ready, I lobbed it to him from about 4' or 5' away. I made it a slow toss so it would be easy for him to catch. He caught it and then it was his turn to toss it back.

I said "Come on...Toss it to me. Bob's up front and he won't be through here for a while, so we won't get caught." I could easily tell he was hesitant to throw it back and again, he said "You won't catch it." ...

Now, as I said earlier, being 'gullible' was one of Don's 'long-suits' and I looked at him with a re-assuring look on my face that I would catch it if he tossed it and I didn't say anything back. I just stood there with my arms outstretched waiting. Finally,

Don's 'gullible side' took over and he lobbed the melon to me from about 4' or 5' away. As it was airborne for just a split second, I turned and walked the other way... It was Don's 'worst fear' about the whole thing and it was happening right in front of his face.

The watermelon 'splattered' in a thousand pieces all over the concrete floor of the Backroom and just as I heard it crashing down, I turned around to see Don standing there with a 'Ghostly Look' on his face and all of the color gone from his cheeks. He couldn't believe he'd fallen for it. One more time, Don's 'gullible side' had gotten the best of him and he was 'had' again.

I took off in an almost 'dead-run' to get away from the 'scene' and I can still see Don scrambling to get the broom and a box to clean it all up before Bob made his 'Rounds" through the store. Bob, however, made his "Rounds" pretty soon after this all happened, so I made a "Loop" by there while Don was explaining why the watermelon was on the floor in a thousand pieces... I heard him say "I couldn't help it, Bob, it slipped out of my hands as I was transferring it to another cart. I just couldn't catch it in time."

Our eyes met as I passed by and I knew he'd covered up the 'prank', so I kept on going. The secret was safe with Don. You can bet though, Don knew from then on that he'd be on the 'receiving end', so he didn't fall for any more of those kind of 'pranks'.

All these years later, I look at carts or bins full of watermelons in a Hy-Vee Store and I think of the night Don fell for it one too many times.

It was the night we played 'Catch'

Well, At Least One Of Us Did ...

"It Was How Big ??" ...

Cash Registers have not always been part of The American Grocery Store Scene. Around the turn of the Century and into the 1920's and 1930's, 'machinery' for Retail businesses was not very prevalent. In fact, there were only a few companies making those expensive machines called 'Cash Registers'. National Cash Register (NCR), Sweda Corporation, Remington Rand Corporation and a few others were starting to perfect the technology that would eventually evolve into the amazing 'Electronic Marvels' in the retail world of today. It has taken over 100 years to reach today's level of excellence.

In 1930, when the 'Supply Stores' started out as the partnership between Charles Hyde and David Vredenburg, there were no 'Cash Register' machines that they could afford on their 'shoestring budget'... heck, they were lucky to be able to pay the bills and have a little bit left over to live on.

What Hy-Vee's Founders used in those days was a piece of carbon paper between two sheets of the sales pad and as each item was sold, the receipt was 'itemized' and the price noted to the right column. When the Customer's purchases were done being written down, the price column was then added down for a grand total...'hand-added' and that meant that the person doing the adding had to be pretty good at Mathematics. Errors could be made easily.

In those very small and primitive Stores of the partnership, their system worked fine and as time moved through the 1930's and rolled into the 1940's Cash Registers became a part of the equipment in the stores. Until then, however, there were no such 'Luxuries'. The new Customers Hy-Vee had won over were used to their ways in the stores and in those small Southern Iowa and Northern Missouri Stores, the communities were not very 'new-fangled' yet anyway. It was a perfect time to upgrade to a more modern era.

Now, the early Cash Registers were not electric. They were 'machines' with levers and gear-wheels inside and as the buttons were pushed on the front of the Register, the levers and gears shifted to make the 'number entered' record on the ink-roller driven paper tape and the total appeared at the bottom...And that whole thing didn't happen until the 'Hand-Crank' on the side of the machine was turned clockwise one full turn. When the next item's price was 'punched' on the front keyboard of the Register, 'another' clockwise crank was made and another number was added. It went just like that for each item sold and it was a 'punch the number—turn the crank' function on every item in every order for the whole day... 'Every Day'.

You can imagine the amount of 'work done' and the 'tired arms' that went home every night from a full day of 'Cashiering and Cranking'. It was a very welcome relief when electricity was added to those

early machines and the 'crank' became internal and was turned by an electrically driven motor. The levers and gears were still in there, but the wretched 'turning of the crank' was now a thing of the past.

The levers and gears in those early Cash Registers were very important in the whole operation. If even one lever or gear malfunctioned, it would make the Register do one of two things... 1. The Register would not work at all or 2. The numbers added would be wrong because of the lever or gear telling it to do the wrong thing. That second type of problem was awkward. You could go a whole day not knowing that the 'adding' was wrong and either the Customer was 'charged too much' or 'the store was 'on the losing end' of the whole thing. Either way, it was bad for business.

As smart people do, Hy-Vee's early pioneers devised some 'systems' to check the addition on a daily or twice daily basis. It's a 'numbers thing', but its accuracy is perfect. A quick routine protected the whole 'Integrity' of the Registers and the 'Integrity' of The Supply Stores.

Here's the function....

On the keyboard of the Cash Register, the addition of 'All the Number Keys on The Register' was made to check addition. For example, by adding 'all the 9's'- 'all the 8's'- 'all the 7's, 'all the 6's" and so forth down to the '1's' and a 'Lone 5', the total was always a '5 followed by all zeroes'... It's true by making this

simple entry, a Register was shown to be adding correctly. It can be done for any number of the numbers as long as the number stays constant all the way through and a 'Lone 5' is added at the end, it will be true. Your total will be a '5' followed by 'all zeros'...

So, a couple of times each day, the Registers were checked and the 'Integrity' of the Registers stayed in place.

It was a 'Great System'.

The only other thing that could cause an error in the totals was 'Human Error' An error could occur by someone just plain ringing in a wrong price. That happened regularly too and sometimes, it was a 'Doozy'...

One such example happened while I was working at the Washington, IA Store as a Part-Timer in 1967. I was 16 years-old, but I will remember it until I am 116 years-old.

The 'Doozy' happened like this.

We had a Full-time Cashier named Sharon. She was a good one too. Sharon was friendly, accurate and she was a lot of fun to work with. Sharon preferred working evenings, so she worked with the Part-time-crew most of the time. We got to know her well and we all loved her.

It was close to Thanksgiving 1967 and the biggest item going out of the Store was, of course, 'Turkeys' and lots of them. Hy-Vee's philosophy of the times of the 1960's and 1970's was to be 'real cheap' on the price of the Turkeys and then hope to make it up on the rest of the order...The Turkeys were sold at a huge loss because of that. Another part of the Philosophy was that 'If you can get the Customers in your Store for Thanksgiving, you'll get them there for the Christmas Holidays too'.... It is a belief that is still 'Alive and Well' in Hy-Vee today.

So, when the weekly Newspaper Ad came out on that Wednesday before this story, Hy-Vee was the lowest price on Turkeys of any Grocery Store in town. The price was '39 Cents Per Pound'...Hen Turkeys or the bigger Tom Turkeys. It was the 'Customer's Choice'...Take your pick.

They were 'Cheap'.

Now, Sharon was usually 'right-on' with her accuracy, but one Turkey got rung up that got into the History of the Washington Store the moment it happened. We laughed about it then and we were still laughing about it the next Thanksgiving.

Because the old Cash Registers had no ability to stop a number that was too large from being entered, the Register would take any number you wanted to put in and that's just what happened on this order.

Sharon's Customer had picked out a nice big fat 24+Pound Tom Turkey and by the time Sharon got it rung in, the price was just under $300 for the Tom Turkey...And yes, it made the total on the order 'look awfully big' when it was totaled up at the end. Obviously, the price for the Turkey 'stuck out like a sore thumb' on the Cash Register tape.

So, the correction was made, but that's when we calculated how big that Tom Turkey would have to be to be that expensive and we started laughing about Sharon's '750 Pound Turkey'. We laughed and laughed and the story grew as it was told. 'Sharon's Tom Turkey' had grown to 'bigger than life' -(Literally) and we had fun with it for years...

Over the years of my Hy-Vee career, I've thought many times about Sharon at Thanksgiving and I always catch myself chuckling inside about her
Tom Turkey...

'All 750 Pounds Of Him' ! ...

"Just Keep On Walking" ...

When we look back at the things that happen in our lives, things stand out that become part of our 'Heritage' and they create a bit of a 'Legend Effect' on the people involved in the story. Sometimes, those 'Legends' can be sad, sometimes they are humorous. Either way, they live on for a long time.

Many times, the funniest things that happen in Grocery Stores are the 'story' that grows out of someone else's agony over a situation. In other words, not the thing that occurred, but how the reaction came across to someone else... Someone's misery is overlooked for the 'story' it brings on. That's what occurred here in this story...

Here's what happened...

In 1968, I was a young 17-year-old Part-timer in the Washington, IA Hy-Vee and something happened out on the parking lot one evening that, by most people's guess, was pretty serious, but the reaction it got from one of the other Part-timers was 'PRICELESS'.

In those days, the groceries were carried out all the way to the Customer's car by a 'Carryout Boy'. There were lots of us in the stores and it was a great way to get to know the Customers and for Hy-Vee to show that we valued the Customer's business. Many times, when we came in the door from one trip to a car, we looked ahead to see if anyone checking out was a friend or the parents of a friend and we tried to

migrate to that order. I usually also looked for the biggest order coming down the Check-out Counter and I went to that counter. I had it figured that the Bosses' would notice I tackled the big orders and I'd get credit for being a good worker. It worked.

So, it was, 'In and Out' through the front doors of the store with carts of groceries and out to the Customer's car and back in again. It was sometimes cold...Sometimes, it was rainy, then sometimes it was hot and sometimes, it was just right. In any weather, the groceries went 'Out' and that's what kept the Customers coming 'In'.

One evening, I had taken a load of groceries out for a woman and I was headed back in. I caught up to another Part-timer, Gary, who had delivered a cart-load of groceries to different Customer's car not far from where I'd been. As we walked in from the far edge of the lot, we talked about small stuff and then it happened.

A lady in a car came driving through the parking lot at a pretty good rate of speed and as we walked, she ran squarely into a light pole base on the parking lot! There was a very loud 'CRASH' noise! The bases on the parking lot lights were made of concrete for durability, but they weren't designed to take a direct hit from a car and she had hit it hard.

It was a loud crash and because there were no seat-belts in most of the cars during that era, the woman flew forward in the car and hit her face on the

steering wheel of the car doing some damage to her face. It wasn't pretty.

I stopped in my tracks, but Gary never missed a beat as he pushed his empty cart and his only comment was "Well, I guess that stopped her!" And with that, he kept on walking into the building.

OMG! ...That was it...His only comment?

I immediately ran over to her car and asked her if she was okay. She sort-of 'nodded' that she was. She really wasn't okay, however, as she had a bloody nose and had cut her lip a little bit. Neither of her injuries were 'life-threatening' or even required a doctor, but she was banged up, the car was crumpled pretty badly and the poor light pole base was broken and chunks of it were lying there on the ground.

It was a mess.

As she sort-of came to the reality of what had happened, she said "I didn't even see that light pole." With that, I hollered at one of the other kids to get me some paper towels or facial tissues and to also call the police for the filing of an accident report. The lady wiped her face and cleaned up a little and by the time the Washington Police Department arrived, she was actually doing pretty well. At this point, I went back into the store and resumed my duties. I figured that the Police Officer would handle it from there.

As I entered the store, Gary came out the front door with another Customer and a grocery cart load of

groceries. He was headed for his new Customer's car and didn't appear at all concerned about the lady who'd had the accident with the light pole. I chuckled to myself as I thought about his response to it all.

From that point on, I knew it was going to have to be something 'pretty big' to get Gary rattled...He seemed pretty calm that night as the whole thing happened. As the story circulated through the store, he was teased about it a lot. For many years, the story lived on in The Washington Hy-Vee.

It was a good one for the Ages...

Yes, it was the story of

'I Guess That Stopped Her !'...

"Hey...Hand Me The Broom !" ...

You can 'Take It to The Bank' that in the nearly 90 years that Hy-Vee has been in operation in the Upper Midwest, there has been a definite 'pecking order' in the Part-time ranks of a Grocery Store. Even in those small antiquated 'Supply Stores' of the 1930's, that 'pecking order' came in the delegation of the duties given to the young people and it became a 'Rite of Passage' on some of the duties handed out in the stores...You know... 'Age Has a Privilege'. In a few jobs over the years, however, some jobs were a 'Size Has a 'Privilege'...If that is what you can call it.

I was a Part-timer in the Washington, IA Hy-Vee Store for a few years in high school and I went from being the 'New Kid' in 1966 as a 'Substitute Carryout' to eventually being in charge of the Frozen Foods department while I was home one Summer from college at now Truman State University in Kirksville, MO. I transferred to the Kirksville, MO Store in 1971.

In between those 'Seniority Chairs', I went through, there were lots of duties to learn and be part of. One of those 'chairs' ended up being decided not by 'Time' or 'Length of Service', but rather by 'How Big a Guy Was'...well, actually 'Was Not'. You see, one of the jobs required a small 'Jockey-size' kid. And for a few years, I was 'that kid'. Oh, I was always glad to do it, but I was always glad when it was done for another year...

Here is "The Dirt" on the job as it happened...

For many decades, Fresh Chickens were shipped to the stores from the packers in wooden crates that were wrapped together with wire. The Chickens came in cartons of about 20 birds and they were all cleaned and in the wooden cartons packed in crushed ice. Now, you may wonder about the crushed ice, but it was correctly 'theorized' in those days that the Chickens would be covered in ice for the time they were in shipment and being stored in the store's cooler. As the crushed ice melted, the cold and almost freezing water would 'bathe' those Chickens and keep them preserved without having to freeze them. Freezing Chickens is safe, but after they are frozen, you no longer have a "Fresh Chicken" and Hy-Vee always sold "Fresh Chickens". It really was effective and a safe way to do it for the time in America's history of food sanitation practices.

So, with 20 Chickens per crate, you can imagine the numbers of wooden Chicken boxes that would accumulate during a 'Big Chicken Sale'. There were massive amounts of them and the store's way of disposing of them, along with all the other cardboard boxes and trash in the store, was to burn them. Each store had a large 8' x 8' x 6' Incinerator attached to the backside of the store and it was fed by a large fireproof door that opened into the Backroom. The fire would get to raging so heavy in there sometimes that the asbestos lining would actually glow after an hour or two of constant use. The smokestack on the

top of the Incinerator was about 20' tall and it could be seen glowing and belching smoke from it each night.

It got hot to say the least.

The yearly job that the 'smallest' of the Part-timers got to do was to go inside the Incinerator and remove all the Chicken wire that had built up in the bottom grates of the Incinerator. You see, the wood would burn and leave ashes, but the wire wrap would melt together into large 'clumps' in the bottom grates of the Incinerator. It would eventually build to a point of hindering the air-flow within the Incinerator.

It was a dirty and filthy job.

So, once each year, the Incinerator would be shut down for a day or two and it would be allowed to completely cool down. Once it was cooled down, I would climb in wearing the oldest of clothes and I'd spend three or four hours unwrapping the 'globs' of melted wire from the steel grates and also inspecting the asbestos walls to make sure they were holding up OK. I didn't really mind doing it, but it was a filthy job...Afterward, I looked like a real 'Chimney-Sweep' of the 'Old Days'.

As the years went along, the Incinerators were replaced with 'Cardboard Balers' and the crushed boxes were then 'baled' for pickup to go to the recycling plants. Also, by then, Fresh Chickens were being shipped in more modern 'Gas Packed Cases'

without crushed ice and the America's cities were requiring that the Incinerators be removed for the betterment of the atmosphere and air pollution reasons.

Incinerators had come to the 'End of The Line' in their usefulness.

I was one of the last 'Little Guys' to have the job of cleaning out the Incinerator at the Washington Store...When I transferred to the Kirksville, MO Store in 1971, the changeover had started.

By the early–mid 1970's, nearly all of Hy-Vee's Stores had stopped using the Incinerators. There were 'Little Guys' in every store that were finally rid of the dirty and sweaty job inside the Incinerator. It was sort of like the old 'Pin-Setter Boys' in the bowling alleys history. You know, before the 'Automatic Pinsetters'. The young men who were the Pinsetters weren't needed anymore for that job. Once again, 'Life and Technology' had come to Hy-Vee and the Incinerators were now gone forever.

An era had passed.

I have been happy to have the days of cleaning the Incinerator as an experience in my years at Hy-Vee. I laugh, once in a while, because I knew that it was one of the only times in my life when I was...

'In the 'Hot-Box'...Not 'On The Hot Seat' !

"Here, Have Some Candy" ...

Since those early days in the 1930's, Hy-Vee's Stores have had 'lots and lots' of young people employed to work in the stores. In those small towns of Southern Iowa and Northern Missouri, the young kids were really happy to get a job of any kind and a job like 'The Supply Stores' provided was like 'Hitting the Jackpot'... It was good work, it was clean work, it was safe work and Hy-Vee always worked around the 'School Schedules' of the kids. That made everyone happy. Hy-Vee has been a great place for kids to work for nearly 90 Years.

In those early stores, there wasn't as much mischief for the kids to get into. The physical size of most of those stores was not much bigger than 1200 square feet and that left 'very little room' for any of the type of Horseplay that kids are known for. Oh, it happened, but it was generally stopped immediately and the young person was again behaving, but still 'always watching' for another chance to have some fun.

As the years and the decades rolled along, the stores were being built larger and there was more 'square footage' in a store. Naturally, as that happened, there were more kids and more Horseplay because of those increased store sizes. The numbers of kids also got harder to supervise and 'run the store' too.

The whole scenario of 'Size and Supervision' would get even more profound as the stores and numbers grew even larger yet in the 1980's, 1990's and into the 2000's. The stories of those 'Horseplay Shenanigans' grew too. One great story about 'Horseplay' came out of a store I worked in and I was in on it.

It 'Played Out' like this.

I was a Part-timer at the Washington, IA Hy-Vee in 1967. I was 16 years-old that year when several of us got into a situation that almost cost us our jobs...How we 'hung on', I will never know, but we did and we were lucky.

One of the nightly duties of 're-stocking' the store for the next day, was to fill the 'Ad Specials' and the 'End Cap Displays'. Both of these were very highly shopped and it was important to fill them for the next day to keep the Day Crew ready to take care of the Customers as they shopped. It was an 'every-night re-stock' on these items.

One of the main items to be stocked each night was an 'End Cap Display' of Brach's Pick-A-Mix Candy. It was bulk candies that were individually wrapped and the Customer simply filled a paper sack with the amount of Pick-A-Mix they wanted and then, it was weighed by the pound at the Cash Register. It was a great item and we sold lots of it.

The full cases of Pick-A-Mix came in boxes of about 30 pounds each and it was the same item in each case. The 'Mix' part of the name came because the Customers "mixed' their selections with each flavor in its own 'bin' and there were about 15 or 16 varieties. When re-stocking the candy, if a full case wouldn't all fit on the display, the partial case was taken to the Backroom until such time that it would fit...It's called 'Backstock' and there is still 'Backstock' on many items in the stores today.

So, one evening, I was busy working in the Backroom of the store and I was loading the partial cases of Pick-A-Mix onto a cart to take it out to the Sales Floor and re-stock what candy would now fit on the display.

There was another young kid sorting the glass 'pop bottles' that had been returned by the Customers for a Deposit Refund of two cents per bottle. He was about 15' from where I was.

When the young kid sorting bottles wasn't looking, I tossed a single piece of candy over and hit him on the shoulder with it. It scared him and we laughed. Pretty quickly, he threw a cardboard 'Six-Pack Pop Carton' over my way and I threw more candy back at him.

As some of the other kids heard the commotion and laughing, they joined in and now, there was a 'candy fight of huge proportion' going on in the Backroom. Candy and Pop Cartons were flying all over.

Soon, the Full-timer who was in charge of everything in the store that night, came around the corner and he even picked up candy and threw it. Why? I don't know, but he got involved and of course, that was the 'Green Light' for all of us and within seconds, it was 'raining' Pick-A-Mix candy'.

By now, candy was laying everywhere. It was on the full stacks of merchandise and all over the floor...Perhaps 500 or more pieces by now. The next thing that happened 'nearly sealed our fate'.

As we saw a shadow of someone coming through the swinging door into the Backroom, most of us 'immediately' turned and tossed a handful of Pick-A-Mix at the door...It just 'peppered' the door and the person coming through.

'Boom', we got him...and then...

Holy Crap! What had we done? It was Jim, the Store Manager...He had unexpectedly stopped back at the store for something.

There we were, six or eight Part-timers and the Full-timer in charge of things, all standing there amid 'candy everywhere' and staring back at Jim...I'm sure we probably looked like deer 'frozen in the headlights of traffic' as we stood straight and not moving or saying anything.

Like us, Jim was not saying anything or even moving.

He stood there looking at all of us through his large black-rimmed glasses. His eyes kept moving back and forth at each of us. We knew he must be 'taking notice' of just 'who' was involved in this 'melee'. After about 4 or 5 seconds, he very solemnly said... "Huh...So, this is what you do when I'm not around?"

And with that, he turned and walked out of the Backroom. The eight or so of us stood there for a few seconds looking at each other and all thinking the same thing... 'Had we had just seen our lives flash in front of our own eyes?" ...There was no doubt about it...We were done...

So, we thought.

To our amazement and complete 'Astonishment', not one word about it was ever spoken to any of us by Jim. We were not sure if he felt his lack of action or words had spoken the loudest or just 'what' the reason was... We just never heard anything.

As the weeks went by and we got past that 'fateful night', we probably had less Horseplay than ever before. Jim's reaction, or lack of, had spoken it all without a word.

When I became a Store Manager, I always tried to remember that night when I was 'up to my ears' in our crew's Horseplay. It had been a good lesson for all of us. Jim's tolerance and patience had 'made

their mark'. We were all 'better people' and I was a better Store Manager because of it.

It was the night we all just about

'Tossed Ourselves Out Of A Job !' ...

“See The Farmer Run” ...

I’m glad I grew up in Washington, IA. I can honestly say I had an upbringing that was ‘pretty close’ in atmosphere as the 1960’s could get to ‘The Supply Store Days’ of the 1930’s. Like those early ‘Supply Stores’, I grew up in Southern Iowa in a small ‘Farm Town’ and what I learned there has served me well for the remaining years of my adult life. Yes, the ‘Traditions and Values’ of a ‘Farm Town’ are ‘Pure and Simple’.

It’s a good life.

Now, Washington is a great ‘Little City’ in Southeast Iowa. Its claim to being ‘The Cleanest City in Iowa’ is a claim that I know has been made for well over 100 years and I believe it’s true. Washington’s biggest industry is Farming. Corn, Soy Beans, Hogs, Cattle and Turkeys are pretty much the makeup of the Farm Industry there. It’s pretty safe to say that more than half the Customers there are Farmers or descendants of Farmers.

In 1967, I was 16 years-old and I was working part-time at the Washington Hy-Vee. In the year of my employment there, I had learned that Farmers of the 1960’s were an interesting group. They tended to be very ‘Down To Earth’ and they were very common in their lifestyles. Most of the men smoked pipes, cigars or cigarettes. Also, I learned that many of them chewed (and spit) tobacco. Between the butts,

cigar stubs and tobacco stains, the evidence was there.

Yes, it was a Farm community.

Another common thing about Farmers of the 1960's was the way they dressed for their chores and light social activities... 'Bib Overalls' were pretty much worn by most of them and it was not unusual for us to see lots of the Farmers shopping in the store dressed in 'Bibs' while shopping with their wives or children. In the Summer months of the year, straw hats were part of the attire too because the Sun can be 'brutal' in the fields.

It was a way of life for the residents of Washington County and all over the Midwest. It was an innocent time in my own 'Heritage'.

Now, Shoplifters represent an 'Ugly, But Colorful' side to the Grocery Business. We were always 'on-guard' for a thief as we did our daily routines and took care of the Customers. Most times, the Shoplifter was there, you just had to know what to look for in the actions of your Customers to spot them. Over time, many in our crew became 'experts' at spotting a thief.

On a hot Summer afternoon in 1967, an incident happened at our Washington Hy-Vee that we still laugh about today. It's classic material for he History Books.

Here's how 'the caper' came down...

I became aware of a man who was being watched in the store as he roamed around. He was dressed in 'Bibs' and a straw hat and he pretty much blended-in to the normal scenery. He 'blended-in' until he kept making the rounds in the store to the carton cigarette display on an End Gondola at the front of the store. 'Trip after Trip' he would go by the rack and take one or two cartons of cigarettes from the rack and put them in his grocery cart. He would then sort of 'mosey around the store' for a bit before coming back for more cartons of cigarettes. He did not know he was being watched, so he made quite a few trips to the carton cigarette rack before he decided to make his exit out of the store.

When he decided to exit, he very calmly backtracked through the store and he walked his empty cart to the area inside the front door where the empty carts were nested together. Then, he headed for the door....

Seemingly, 'Empty-Handed'.

As he started to exit the store, Lynn, (one of the crew following him) hollered at him to stop and that's when the chase ensued. Out the door and across the parking lot he ran...or at least that's what he tried to do. He was running like a man with two 'Sticks' for legs and he could not bend his knees to run. He was running as fast as could 'stiff-legged' to try to get to his pickup truck so he could make his getaway.

Lynn quickly apprehended him and led him back into the store to wait on the Washington Police Department to come and get him. When the Police arrived, it was then that his 'Modus Operandi' was discovered. He had tied the legs of his baggy Bib Overalls tightly around his ankles with twine and then cut holes in the front pockets of his 'Bibs'.

As he sauntered around the store, he would take the cartons of cigarettes and slide them through his 'holey pockets' and into the legs of the Bib Overalls. With the legs being tied, the cigarettes just kept 'stacking-up' in the legs of his Bib Overalls. When they got full, he decided he better head for his pickup truck.

When the twine around his ankles was cut loose by the Police, it became clear why he couldn't run. He had about 30 cartons of cigarettes in the legs of his Bib Overalls and that's why his knees wouldn't bend. His 'genius idea' had just failed and he was off to jail. We were in awe of the whole thing.

The story went around Washington like a 'Wildfire' and his name was discussed a lot. It was not only expensive for him in court, but he was talked about by everyone in the county. The embarrassment had to be terrible for him and for his family.

To this day, when I see someone in a Grocery Store

that is wearing Bib Overalls, I try to imagine what they'd look like running across the parking lot 'stiff-legged' with the legs of his 'Bibs' full of carton cigarettes.

It was the day

We chased a 'Stick-Man'

Across The Parking Lot ! ...

“If you are right 51% of the time, you’ll be successful in the Grocery Business.”

Dwight C. Vredenburg

President, CEO and

Chairman of the Board

(Deceased)

“Somebody Stole My Car !” ...

Hy-Vee’s ‘Roots’ grew in ‘Rural Towns’ in Southern Iowa and Northern Missouri. In the 1930’s, most of those towns were very small in size and population and ‘Life’ in those towns was a very ‘Clean Living’ with lots of really great people. It was pretty common for a store’s clerks to know every Customer coming in and of course, that meant that you also knew things about them and their families... Sometimes for a few Generations of the family.

From the 1930’s until around 1960, Hy-Vee stayed mostly in those smaller towns. Hy-Vee’s Heritage is in those towns. After the early 1960’s, however, Hy-Vee’s executives felt the Company was strong enough to enter some ‘Metro Markets’ and ‘compete’ their way in. That subject is in another story coming later in this book, though.

Rural Life in the Midwest is a ‘Life All Its Own’. Farming and raising livestock and growing lots of your own food for your family’s personal consumption, meant that the items you’d sell in a store were ‘totally different’ than what’s in the stores today. The people shopping in the stores today, however, are not a lot different in ‘what’ they want from their Grocery Store....

It was then and it is now that Customers want to ‘Go Where They Are Invited’ and they will ‘Stay Where

They Feel Welcome'... So, with these two simple things, Customers will be loyal forever to a store.

Perhaps the biggest difference today, compared to more than 50 years ago, however, are the 'habits' of people today versus those years.

Yes, 'Things Have Changed'.

Here's a story of how those 'habits' in the lives of some of the people in those earlier times at Hy-Vee caused some commotion and their 'simplicity' caused a problem!

It happened like this.

I was working Part-time at the Washington, IA Store. I worked in that store from 1966-1971. In 1967, we had something happen that I am sure 'could' have happened in another town, but I have never heard of it again since.

We were busy one afternoon in late Summer of that year and all of a sudden, one of our very good 'Farmer Customers' came running back into the store hollering that "His car had been stolen!" ... He was frantic and really 'wound-up' over it.

Immediately, it got everyone's attention.

Of course, we all offered to help our Customer with 'The Stolen Car' and he kept going on and on about "Who" and "Why" someone would target his car. He said the best thing we could do to help was to call

the Washington Police Department and get them on the scene so they could help him with his predicament and find his car. So, as he sat there waiting for the Police to arrive, we took his cart-load of groceries and pushed it into the cooler for safe-keeping of the perishable items he had purchased.

When the Police arrived, he told them his story and they walked out together as he showed them where he'd parked his car on the Hy-Vee parking lot. When he came back in, we got our Customer some coffee and asked if he wanted to call someone to come and get him, but he said he'd prefer to wait a few minutes to see if anything developed with the Police before he "bothered" his wife to make a "Trip to Town".

We got him a chair and he sipped his coffee as he sat and waited. He was calming down pretty well by this point.

Now, when the Police left the store, they radioed ahead to Police Headquarters about the description of the car. You know, 'Year, Make, Model, License Number and Color'. All of that information was then conveyed on to the Washington County Sheriff for their help too. Everyone would be 'on the look-out' for his car. In a town of 6,000 people like Washington, 'If it was in town, they'd find it'. Stolen cars just didn't happen around Washington in 1967.

So, after about 45 minutes or so, we got a call from the Police Department Dispatcher that our Customer's car 'had been located' and the Police

were on their way back to Hy-Vee 'Following our Customer's car along the route'. That comment by itself had us all a little curious...

What was going on?

Sure enough, in a few minutes, there came his car onto the Hy-Vee parking lot and immediately behind it was the Police Squad Car. They both parked and got out of the car. They didn't come into the store though as we thought they would, but instead, they walked down the parking lot about 15 or 20 stalls and stood by a 'another' car there.

Not just an ordinary 'other car', however, but one that looked 'VERY FAMILIAR' to our Customer...In fact...it was 'Identical' to our Customer's 'Stolen Car'. It was then that we got 'The Rest of The Story' and that story 'Marched Right In' to the History of the Washington Hy-Vee.

Two men, both from Washington County, had each purchased cars that were almost identical in every way... Year, Make, Model and Color. So, from a quick glance at either, you'd swear it was the same car and our 'car thief' was 'no thief at all'.

It was an 'Honest Mistake'.

You see, what made this situation so funny and ironic was the fact that those 'Clean Lives' that are lived in those small rural areas had 'given way' to some bad habits over the years...Keys being one of them.

In those days, most Farm families left their keys in the ignition and also one in the trunk…You know, "No need to fumble for keys, when you can just leave them in the car" …The 'Fickle Finger of Fate' had caught-up to them both. Both had left their keys in the car and they even parked fairly close to each other. So, our 'car thief' merely walked out with his groceries, got in and took off.

In the wrong car…

Now, all these years later, you wouldn't be able to do that, but those were the 'Ways of Rural America' in 1967. Innocence at its best.

The 'Car-Caper Whodunit' had been solved…

It was an innocent case of

'The 'Olds' Switch-A-Roo !'…

“Sell what your Customers want to buy, not what you want to sell.”

David M. Vredenburg

Hy-Vee Co-Founder

(Deceased)

“It Got How Deep ??” ...

So many things have changed in their packaging over the nearly 90 years since those primitive ‘Supply Stores’ started in 1930 by Charles Hyde and David Vredenburg. With Hy-Vee and America, it has been a real ‘Journey’ through those years to see all of the ‘new innovations’. Some of those changes were done to make the products ‘look’ more attractive. Some were changes for ‘storage’ purposes and some were done for ‘sanitation and safety’ reasons... You know, because of germs and possible contamination.

Until the mid-1960’s, a Customer could still go into most Hy-Vee Stores and fill their own jug with bulk vinegar. One-hundred pound bags of sugar were an everyday item along with 25 pound bags of flour. There were even 100 pound bags of Rock Salt for those ‘new-fangled’ Water Softeners. Frozen Cherries and Strawberries were sold in 25 and 30 pound cans and the ‘Farm Communities’ were especially known to do the ‘Home Canning’ that would take place each year to keep the ‘Garden Harvest’ for those cold Winter months that would come again soon... as they did each year.

I can easily remember the hundreds of cases of canning jars and lids. ‘Kerr’ and ‘Ball’ were ‘household names’ and everyone wanted those two ‘trusted names’ on their Mason jars and canning lids.

All of this was very big business.

Now, 'safety' was a big reason for many of these package changes that were happening. All or most of these items eventually would go by the wayside and packaging of different kinds took over. By 1980, as America's 'technology' took over, so did the 'Safety Standards' that went with these items. America was on a 'quest' to protect its citizens.

Fresh Chickens were an area of real concern for the safety factors of selling food during those early years. Fresh Chickens are known for high amounts of bacteria and in some cases, Salmonella. The Stores of the 1930's, and on through to the 1980's, bought their chickens for resale from 'local' or 'regional' suppliers that brought these Fresh Chickens into the stores. Fresh Chickens were shipped to the stores in wooden crates that were held together with wire edging and clasps. This was necessary because the technology of 'Safe Chickens' then was to put the cleaned Chickens in these crates and then crushed ice was packed around the chickens to keep them cold. The idea was that as the ice melted, it would run all over the chickens in the crate and 'bathe' them in icy-cold water. In doing that, the Chickens would stay as close to 'germ free' as the technology would allow for those days. The wood could endure the wetness whereas cardboard could not.

It wasn't a perfect solution, but it worked 'for the times'.

In 1970, I was working at the Washington, IA Store when something happened that would be talked about in that store for many years to come. It wasn't funny then, but as things do, it has got funnier as the years rolled along.

The story 'floated around' like this.

The young man whose job it was to 'clean-up' and 'close-up' the Meat Department in the late evening was named Mike. Mike knew his routines well and he handled all of them very efficiently. One of those duties was to 'bag' whole Chickens and stack them in grocery carts in the cooler for the Chicken Sales in the weekly ads. It simply meant that the wooden crates of chickens were opened and the 20 or so chickens per crate were each then slid into a clear plastic bag and the end of the bag was stapled shut to keep them airtight. Then, when the Chickens were all bagged up, they were sent across the scale for a price tag to be printed and that tag was then stuck onto the bag for the Cashiers. Hundreds, if not thousands of Fresh Chickens would go through on a 'Big Sale' and it was a lot of work.

The 'clean-up' part was the worst part. The cold, wet and smelly wooden crates had to be emptied and the ice inside was dumped for draining. The ice went into a floor drain and the wooden crates were burned in the store's raging inferno called the 'Incinerator'. It was basically a big 8' x 8' x 6' 'asbestos-lined oven' with a tall chimney on it and everything from boxes to trash and paper of all kinds was burned.

To rid the wooden Chicken crates of ice, the stores were equipped with a large floor drain near the Chicken Cooler and the water from the melting ice would go into the drain and go down the sewer to the city water system. It could speed things up when the hot water heater on the edge of the floor drain was turned on full blast and hot water was used to help melt the ice. Nearly every night and especially on nights of the "Big Chicken Sales', the hot water heater ran seemingly all night... And that's where this story is headed.

So, on the night of this story, Mike bagged a lot of Chickens and finished his duties. He cleaned everything up and went home for the night.

Very early the next morning, the store's 'Morning Crew' came in to get started and got the 'shock' of their lives...There was about one to two inches of water all over the backroom floor and it was creeping out onto the main sales floor of the store. The hot water heater had been left on 'full blast' and it had been on all night. It had overflowed the floor drain itself and when the floor drain couldn't handle any more, it backed up...EVERYWHERE!

Now, by itself, an inch or two of water doesn't seem so bad. But now try to envision 'every' stack of merchandise in the Backroom having the 'bottom case' wet and starting to fall over from the loss of strength. Cereal was ruined, paper goods were ruined and the water that had run into every cooler and Backroom Freezer was now cold or frozen. It was an awful mess. And not only were the cases of merchandise wet, each stack had to then be 'dismantled' to get to the bottom case and then re-stacked. Imagine the number of hours of 'Labor Cost' invested in it.

So, Mike was immediately called to come in and help clean it up. So were many of us who could get there quickly. There were at least six or eight of us that were 'invited' to clean up this huge mess and it really was 'HUGE'...

Now, 'nerves were frayed' and the moments were still really serious, but I will remember all of my life the sheepishly nervous way Mike asked the Store Manager, Ivan, "Are you going to fire me, Ivan?" We all sort of 'perked up' to hear Ivan's answer.

Without even looking up from the floor mop he was swinging across the wet floor to soak up the water, Ivan said to Mike "At least not until you get it cleaned up." ... And with that, everyone lightened up and we all laughed out loud. We knew Mike's job was safe and that he'd be forgiven.

From that day on, "Not Until You Get It Cleaned Up"

was bantered around to poke fun at Mike and 'take a shot at him' in a joking way. Mike was good-natured and the teasing seemed to happen often.

It became known as the day

'The Chickens Got Their Revenge !'...

"Brrrrr... It's Cold In There !" ...

The Part-timers in a store add so much to the 'Excitement Level' in a store and the fact that they think they are pretty much 'invincible' makes it that much more fun because they are willing to do things that others wouldn't do for fear of 'The Consequences'. Some of the antics of the Part-time crew happen on the 'spur of the moment' and they do get out of hand pretty quickly.

I was a Part-timer in the Washington, IA Store and one night in the Fall of 1967, we (a couple of us) did something that we still laugh about today. It involved the Full-timer (Man-in-Charge) of the store for that week of night-shifts and if it would have been me that it happened to, I would have been furious.

In the 1960's, supervision at night in the Stores was pretty loose. You had a 'Full-timer' (Bill in this story) and about 8-12 Part-timers and a few Cashiers. It was Bill's job to keep 'Law and Order' while making sure the duties all got done and that the store was ready for the Janitor that came in at 8:30 PM. The pop bottles all had to be sorted, the shelves had to be stocked full with the items that would fit on them, the trash had to be emptied on the Cash Registers, the paper sacks had to be filled (we only had paper bags at the time) and all the Ad Items ('The Specials') had to be filled for the next day's business. It was actually a lot of work to do each night.

Bill was a 'tall and lanky' guy with a short haircut and his very dark hair had a little bit of curl to it. Like most of the Full-timers of the era, Bill smoked cigarettes and he smoked a lot in the Backroom of the store. Bill had a big wide grin that showed his teeth a lot and when he laughed, his cheeks kind of squinted his eyes to 'almost closed'. Everyone liked Bill and he'd been around Washington all of his life, so he knew everyone in town.

Well, Bill was a pretty good 'Sport' about things and he liked a good 'practical joke' about as well as anyone, so we (a few of us Part-timers) got together and figured out a 'plan' that would be a prank on Bill and that prank would allow us to 'run wild' for a bit. 'run wild' meaning just not having to work as hard and also 'loafing' a bit. That 'running wild' would be fun for as long as it would last.

Here's the story...

The Backroom Freezer sat in the Backroom of the store along the North edge of the building and the sales floor was adjoined to that area with a swinging door between the two areas. The hallway that was adjacent to the door to the Backroom Freezer was only about 5' or 6' wide with some merchandise stacked along the wall to make it even narrower. When you reached the end of the hallway, the Restrooms were there. Another turn yet, took you farther into the Backroom.

Now, we decided that we had to have a 'reason' to get Bill into position for the prank so we decided that we'd tell him that there was one particular flavor of Hy-Vee Ice Cream that we couldn't find in the Backroom Freezer while we filled the Ad Specials. It was a 'bogus' excuse, but it worked for us and we were able to get Bill to fall for it.

Bill said he knew where that flavor was at in the freezer and he'd go get it. Like us, Bill knew that the freezer was quite full and he took off for the freezer in the Backroom. As soon as he entered the freezer and the door closed, we waited for him to get clear to the far back corner of the freezer and then one of us tossed a couple of wooden pallets on the floor and they wedged in the narrow hallway there so as not to allow the freezer door to open...One more thing and the plan was 'perfect'... We flipped the light switch off in the freezer.

Then, we went about our plan of just doing nothing... 'running wild' so to speak...

We had decided that we'd let Bill out if something important happened and he was needed for the operation of the store for a problem that might arise for helping a Customer. Otherwise, Bill was trapped in '0 Degrees' and in total darkness too. The only heat or light he may have had were 'if' he used his cigarette lighter to help him see.

So, the time started going by and we had our laughs and our 'run of the place' for a little under an hour

before we figured out that we shouldn't 'push our luck' too far. We quietly went to the hallway and picked up the two wooden pallets and leaned them against the wall where they had been and then we flipped the light on and 'ran like crazy'.

Bill came out of the Freezer like a rocket and he was obviously 'frozen to the bone'. He came running into the Backroom where we were gathered and it was all we could do to keep straight faces when one of us asked... "Where have you been?" All Bill could do was 'stutter and stammer' about being in the Freezer for an hour with no coat on and we just had to stand there 'playing dumb' to what had happened. We made some small talk that we just didn't know where he was and we'd been "Up Front" bagging groceries. After a few minutes, Bill warmed up and the fun was over. We were now behind on the duties we needed to get done, so we really hustled and got caught up.

As far as we know, Bill never figured out just 'who' had done 'what', but it was a 'narrow list' of names and since we had sworn ourselves to secrecy, we made sure he didn't find out. You can bet we laughed our heads off after work.

It was the night

'We Gave Bill The Cold Shoulder !'

(and Other Parts too) ...

The Big Chicken Sale...

'Business Hours' are a part of the Grocery Business that has evolved over the 90 years of Hy-Vee's History. During the early days of 'The Hyde and Vredenburg Supply Stores' of the 1930's, the hours a store was open were pretty much an '8--5' schedule. The stores were always closed on Sundays and holidays...All holidays.

As the decades would roll along, longer hours were added for America's stores and now in the 21st Century, 'Open 24 Hours' is advertised and posted in the majority of large Supermarkets all-over the country. Christmas Day is still 'universally' looked at as a day to close, but it's the only one.

As the stores in Hy-Vee evolved in size and variety of merchandise, we saw 'lots' of things happen around those 'later closing times' that were strange, unusual and sometimes funny... That's what this story centered around and it is as funny today as it was when it happened all those years ago.

Here's how it all came down...

During the 1960's, it had become common for the smaller 'Farm Towns' in Iowa and surrounding states to be open until 8 PM or even a little later on one or two nights of the week. Sundays were still a day of being 'closed', but that would also change in the next few years.

While I was a Part-Timer at the Washington, IA Hy-Vee Store from 1966-1971, Washington was pretty much 'typical' of other stores of the day. We were open until 8 PM daily and closed on Sundays and Holidays. That was our routine.

The Chamber of Commerce in Washington had decided earlier that Spring to ask the stores around the City Square and other prominent locations in town all to stay open until 9 PM on Thursday evenings. This was to try and get the rural families to 'come to town' and shop a little longer.

Thursday nights seemed to be working well for us at Hy-Vee and we saw a pattern of people coming to Hy-Vee 'late' on Thursdays after they had shopped for other things or 'whatever' they had done 'Uptown' on the City Square where most of the local businesses were at the time. I say 'Whatever they had done' because that's what this story is about the 'whatever' part. Sometimes, the Customers were at 'other' businesses near the City Square.

One Thursday evening in late Summer of 1967, I was working until 9 PM when the store would close. As I said, we seemed to get some 'Late Shoppers' on Thursdays and we always expected them to show up around 8:45 or very close to 9 PM. It was consistent that way. We would always let them shop until they were done, however, as that was 'How it was done' in those days.

So, we were running around the store getting the last-minute duties done. We were doing things like finishing the stocking of the shelves, sorting the pop bottles, filling the ad items, filling the paper sacks on the Registers, sweeping the floors and any other thing that needed done late of an evening to prepare the store for opening the next morning at 8 AM. We also tried to get out of the Janitor's way when he came in just after closing time.

Everyone was busy.

At about 8:45 on this particular Thursday evening, I rounded the corner on one of the aisles going to the Front-end of the store and I noticed a man entering the front area of the store by the doors. I could tell by his 'Swagger and Stagger' that he was not sober and I kept a close eye on him as he came in.

This man spotted me and very quickly, he said in a very slurred voice "Where's the Chicken? That Old 'B*#@h' sent me in to get some Chicken."

Instantly, I knew it was my 'big chance' to have some fun.

"Well," I said "You're in luck. We have Chickens on sale today and you can take her lots of Chicken. I just know she'll be really happy if you stock up while the big sale is on. They're only 19 cents per pound and that's a 'Great Buy', but you have to get 'em tonight to get that price."

I could see him thinking as he 'swayed back and forth' and looked at me. Finally, in his slurred voice he said "Okay, how many should I get? I don't know why she can't get her own 'D@%N' Chicken. How many ya' got there?"

Boy, was I having fun now...

So, with a 'Devilish Smile', I said "Heck, just buy 'em all. You'll be a real hero with her. You won't have to come back for more Chicken for a while, either. Go ahead, take her a bunch."

He nodded approval, so I grabbed a grocery cart and we started loading the Whole Chickens into it. We loaded all of them in the case into the cart. I got the Chickens 'rung up' on the Cash Register. I doubled up some big paper sacks for strength and I bagged them all up in four 'very full' paper bags.

They were heaped full.

Then, 'out the door' he staggered pushing his cart with 37 Chickens in four large bags. As he walked out the door, he said to me in that slurred voice "That Old 'B*#@h' wants Chicken, I'll take her Chicken."

I followed behind him a little to make sure he got to his car okay. As he reached his car, he stopped for a moment while he urinated all over the left rear tire of his car. Then, he loaded the four bags into the back seat of the car, climbed into the Driver's Seat and 'took off' for home.

Knowing full-well that his wife was going to be getting the 'Surprise of Her Life', I took the cart and returned inside. Then, we all headed home. For the next three or four days, I 'held my breath' that we wouldn't hear from her. Lucky for me, no call ever came.

It was the night our Customer

'Played 'Chicken' With His Wife !'

“A quick nickel is better than a slow dime.”

Charles L. Hyde

Hy-Vee Co-Founder

(Deceased)

"Just Put 'Em In The Trunk" ...

From the 1930's until the late 1970's the position of 'Carryout' was a position that was the entry level position for most 'Young Kids' that went to work in the stores. It's been going on for nearly 90 years and it still holds true... 'When the Customer buys their groceries, they still have to get them home.' That's where the Carryouts came in. We made that easier for them.

Now, the cars of the 1920's and 1930's were rather small and the Carryouts of that era would bag the Customer's groceries and then carry or push the groceries right to the Customer's car which was usually parked in front of the store on the street. Taking the groceries right to the Customer's car was very 'Labor' intense, but it provided lots of the 'Service' that Charles Hyde and David Vredenburg wanted to give to their Customers in 'The Supply Stores'. Bicycles were even used in those small towns of Southern Iowa and Northern Missouri for 'Delivery' in those early 'Supply Stores'. A story still goes around about a motorcycle and side car being used to deliver groceries in a Southern Iowa Store of the 1930's.

As the years rolled along through the 1940's, 1950's and into the mid 1960's, the parking lots got larger and parking became confined to an area very near the store. Because those years prior had seen the stores on the 'City Square' or in an area where there

was no parking, the new 'Parking Lots' required more 'conversation' by the newly created position of 'Carryouts' and more training on that 'Customer Service' to the Carryouts. The growing Company was striving for the best Customer Service possible. The 'training' was added and the 'bond' between the Customers and the store's crew got stronger yet. Everyone was learning that the store crews would be very friendly at 'The Supply Stores' and later Hy-Vee.

Many times, the young Carryouts knew the person coming through the checkout lane. Or sometimes, they would try to look for and take care of an order they wanted to take out to the car...You know, a friend or a good-looking girl etc. It was usually a decision made when you came in from a previous run and you started bagging the order of the person (or persons) you wanted to carry out the groceries for.

It was almost a 'social event' for the Carryouts.

The practice of 'to the car' was used until around 1970 when Hy-Vee decided to have a 'Drive-Up Station' where the Customer was given a 'cart number' and then they 'drove-up' for their groceries. That 'system' gave way later to today's practice of the Customer pushing their groceries to their own car.

The 'Carryout' system was where I started and it offered so many fun stories about things that happened. It was an 'interactive' system and gave

much more opportunity to have fun with the Customers.

One great story about being a 'Carryout' happened to me while I was a Part-timer at the Washington, IA Store. It was a 'spur of the moment' thing, but its memory has lasted nearly 50 years with me. It was fun.

Here's how it all happened.

Late one evening in 1968 at our Washington Store, the groceries were to go out with a guy we all knew to be a pretty good 'Drinker' and a pretty good 'Jokester'. So, I bagged the order and started out to the car with 'The Jokester'. As we walked out of the store moving toward his car, we talked and made simple jokes along the way. He really was a good guy.

About halfway out to the car, 'The Jokester' proudly announced to me "Just put 'em in the trunk." and he took off for the Iowa Liquor Store that was right next to Hy-Vee. The key was in the trunk-lock (as was common in Farm Communities in those days), so I opened the trunk. Wow! The trunk on his car was 'HUGE' as were most of the trunks on the cars of the 1960's. Those cars were large and had 'huge' and 'deep' trunks. They would hold a lot of stuff.

Then, it hit me like a freight-train...He'd said "Just put 'em in the trunk." ... So, that's what I did to 'The Jokester'--- I called out to another Carryout that was nearby to help me. We tipped the cart on its side and

laid it squarely into the trunk and closed the lid, complete with the groceries inside it. It was the perfect way to handle 'The Jokester' and would he ever be surprised when he got home.

To get caught at this would have been 'Certain Death' for my job, so I held my breath for several days and when any discussion about 'The Jokester' bringing the cart back came up, I just acted like I didn't know anything about it. There were only two of us who knew who had done it and 'we weren't talking'.

Soon after, it all calmed down. It was great while it lasted though. It still comes to my mind when I see one of those older cars with a 'huge trunk'...

It was the night the joke went home with 'The Jokester', but

'The Joke' Coulda' Been On Us !...

The Karate' Kid....

It's pretty safe to say that people everywhere like a 'Good Time' and lots of times, those 'Good Times' are at the expense of another person. Those times can be fun to be both a 'Spectator' and a 'Participant'... That perspective, however, depends on 'What' happens and 'Who' it happens to.

Since the early 1930's, when Hy-Vee started out in those small little 'Supply Stores', there have been 'lots and lots' of examples of ornery activity that lurked around each corner of the store...Jokes have been played on people...Pranks have been pulled on people and 'sometimes', the things that happened were 'Painful'...Both in 'Embarrassment' and also in 'Just Plain Hurting'.

In my 'Hy-Vee Career' that began at my age 15 in 1966 until my retirement from Hy-Vee, I have witnessed many things in the 'Fun Stuff' category of working with large numbers of people. With all those folks all under one roof, those times have produced some really funny stories for 'The Storytelling' History Book of Hy-Vee.

One such story happened while I was working at the Washington, IA Hy-Vee Store in 1967. It was the result of a lot of 'Boasting' and 'Showing-Off'.

It went like this...

One of the Full-timers at the Washington Store was a guy named Hubert. 'Hubie', as he was sometimes called, had started to be a 'show-off' and he was letting it be known that he knew Karate. How much he knew, I am not sure anyone really ever figured out, but he started breaking wooden slats from crates and he was breaking small boards that would show up and he made a 'big production' out of all of it. He had told everyone the 'How-to's' of Karate and the 'Mental Parts' of it all and he pretty-well had himself convinced that he knew what he was doing...Nobody else perhaps, but he had himself pretty well believing he knew it.

Now, in a large group of people like a Hy-Vee Store, you can be assured that the type of 'Martial Arts' that Hubie was putting on display would eventually be questioned by somebody and there would be a 'show' to prove his prowess in Karate...

And there was one coming down the track.

The guys Hubie worked with in the Produce Department had listened to his story of the Karate for quite a while and they were about ready to have him 'Put Up or Shut Up' on his skill. So, at the Breakroom table one day, Ed and Jim sort of 'challenged' Hubie to a 'demonstration'. Well, it got talked about for a few days and then the whole thing came to life.

A few days into "The Challenge", Hubie decided that 'This was the day' and a time was picked that would ensure a pretty good crowd. When the time chosen

came around, Hubie received some 'prompting' to get it all underway in front of everyone.

It was decided that a broomstick would be a good thing to demonstrate on and 'The Show' was on...We were going to see Hubie's Karate in action.

A stack of full cases of canned goods was used on one side of the broomstick and a 'Low-Boy' stock cart was used on the other side. Now, a 'Low-Boy' was an 'L-Shaped' four-wheeled cart that was made of very heavy steel and was built to carry lots of full and heavy cases of product from the Backroom to the Sales Floor for stocking the shelves. It had a handle at the back and a small wire basket to carry odds and ends in. Overall, a real 'workhorse' piece of equipment.

With a group of near a dozen people watching, the broom handle was placed between the cases of canned goods and the 'Low-Boy's' handle that had been backed up to line up straight with the other side. Hubie was busy adjusting the distance a little for his Demonstration of Karate and finally, he had everything ready for his 'Karate-Chop' on the broomstick.

After a few comments from him about the importance of the 'mindset' and 'concentration', Hubie was ready to go. He looked down intently at the broomstick and he raised his hand in the air like a 'Tomahawk'. Suddenly, he let out some kind of a 'War-Hoop' and he started his downward 'Chop'.

What happened next is 'The Story' that came out of all of this...Jim and Ed were standing on the end of the broomstick that was supported by the 'Low-Boy' and just at the same time Hubie started his downward 'Chop', Jim shoved the 'Low-Boy' closer to the Canned Goods Stack with his foot and Hubie 'Karate Chopped' the handle on the 'Low-Boy' cart...

'EEEEE--YOUCH!'... Man, it had to hurt...

As Hubie 'danced around wildly' shaking his now 'really sore hand', Jim and Ed, along with everyone else, were laughing so loud, you could probably have heard it clear out of the Sales Floor of the store.

It took about 10 minutes to get everything and everyone back to normal. Hubie's hand eventually did quit hurting and everyone quit laughing about it all, but it lasted several days and weeks afterward... Poor Hubie had 'once again' fallen victim to Jim and Ed and the 'Fun' they always had with anyone they could 'pull one over on'.

And it had been a 'Good One' too....

Nowadays, when I hear someone talking about Karate and I see the demonstrations put on from time to time, I always think about the time I witnessed a 'Spectacle' of a Karate Demonstration in the Backroom of the Washington Hy-Vee.

I would imagine everyone else there that day remembers it too...Especially Hubie.

It was the day

The 'Karate Kid' Got KO'd

By The 'Low-Boy'...

“To sell anything, you must first invite your Customers in with a good ad.”

Dwight C. Vredenburg

President, CEO and

Chairman of the Board

(Deceased)

"Oh Well, It Will Heal" ...

Nearly 90 years ago, the 1930 partnership of Charles Hyde and David Vredenburg saw their 'Supply Stores' as more than 'just a job'. They saw those small-town stores in Southern Iowa and Northern Missouri as a business that could 'be part of the Community' too. Not only did they view the stores as a source of food and supplies for the towns, but they knew that having the 'right people' in those stores would 'tie' the Customers to the stores and that would equate to 'Solid Business' over the years.

And they were absolutely right...

Now, all these years later, it is 'still' a Cornerstone of Hy-Vee's Philosophy to be 'part of the Community'.

Cashiers at Hy-Vee are hired for reasons that are completely different than you might imagine. Some people think it's only to have them at the Cash Registers to ring up the groceries being purchased by the Customers, but the equally (if not more) important reason is to be a 'familiar face' to the regular shoppers that come and go in the stores. Every store is that way, but it is especially true in the stores located in the small rural towns...In 1930 and now...

Hy-Vee has had so many variations of the descriptions above, but those two factors are just about it. 'Accuracy' and 'Personality'. If the Customers in a store are predominantly Seniors at a

given time of the day, then it made sense to have them greeted and assisted by someone with similar attributes. If it was a college atmosphere and the Customers were mostly College Kids, then it made sense to have them greeted by College Kids of their own age. It isn't Rocket Science, but it does get a bit complicated sometimes trying to sort it all out as to 'who' and 'when' they will be Cashiering.

It is a Science for sure ... 'The Science of People'...

A story I will always remember is one that I still chuckle over today and it involved a great Cashier named Lois and a great friend named Randy.

Here's the Story...

In the Summer of 1971, I was working at the Washington, IA Hy-Vee while I was home between my second and third year of College at now Truman State University in Kirksville, Missouri. I was glad to be home and see everyone. I knew almost everyone that came into Hy-Vee because I had worked there for over four years already and in a town of 6,000 people, you do get to know nearly everyone. It sure gives the job 'personality' and I loved that part of the job.

Now, Randy was a classmate of mine from high school. He was about as friendly and enjoyable to be around as anyone you could ask for. He had a smile that seemed to cover his whole face when he 'flashed it' to others. He had stayed there in Washington and

was working with his Dad in 'The Family Business'. It was a good business and he had a good future ahead of him there.

Randy really enjoyed hunting and the rural areas around Washington County offered lots of places to go hunting and 'get to the Outdoors' for some activity. Deer, Pheasants, Rabbits, Squirrels, Quail, other animals and birds were the main items hunted for around the County. Lots of them...

After all, it's 'Rural America'.

So, while out hunting one day in a field in the County, Randy attempted to cross a wire fence with his shotgun in hand when the gun discharged hitting him squarely in the foot and ankle area. It was necessary to remove his foot, ankle and quite a bit of his lower calf in the repair of the wounds. Obviously, it was bad and yet, it could have been worse. Randy was a guy who always looked at his glass as 'Half-Full'. He viewed it that 'It was what it was', however, and he felt lucky to have survived the ordeal.

He was handling the whole thing very well.

As I said previously, the Cashiers were hired for their accuracy, but also for their connection to the Customers and Community. Lois was no exception. Lois was very friendly and a very popular Cashier. She was a very accurate and talkative Cashier who had lived in Washington for many years. She was

also the mother of some 'past high school aged' children that we all knew.

Sometimes when Lois talked to people, however, the words just sort of 'rolled out of her mouth' and occasionally, she had spoken before she thought about what she was saying.

It could be comical to say the least.

So, on the day of this story, Randy had come to Hy-Vee to do some shopping and he was in the store for a little while gathering his items. He made his way around the store on his crutches, with one pant-leg hanging empty from the hunting accident. As usual, he was friendly and when he went through the Check-out Line, he was smiling and talking to everyone he knew. Almost everyone knew who he was and how he had been injured...

I say 'Almost Everyone'...

Lois was mentally consumed with her previous Customer's conversation that she sort-of 'spaced-off' for a moment. As Randy stepped up to be the Customer that Lois was now checking out, Lois tilted her head back, looked down her nose at him through her Reading Glasses and said "Hi Randy, I heard you hurt your foot. Well, just stay off of it for a while and it will heal." ...

Say Whaaaaat ??...

You could have heard a pin drop because it was obvious there was no foot in there to heal and everyone knew it ...Except Lois. So, Randy looked at me and I looked at him and then we both looked at everyone else. Then, we all burst into laughter because it really was unexpected and it was comical. Lois only caught on because of the laughter and when she realized what she'd said, she turned red and sort of suffered through it. She was a great gal to have at Hy-Vee.

After that day, Lois made sure she knew 'who' she was talking to and 'what' she was talking about because on this day she had really opened her mouth and inserted her own foot.

It was the day that Lois tried to

'Talk Randy's Leg 'Back On'...

“You’ll only be as good as the people you surround yourself with.”

Dwight C. Vredenburg

President, CEO and

Chairman of the Board

(Deceased)

"HELP ! ... It's After Me !"

Hy-Vee's Heritage from 1930 in Beaconsfield, Iowa goes back to the small 1200 square foot stores that peppered the Midwest in every community around. Larger Supermarkets would eventually show up, but it was many years in the making and it would take literally thousands of 'New Innovations' to make it to the present day '21st Century 'Super-Stores' with every gadget and modern piece of equipment 'known to man'.

Hy-Vee opened the Ankeny, IA #1 Store in 1967 and it did very well from the first day. It began in a growing Des Moines Area suburb and the store and the Community grew fast together. The store has continued to be a huge success over the nearly 50 years since it opened. This story involved the Ankeny Store.

Here's what happened.

One 'new innovation' in the Grocery Industry that came along near the time of the Ankeny Store was known as a 'Garb-El'. The 'Garb-El' was an 'Industrial Size Garbage Disposal' and it was a really new item for helping to keep up with the trimmings from all of the Fresh Produce in the stores. No longer did the Produce Clerks have to 'box' all the trimmings and with the 'Garb-El', when Produce Items started going bad, they simply put it down the 'Garb-El' and it was gone in an instant.

The use of the 'Garb-El' saved 'time and effort' and it really seemed to increase Hy-Vee's Productivity, known then as 'Man-Hour Production'. In other words, 'How many $$ of Sales were made for each Hour spent on Labor or Wages'. Obviously, this old 'Man-Hour Production' number was a benchmark that every store could use to keep up with every other store. You know, sort of like 'competition' to be the best and the most Productive.

So, the newly invented 'Garb-El' was placed initially in a few Stores and due to its location to local 'Garb-El' service company personnel for repairs, Ankeny was chosen as a store for installation.

Well, a home garbage disposal works on a principal of flushing water behind the garbage being ground up and it all goes out as a 'soupy liquid' in the exit lines of the house's plumbing. So, with that established principle on how it all worked (or should have worked), Hy-Vee decided the installation of the 'Garb-El" could be tapped right into the existing sewer lines for the store in the Produce Trimming Room. It seemed like a good idea...at the time.

Now, like some 'new innovations', there are some 'issues' to be worked out with them and the 'Garb-El" had an 'issue or two' that showed up rather quickly. Those 'issues' reared their ugly heads and to this day, the stories still go on among the 'Old-Timers' who were around.

Not long after the 'Garb-El' was installed and became operational, the Store Manager, Dick, and the Produce Manager, Glenn, both were alerted that there was a 'HUGE PROBLEM' in the basement of a neighbor's house not far from the Store. It seems that when the 'Garb-El' was installed, the exit line to the sewer was not changed and all of the now 'soupy green garbage' was going through a sewer line that was not big enough to handle it all. And doing what liquids do, this 'soupy green garbage' started backing up wherever it could go to a low-spot in the system. In this case, it was the neighbor's basement. It was a 'Grand Mess' for sure.

So, clean-up people were sent to the neighbor's house and the whole 'soupy green mess' was cleaned up and they went back to the store to try and figure out how to resolve it. Eventually, new larger sewer lines would have to be run that could handle the 'soupy green mess' from the 'Garb-El'.

As problems do, however, they don't ever wait until a problem is 'rectified' or for 'a convenient time' to become problems and before the sewer line was replaced, 'something else' happened in the Ankeny Store and the 'next problem' caused by the 'Garb-El' is 'The Story That Lives On' in the Ankeny Hy-Vee's History.

It's A 'Really Good One' too!...

It seems that one of the Full-time Cashiers had gone into the Ladies Restroom and had sat down on the

toilet to 'use the facility' and while she was sitting there, the pressure had built up so badly in the small and inadequate sewage line, that the 'whole mess' came 'belching out' and it 'belched out' of the toilet in the Ladies Restroom. Yes, 'Straight Up'!

The Ankeny Hy-Vee Produce Manager, Glenn, said that the Cashier came running by him as she ran out of the Ladies Restroom pulling her pants back up and she was 'shrieking' as she ran. The 'soupy green mess' had 'erupted' straight up her back as she sat there on the toilet and she now had all of it 'streaked up her backside'.

That's when the 'Garb-El' was 'shut-down' and not used again until new larger sewer lines were installed that could handle the volume of the 'soupy green mess' that was going through them. In all new stores thereafter, 'larger' sewer lines were part of the blueprints for successful operation for the 'Garb-El' in the Produce Department.

Now, for years, it has been a very funny story to every person 'except' the Cashier who got the 'green stripe' up her back as she sat on the toilet. She probably would trade that experience with anyone who would trade her for it.

It was the day ... 'The Crapper Shot Back'

"How Was It Spelled ??" ...

In those early years of 'The Supply Stores' now called Hy-Vee and well on into the 1990's, each Store Manager was responsible for writing and producing the Weekly Ad that would run in the town's local Newspaper. The Store Manager would make the item selection for the ad Items and then work with the local newspaper personnel to get the ad layout done with the pictures of the items included for the 'Run of the Press' Ad. It was also known as an 'ROP ad'.

These ads would usually run to begin on what is called 'Best Food Day' (usually Wednesday) and on Best Food Day, all grocery competitors would run their ads on the same day to try to get the best 'draw' into their stores. Major Food Manufacturers and other companies that supplied the stores would coordinate their 'Deal Allowances' and 'Coupon Offerings' to print or take effect on Best Food Day each week. Overall, it organized the shopping in a community pretty well

Now, because the ads were 'Run of The Press' (aka ROP), there would occasionally be 'misprints' or 'misspellings' that would be so funny or cause such a 'stir', that they became nearly 'immortal' in that town. Years after, people would still refer to them and say "Remember the time?" ...

It was like 'Folklore' in many cases.

Some good examples of these ads that ran were simple misspellings like 'Moosetraps' when it should have been 'Mousetraps' and 'Druncan Hines' instead of 'Duncan Hines'. 'Popcorn' turned into 'Poopcorn' and so forth. There are several more really good examples.

It got rather wild sometimes and Store Managers 'cringed a bit' as they opened the Tuesday evening newspaper to read for the first time the ad starting on Wednesday morning.

In the late 1960's, Hy-Vee's Store in Tarkio, MO (Northern Missouri) became famous for an item that ran in their weekly newspaper ad. It took 'months' for it to settle down after it ran in the newspaper one Tuesday afternoon in Tarkio. It was an 'accident' that couldn't have been better timed if it had been planned.

It 'ran' like this.

One of Hy-Vee's early merchandising ideas involved Cut-up Chickens. An 18-piece 'Family-Pack' had been developed using a specified number of 'cut pieces' of the Chicken. It included the Breast, the Drumsticks, Thighs, Wings and then some 'extra' pieces of each to get the number of pieces to the '18 piece' count. The extra pieces were more Wings, Drumsticks, the Back and Thighs and the Neck. It was basically 'rearranging' the piece count' of dozens of Chickens to accommodate the packaging for higher profit. This package could be sold for a very low price per pound and that allowed for selling the remaining extra Breasts, Thighs and Drumsticks in packages containing only those pieces for a higher price per pound thus making 'more money' on the overall sale of the entire Chicken Program. Sometimes even 'oddball numbers' of parts were packaged together and called just called 'Chicken Parts'.

It was and is called 'Merchandising'.

'Merchandising' the Chickens really did work very well and Hy-Vee used this program until the end of the 1980's when 'pre-packaged' (from the supplier) Chickens came into the market. These were cut, wrapped and ready for the case right out of the box with no special work involved beyond weighing. They are packed in a safe 'preservative gas' and they are called 'Gas Pack Chickens'. They are much more sanitary and safer by far than the old 'Ice-Pack' Chickens of the decades prior.

So, on the day of this 'famous' weekly ad in Tarkio's History, the ad came out, as usual, in the Tuesday afternoon newspaper and the paper was delivered all over town. In reading the ad, the Store Manager discovered (to his horror) that the newspaper printing had misspelled the correct item 'Chicken Parts' and it was turned into 'Chicken Farts'...

The 'Rest of The Story' became Legendary.

As usual in the smaller towns of Northern Missouri and Southern Iowa, the old Farmers in the area had

gathered the next morning for coffee at the 'local café' and they 'hooted and hollered' over the misprint as they had read the ad from the paper from the night before. It was so funny that several of them 'went into action'. They couldn't let this opportunity go by without somebody 'getting roasted' over it.

So, they devised their 'plan' and a group of them went over to the store and presented themselves at the meat case. When the Meat Department Manager came to the case to greet them, they proudly announced "We came to get some of those Chicken Farts".

You can imagine their laughter as they asked.

But, not to be outdone, the Meat Manager calmly said he'd go get some and be right back. He then went to the Cooler where he very carefully 'blew air' into three or four small clear plastic bags, sealed them with a knot and then wrote "Chicken Farts....$.29 per pound" on each bag with a red marker.

Shortly, he returned to the men that were waiting and he said "Sorry for the delay---I had to catch the chickens and squeeze them extra hard to get this much."

I was told that you could hear the laughter all over the store.

No one is really sure who had more fun with it---the Farmers or the Meat Manager, but the story still gets

repeated occasionally by the real 'Old-Timers' still around.

It was the time that the 'Fowl' Smell in

The Air Was 'The Smell Of FUN !'

“Cheerfully give refunds or don’t give them at all.”

Dwight C. Vredenburg

President, CEO and

Chairman of the Board

(Deceased)

“Just A Little More...Oh, No...No !” ...

Hy-Vee’s Stores of the 1950’s and the early 1960’s did not yet include the Bakeries or Deli/Kitchens that were added in the late 1960’s and into the 1970’s. The older stores were designed and constructed with the usual front doors of ‘In’ and ‘Out’ and the immediate turn to the left or to the right upon entering the store lead right down Aisle One and deeper into the store for shopping. Turning to the left meant your Store was a ‘Left-Handed Store’. Turning to the right meant your store was a ‘Right-Handed Store’. It was a ‘technical designation’, but it meant something during those years.

The Meat Department was in the back of the store and the Produce Department was in the farthest last aisle of the store after going by the Milk and Dairy items... then on to the Bread... all before going to the Check-out area for payment and leaving the stores.

The ‘very primitive’ Frozen Food Department was generally, somewhere near the last part of the store and it was close to the location of the Ice Cream, which was designed so the frozen items wouldn’t melt before finishing the shopping.

The store design ‘usually’ included an ‘even number’ of aisles so that following the shopping pattern of the aisles was leading Customers down the ‘Odd Numbered Aisles’ toward the rear of the stores and the ‘Even Numbered Aisles’ brought the Customers

back to the front of the store. The last aisle was usually an 'Even Numbered Aisle' with Produce and Bread to be added to the cart last so as not to crush them with other items.

It all worked very well.

Aisle One of the older stores was pretty much canned goods and juices in the aisle. Almost always, Aisle One was the Canned Vegetables in alphabetical order along the wall and Juices on the opposite side of the aisle in sequences of Fruit Juices and Vegetable Juices, separated, but next to each other.

Sometimes, Candy would be at the end of the Juice side for an 'Impulse Item'. It was a pretty good layout. It also served a good purpose of getting some tough durable items in the bottom of the carts first so they didn't crush other items in the shopping pattern as the customer shopped.

With the addition of the Bakery and Deli/Kitchen to the stores in the late 1960's and 1970's, it was necessary to add on to the buildings to fit the two new departments into the stores. Newly constructed stores had the two new departments added into the blueprint and they were then built that way. Hy-Vee was evolving into a 'One-Stop Shopping' Store.

When an addition was made to an existing store, however, construction was done to add the new outside walls of the addition and finish the new departments in their entirety before the old exterior

wall was removed. It was always exciting because the Customers and employees watched for months as the building changed and the excitement grew with the anticipation of the new items that would be featured. It also kept the mess under control and separate from the other parts of the store for a while longer.

When the new area under construction was done and it was then necessary to 'knock-out' the old wall, it was necessary to 'reset' or 'rearrange' the items in the older part of the store to allow more room and expand on sections too. The new areas usually included space for some new dry grocery shelving and Frozen Foods cases etc. It was an 'expansion' and in lots of store expansions, the Shelving Gondolas had to move in order to match the blueprint and the new space for the 'new addition'. It was a very exciting, but stressful time for all involved.

It got 'real stressful' in one Store. It went like this.

In the early 1970's, the Iowa City, IA #1 Hy-Vee Store made the 'Journey' of the addition of space to add a Bakery to their Store. There was not enough room to add a Deli/Kitchen at the time, but it was decided that a Bakery would enhance their store and so it was done. Space was added to the store by taking out some of the parking lot and when the new area was all done, the old wall was torn down and the expansion into the 'new area' began.

The new blueprint called for the Shelving Gondola that ran along the old Aisle One outside wall to be moved backwards about eight inches to give more room down the aisle for shoppers to use. Now, that would usually mean taking all the items (in this case, Canned Goods) off of a full 48-foot or 56-foot length of shelving, moving the shelving and then, fully re-stocking the shelves with the products.

Basically, it meant a couple of days to move it.

The story of the 'The Great Crash', came as the result of a decision made by Doyle, the Assistant Store Manager. Doyle was in-charge and working with the crew of sales people who'd come to the store to volunteer their time and help move the Shelving Gondola with the Canned Goods on it. The Store Manager was at the Weekly Managers Meeting at Hy-Vee's Headquarters in Chariton that day and he was not there for the move.

It was at this point, 'The Big Idea' was hatched.

Doyle sent everyone out to their cars to retrieve the 'Jack' that was in their car trunks for changing car tires. When the 'Jacks' were all 'retrieved' and back into the store, each person was instructed to position their 'Jack' at a point on the shelving gondola right below the upright support pole on the front of the Shelving. The support poles were about four feet apart.

Now, with all the 'Jacks' in place and the shelves still full of thousands of cans of Fruits and Vegetables, the object of the effort was to start working the 'Jacks' together and 'at the same time', each person was to move their 'Jack' so the Shelving Gondola moved slowly backwards the required number of inches to match up with the new plans.

As the Shelving Gondola started moving so slightly and backwards, 'something' went terribly wrong and the entire 48' Feet of shelving tipped over backwards sending thousands of cans 'flying everywhere.

Now, they had a mess of 'HUGE' PROPORTION'.

With everyone standing there wearing 'looks of disbelief' on their faces, there was now a 'mountain of canned goods' surrounding a 'pile of shelving support poles'. The next two days were spent picking everything up and loading it all into grocery carts to get it out of the way for the shelving support poles being 'set-upright' in their new position in the aisles and then the Canned Goods were all stocked to their original places.

It was a lot of work and it did eventually get rather humorous as it became known as

The Day The New Addition

'GOT ALL JACKED–UP'

“Always do what’s right.”

Ronald D. Pearson

President, CEO and

Chairman of the Board

(Retired)

"Box-Boys...Where Are You ??" ...

The reference has been made to the 'Southern Iowa and Northern Missouri Heritage'. Hy-Vee has it and I never found that to be so true as the things I learned when I transferred from one store to another in my college years.

Wow! Did I have a lot to learn!

Now, I had worked through high school at the Hy-Vee in my hometown of Washington, IA and that had provided me with a great job and lots of fun experiences and friends. It was a wonderful way for me to find out that I wanted to be 'A Hy-Vee Guy' with my 'life's work' so, when I graduated from high school in 1969, I chose to go to college in Kirksville, MO at now Truman State University. I continued to work at the Washington Hy-Vee on weekends for a while and eventually, I made the move after asking for a transfer to the Hy-Vee in Kirksville, MO.

I was so excited when I was hired Full-time at the Kirksville Store. I was hired because I had Hy-Vee experience and I would also be rather inexpensive help for them because I was in school too. I had become a Full-timer at $2.30 per hour.

It was 'PERFECT'!

On that hot day of August 13, 1971, I started at the Kirksville Hy-Vee. I drove my old 1963 Mercury Convertible down the 120 miles from Washington to

Kirksville. As I drove, I listened to President Richard Nixon on the radio about curbing inflation by way of Price Controls. I listened to the entire speech he made regarding the move. I knew it was a 'major step' for America and I would learn later just 'how major' it was.

It was 'History in The Making'.

I started at 2:00 PM that day stocking shelves on the 'All-Night Stock Crew' there and I was assigned to stock in the Canned Goods aisle of the store. So, with that drive to the Kirksville Hy-Vee, I mulled over all of the 'Day's Happenings' as I stocked. I was amazed too at the differences I found in the Hy-Vee I was used to in Washington and the things I had already found to be different in the Kirksville Store.

For one thing, the Sales Volume was a big change as the Kirksville store was probably doing three times the Sales Volume that the Washington Store did. Another big difference I saw was the prices on the merchandise. I was used to prices that were higher than what I was seeing and there were larger 'shelf sets' on the shelves to hold the larger quantities of those items. I can remember Hy-Vee Canned Vegetables being priced at 5 cans for $1. Wow! ... To me, that seemed cheap. Hy-Vee White Bread was 15 cents for the one pound loaf and there were many other differences in the prices too.

Soft Drinks, Beer prices, and Meat prices all seemed to be cheaper and I think it was my first experience

in seeing that 'Volume Cures a Lot of Ills' in a store. In simple language, 'The more business you do, the cheaper you can be'. I was seeing it first-hand. It was part of 'The Education' one can get from working in different stores in different towns. I began to see that I was getting my 'Education'...Both at college and at Hy-Vee.

As I interacted with the crew, I found out that there were lots of people from all over Hy-Vee's Territory. Most of them were there, like me, to go to college and 'work their way through'. I felt a 'kinship' with them right away. We were all glad to be there and have a job.

We all found ourselves working some tough schedules. I remember for about a year and a half, I worked from 5:00 PM until 5:30 AM four nights per week and then I was in school 7:00 AM to 3:30 PM five days a week. They were very odd hours during our time there and they were hard too, but hey... 'It paid the bills' and my ultimate goal was a 'Career with Hy-Vee' and to get a Degree in Business in the process.

It worked...

Now, as the Customers came in that first day, I found it to be my first experience with "The Missouri Drawl" and I wondered to myself... "Will I get that Drawl while I'm living here?" I chuckled. I heard talk of "Wee-uns" and "You-uns" and then came my favorite... "Sodee-Pop". It was immediate that I

noticed that one and I would go on to learn so many more differences between Southern Iowa and Northern Missouri. It was a simple 120 miles, but there were many differences for sure. It was like 'moving to another world' and you know? ...I Liked It.

So, we stocked shelves and helped Customers find things and I listened to the voice on the loudspeaker call help to the Front-end in voice with a bit of a 'drawl'. I heard the voice say "We need all 'Ones' up front." I stopped for a second and then I thought to myself... "Well, I'll learn it all as I go along".

A short time later, I heard the same male voice come on the loudspeaker and say "We need all 'Ones and Two's up front." Again, I had to think for a minute and I came to the conclusion that there were different designations of the crew and depending on your 'number', that was how you were called up front over the loudspeaker. I decided I could get used to that as well. With me being used to everyone being called up by name, I knew it would be a change, but 'Yes' it could be learned and then I went on 'stocking the shelves' as before.

About a half an hour later, I heard the strangest thing I had ever heard on a store loudspeaker before and I completely stopped what I was doing and listened to see if it was someone 'playing on the microphone' or 'God Forbid', it was another 'new way' I was going to have to learn.

A very strange male voice came on the loudspeaker and I heard him say in a very odd and almost 'EERIE' way... "Box-Boys ... Where Are You?... Our Customers Are Waiting..." And immediately following that statement, there was a shrill 'whistling'. You know, like 'whistling for the dog to come'. I later found out that it was the Store Manager, Adam, and he'd gotten into the habit of doing that to 'show-off' a little humor to our Customers.

For the first time in the two hours I'd been there, I found myself saying "What on God's Earth does that have to do with a Grocery Store?" I was taken back a bit, but again, I returned to stocking the shelves. Many other 'new things' would end up on the 'list of stuff' I'd learn while I was there at the Kirksville Hy-Vee.

We stocked until 3:00 AM the next morning and by then, we had gone clear through the store and stocked the entire truckload of groceries that had come from Hy-Vee's warehouse in Chariton, IA earlier in the day.

We were tired.

I remember going back to my rented place there in Kirksville and sleeping until almost noon. I was due back into work at 2:00 PM and I'd been told we'd have 'another truck-load' to put on the shelves...I was amazed...

I'd made the move to 'bigger things' and I knew I was about to add 'yet another' chapter to my Hy-Vee career. Little did I know then that I'd eventually have 'Chapters' in eight different stores.

Over the years, I have thought to myself that I would like to have had a video of my facial expression when Adam 'whistled for the Box-Boys'.

All I could think about at that moment was...

'WOOF-WOOF'...

'Who Let The Dogs In ?'

'Four-Wheeling In A Two-Wheeler !' ...

Machismo seems to take over in a Hy-Vee Store wherever you get young men working together and somebody starts bragging or telling about something they can do better than others can do it...Yes, that 'Macho Feeling' seems to just 'blossom out' and before you know it, there's a great story coming out of it.

I was a Full-timer at the Kirksville, MO Hy-Vee from 1971-1973. I was a College Student at now Truman State University. Many of the Hy-Vee Crew there at the time were College Students and we all got along very well. In fact, we all got to be close friends.

In the Spring of 1973, I put myself in a position that was nearly always 'remembered' and laughed about when groups of the old Kirksville crew gathered for a party. It is a really great story and it should live for a long time into the future.

Let me tell you how it all happened...

One day, the Breakroom 'conversation' had focused on the new 4-wheel drive K5 model Chevy Blazer that one of our Full-timers, Jim, had recently purchased. It was touted proudly, by Jim that ... "Hell, it'll go anywhere!"

Stories of Jim taking his new Blazer out into Thousand Hills State Park to go 'Mudding' were all over the Store and the vehicle was becoming

somewhat of a 'heroic figure' among our crew. I had ridden in the Blazer at the State Park and I have to admit, that it did go through about all levels of mud and it sure was lots of fun.

So, in the Breakroom one morning, the Blazer's owner, Jim, was again talking about going 'mudding' and the subject of "Could it climb the hill behind the store?" came up. Now, the hill back there had been created alongside of the Highway 163 Business Route and it ran up the backside of the store. It must have been about 150 feet or so from highway level to the 'Back Lot' of the store. The incline was very steep and there had been virtually no plant growth on the hill since it was completed. The rains from the previous day or so had the hill in a 'pretty muddy' condition.

At this point, when the subject of 'The Blazer' and it 'Climbing the Hill' came up, all the guys were offering their opinions as to whether it 'would' or 'wouldn't' climb the hill from the highway to the store. I couldn't resist, so I finally said "Oh, baloney, my old Comet could make it up that hill!". I had a 1963 Mercury Comet convertible with a small V8 engine and an automatic transmission.

And that's how my mess started...

A 'Bunch of Guys', 'Pride' and 'My Big Mouth'... Yup, that's all it took. The look of a dare and not wanting to back down glared at everyone listening. So, with that, we all took off out the back door. Jim got 'The

Blazer' and I got the Comet and 'The Duel in the Mud' was on.

The situation was like this. Each of us would take a 'running start' and leave the highway driving up the hill to the Back Lot of the store. It really did look easy... However, the only easy part was the 'talking about it' part. The results turned out to be anything but easy.

So, there we were, Jim and 'The Blazer' and me and my '63 Mercury Comet---along with about 15-20 of the guys from the store. Everyone was 'hooting and hollering' as Jim and I made our way around and down to the highway. We put on a pretty good show as we 'honked and waved' and 'revved' our engines. We were having a great time as we 'showed-off' for the rest of them.

It was pretty ridiculous actually.

Jim decided he would go first. He left the road at about 40 miles per hour and after 'throwing mud' (and a deafening roar) everywhere, he made it up the hill to the cheers of the rest of the guys. He had a big wide grin on his face as he got out of 'The Blazer' and waved at me.

Now, it was my turn...I was doomed.

So, I left the highway at about 40 miles per hour and I think the first half or two-thirds of the trip was completed with basic 'Physics'--you know, 'Mass Combined with Motion', but that was about all it was.

Quickly, it became mostly 'Speed and Mud'...And of course, with the 15 or 20 guys watching and laughing.

The Comet soon reached a point about 20 or 30 feet from the top of the hill where it became so 'deeply embedded' in the mud that it was absolutely not moving another inch. So, I shut it off and got out.

I would bet the roar of the guys could be heard for a quarter-mile. There were 15 or 20 guys "hooting and howling' at the tops of their lungs. It really was pretty funny, so I joined in and we all had a great laugh. At that moment, the story had just joined the 'History Books' as one that would live-on for a long-long time in the Kirksville Store.

But then the 'Real Humiliation' came...

I had to borrow about 4 large 'tow-chains' from the various guys. We hooked them 'end-to-end' and I proceeded to have Jim and 'The Blazer' pull 'The Comet' and me to the top of the hill. The engines were screaming and my tires were flying and 'throwing mud' everywhere. When we got to the top of the hill, the Comet was covered so heavily in mud that I don't think you could tell its true color.

We made it, but I still laugh when I think about

Two-Wheeler 'Mudding' At Hy-Vee ! ...

“I’d Say...About This Tall” ...

As Hy-Vee evolved from those primitive ‘Supply Stores’ of the 1930’s into the modern ‘State of The Art Stores’ that are built today, ‘Growing Pains’ in the stores happened all the time as the stores grew in Sales.

Now, after the nearly nine decades that Hy-Vee has operated in America’s Midwest, one thing that is certain in Hy-Vee is that not every store is like another. The ‘Demographics’ are different, the ‘Climates’ are different, the ‘Economics’ are different based on clientele and the stores are not all built to the same blueprints. All of this combined with the fact that each Store Manager runs his own store and has complete Autonomy.

Hy-Vee is ‘unique’ to say the least.

It’s a proven fact that when a store needs more space and an expansion is necessary, many times, it’s easier to build a complete new store than it is to try to ‘change’ the existing store to what you want. Walls need to move, Plumbing needs moved, Refrigeration Lines need moved and that all means trying to do it while a store is ‘Open for Business’.

That’s where the hard part comes in.

‘Small Projects’, however, are routinely done to accommodate an individual store’s needs and many times, that configuration is left up to the Store

Manager to get it done locally and with a minimal amount of expense.

One such example proved to be a 'Good and Bad' thing all rolled into one. I was there when it happened and this is how it all came down.

Or up, in this case...

In 1971, I was working at the Kirksville, MO Hy-Vee while going to college and the store was doing lots and lots of Sales Volume for the space the store had to offer. It was one of Hy-Vee's larger Sales stores and it was highly profitable. Our store in Kirksville was 'bulging at the seams' and some things had to be done to help. Our Store Manager was a sharp operator named Adam. Adam had 'Opened' the Store brand new just 10 years earlier and he'd been very successful at running our store during all of those years.

It was a constant effort to know where to store any excess stock in the store and the old saying about "Higher Inventory Equals Higher Labor Cost" was holding true in our case. If you got a large amount of an item in on the Hy-Vee truck, it just plain got in the way to stack it all up in the Backroom until it was sold. So, needing a 'solution for space', we found an 'unused space' in the Backroom. Along two walls of the Backroom, we decided that there was enough space to put some small 'decks' suspended from the ceiling with steel rods and plywood flooring. These would be used for the storage of the 'highly

breakable' potato chips that carried the Hy-Vee label and needed to be handled as few a number of times as possible to keep the breakage to a minimum. Nobody likes broken potato chips and we hoped that system of storing them would prove to be our answer. We were committed to keeping our Customers buying the Hy-Vee Potato Chips repeatedly, with confidence, because they were nice and pristine in shape.

So, as 'Hy-Vee People' do, when we observed how well this system for the Hy-Vee Potato Chips was working-out for us, the 'minds' started looking at another similar problem that was occurring and causing breakage too... Cookies and Crackers.

Like Hy-Vee Potato Chips, the Cookies and Crackers carrying the Hy-Vee name came in on the Hy-Vee delivery trucks from the Hy-Vee Warehouse in Chariton, Iowa. Storing them in the Backroom also had a 'breakage issue' and just like Hy-Vee Potato Chips, nobody likes broken cookies and crackers either.

Then, an idea was 'hatched'...

In looking at the Backroom and the layout of it, it was observed that an area over the Backstock (excess stock) of Cleaning Supplies was perfect for a deck to be 'hung from the ceiling rafters' like the Hy-Vee Potato Chip decks had been along the walls. This new deck could be 10'x10' and it would be perfect for the excess inventory of Hy-Vee Cookies and Crackers. The new deck would be a huge help for

times when either Hy-Vee Cookies or Hy-Vee Crackers were in the weekly Newspaper Ad and then the needed quantities were large.

A local Carpenter 'Fix-it Man' was called and he reported to the Store. Our Store Manager, Adam, took him to the Backroom and they looked at the construction of the Potato Chip Decks he'd built just a short time before. Then, Adam took him to the Backstock area for the Cleaning Supplies that would be used for the Hy-Vee Cookies and Crackers deck and they surveyed that area. They agreed it would be a great idea and the 'Fix-it Man' said it would be easy to do.

So, the 'Fix-it Man' made a list of the supplies he needed and he went off to the lumber yard to get those items. It wasn't a hard task, but the weight on this deck was going to be more than the Potato Chip decks, so he needed more in the way of materials. When he returned, he unloaded the items and since it was late in the day, he said he'd return the next morning to start on the project.

Our next task necessary to prepare the area was to move everything currently stacked on the floor there to another area to make space available for him to work easily with his ladder and so forth.

We moved it that evening and we were ready...

As he said he would, the 'Fix-it Man' returned the next morning to build the new Hy-Vee Cracker Deck. He

'measured and cut' and he had the whole project organized, laid out and ready to install, but the only remaining decision left to make was 'just how high off the floor' did Adam want the Cracker deck? The steel rods were threaded and they could be hung and then cut-off at the desired length.

So, the 'Fix-it Man' sent word to the store's Office that he wanted to see Adam in the Backroom. Adam then made a trip to the backroom to find out why he was wanted back there. After explaining what he needed, the 'Fix-it Man' waited on Adam for the answer of 'how high' off the floor the deck should be.

Adam's mind was busy on 'Office Stuff' and not really giving it much thought, he just simply walked to the center of the proposed new deck area and he put his hand flat on the top of his head and then walked out from under his hand and he said "I'd say about this high off the floor." So, the 'Fix-it Man' measured Adam's hand off the floor and that was it...

It was decided.

The only problem with the whole calculation (or lack of) was that Adam was not a tall man and his measurement of 5'7" off the floor was not high enough for most people to comfortably be able to walk under the new Hy-Vee Cracker Deck without hitting their head on it.

It would be a safe bet to say that 'hundreds' of clerks (myself included) in the Kirksville Store hit their head

on that Hy-Vee Cracker Deck over the next 20 years before a completely new store was built to replace the old one. The 'Cracker Deck Idea' was great...

There were a couple of "Side Effects", however, ...

They were "Feet and Inches" ...

It was a quick decision that

'Decked A Lot Of People'...(Literally)

"But, Officer, He's On A Leash." ...

As Charles Hyde and David Vredenburg knew all along at the outset of their partnership in 1930, small towns produce some wonderful people and some wonderful memories of the things they do. 'personality' adds so much to the 'day to day' routines

As the years rolled along in Hy-Vee's Heritage, transporting cash, checks and receipts to the Bank at night started to take a more important a bit of strategy. To keep from being robbed and also to make sure the money and receipts made it to the Bank safely, some towns had employees follow each other to the Bank for some extra coverage, some towns started 'wiring' their store's Safe with an electronic alarm and the money was left in the stores overnight, and some stores even got Police escorts every night so the money and Hy-Vee People were assured of being safe on the trip to the Bank.

The Kirksville, MO Store Manager, Adam, had made an arrangement with the Kirksville Police to take the 'Night Manager on Duty' to the Bank and deliver him back again to the store. It really worked out well and it was a very safe way to do it. It was simple. A call was made to the Police Department at the time each night as the trip to the Bank was needed. A Police Squad Car would show up very quickly at the store's front door to pick me up (or someone else on duty) and the trip 'to and from' the Bank was made. We got

to know the Officers pretty well on these trips. They were great guys.

Now, in every town, there are 'Town Characters'. Some are sane, but 'just fun-loving' and then sometimes, you'd swear that some of them are 'just 'plain nuts" ...

On one trip to the Bank in 1972, I met one of them in 'the latter category'...His name was Angelo.

Angelo was a 'pretty well-known character' around Kirksville and the Police Officers knew him and his 'antics' all too well. He was known to have done lots of 'on the edge' type of stuff and he was always the center of a call to respond to where he was and to what he was doing.

It was almost always fun.

So, one night, I wrapped up the bags of money I needed to take to the Bank and I made the usual call to the Kirksville Police to ask for the ride to the Bank. I waited about 10 minutes and then Officer Davey showed up with his Officer Partner in the Squad Car and we took off. It didn't matter what came up while we were on the way to the Bank, the Bank stop was always taken care of first. Sometimes, however, after the stop at the Bank had been made, we'd get in on a 'side trip' that was really fun for us and usually fun for the Officers too. We'd stop a motorist for speeding or we'd help someone with a breakdown.

Whatever it was, it usually was a short 'side-trip' and we'd be back at the store soon.

Now, Angelo's 'pranks and antics' were known to cause turmoil, but they were never really illegal stuff. They were just plain nuisances for everyone involved. His reputation was a long and interesting one. Why, he'd even been known once to entice a well-known local 'female character' into having sex with him through the bars of their adjoining cells on a night they were both held for a short time and then turned loose again. Angelo just had it in him to do anything that his 'little mind' could conjure up.

So, as we made the stop at the Bank, I deposited the money bags in the Night Depository Drawer. I had just climbed back into the back seat of the Squad Car, when a call came in to Officer Davey and his Partner that Angelo was at the downtown movie theater... "Scaring the heck out of people' going in and out of the theater." Officer Davey turned and asked me if I had a few extra minutes that they could respond. Knowing it would be fun, I quickly said I had the time and that I could ride along to the call.

With that, we took off for the downtown area to see what Angelo was up to. With 'lights on' and no siren, we headed downtown and as we got to the movie theater, there was a rather large crowd gathered there. Through the crowd, we could see Angelo moving about and laughing very hard as he moved.

As he moved about, so did the people in the crowd... Rapidly and rather 'Herky-Jerky' in those movements.

Then, we got a glimpse of what he was doing.

Angelo had about a 6' snake tied up in a crude type of 'leash' and he was letting it 'slither around' close to people as they tried to enter or leave the movie theater...It really was funny and even the two Officers I was with laughed out loud when they saw what Angelo was up to. Even though this 'Snake Charming' by Angelo was funny, it couldn't be allowed so the Officers moved to the center of the crowd to where he was and said "Angelo, the snake has to go."

It was Angelo's response that is so etched in my mind. He looked straight into the face of Officer Davey and he said "But, Officer, he's on a leash".

Lots of the people in the crowd laughed and with the threat now gone, one of the Officers got a cloth bag out of the trunk of the Squad Car and they asked Angelo to put the snake in the bag. They said they'd "Take it and turn it loose" in a wooded area on the edge of town.

Reluctantly, Angelo unleashed the snake and slipped it into the cloth bag. A piece of string was used to tie it shut and the bag was placed in the trunk of the Squad Car.

Angelo was told to go home and he left. We headed back to the store laughing and talking about Angelo and his snake.

For a long time after that, we joked about

Going 'Snake Hunting' On The Way Back From The Bank ! ...

“Our Customers pay the bills.”

Dwight C. Vredenburg

President, CEO and

Chairman of the Board

(Deceased)

“No Boys Back Here” ...

Store microphones and loudspeakers in the ceilings of Hy-Vee Stores for communications were a great innovation of the late 1940’s... Until then, the primitive 1200 square foot ‘Supply Stores’ of the 1930’s were small and there weren’t as many Customers being taken care of at any given time like there would be later on in Hy-Vee’s growth. In those days of the 1930’s and even into the early 1940’s, if something needed checked on for a price or if the phone call that was coming in was for someone in another Department, it was simply a ‘hollering around the store’ that passed the message along...It meant that no matter what the subject was, everyone was going to be in on it...And it sometimes got really funny or embarrassing.

In the early 1940’s though, things were changing. The stores were getting larger physically and ‘innovation’ took over. With the advent of the store microphones and ceiling-mounted loudspeakers in the early 1940’s, they became a ‘time-saver’ and ‘a nuisance’ all at the same time. It seemed that ‘invariably’, one person would start to ask something over the loudspeaker to someone in another area of the store and ‘another somebody’ would pay no attention to the already started conversation and they too, would start out talking over the loudspeaker. Obviously, it could get ‘pretty funny’, ‘pretty embarrassing’ or ‘pretty maddening’... depending on what part of the equation you were in.

The typical questions or comments over the loudspeaker were things like "We need more help up front please" or "We need another Checker up front please" and also things like "John, phone call on line #1 please". Almost every conceivable thing was said at one time or another and 'once in a while', laughter could be heard everywhere in the store because of the 'comment' and the 'response back' made over the loudspeaker.

Mostly, 'the response'...Yes, the 'fun part' was 'the response'.

Another irony was that it seemed like a 'select few' were the ones that said the most annoying or interesting things on the loudspeaker for 'God and everyone else' to hear. In most cases, if they had just stopped to think of what they were going to say and how they were going to say it, things would be fine, but, "Noooooo" ... What was said was usually a real 'Zinger' and it lived for a long time in a store's history.

Here's how this story got 'blurted out'...

While I was a college student and working in the Kirksville, MO Store in 1972, something happened that created a real 'roar of laughter' and a real 'roar of anger' at the same time. It wasn't an honest mistake, but nonetheless, it happened and it was 'one for the ages'.

Elaine was one of the Full-time Cashiers and she had a habit of asking things in an annoying way over the

loudspeaker and it was generally the 'Men' in the store who hated the way she said these things. She was loud with her voice and her 'tone' just sort of got people 'riled a bit'...It was 'innocent' on her part, but you never knew 'when' something was going to come across the loudspeaker from Elaine that would be the 'Talk of The Day'...and the 'response' was even better.

Now, Elaine was always busy at her Cash Register checking the Customers through because she was very popular with them. She was usually busy taking care of the people who wanted 'only Elaine' to help them. That 'loyalty' was one of the big benefits' of having long-time residents and friends of lots of people working in the store. Elaine was loved by all and she was a 'Great Hy-Vee Friend' to everyone.

On the day of this story, a Customer came through Elaine's Cash Register lane to 'check-out'. She unloaded her groceries onto the conveyor belt that would move them to Elaine and as she finished, she said "I really wanted some of those Oscar Mayer Hotdogs that are in the ad, but the shelf was empty."

So, not missing a beat, Elaine said "Well, let's check on those." And she leaned into the microphone and blasted out "Boys, do you have any of the Oscar Mayer Hot-Dogs that are in the ad?" and then she stood up straight and looked at her Customer while waiting for the response to come.

And was it ever coming!

You see, the response that was coming had been brewing for quite a long time in the Meat Department as Elaine always referred to them as "Boys" ... They hated her calling them "Boys" and 'Today', they were going to change that.

After a few seconds of waiting and a 'small-talk comment' or two with her Customer, Elaine got a response to her question. The Meat Manager, Jim, came on the loudspeaker and said... "We don't have any boys back here, Elaine."

Instantly, the 'whole store' erupted in laughter and I remember watching Elaine as it happened...There was not one hint of humor on her face as she 'apologized' and 'very courteously' finished taking care of a 'now embarrassed' Customer who was going home without any Hot-dogs and was 'embarrassed' on top of that.

You could easily see that Elaine was furious. She might just as well have had 'Mad' stamped on her forehead. I didn't blame her for being upset.

Soon after, the moment presented itself for her to make a quick exit from her Cash Register and Elaine slipped away to the back of the Store where she confronted a 'Meat Department full of laughter'. There were 'words' exchanged between Elaine and Jim and it wasn't a pretty sight to see or hear.

Everyone in the Store had ‘heard it’ and everyone in the store had ‘laughed at it’...

Everyone except Elaine.

From then on...Things were asked a bit differently over the loudspeaker.

It was the day the Meat Department Guys

‘Separated The Men From The Boys !’

“There is no one key to Success...It is a whole ring of keys.”

Dwight C. Vredenburg

President, CEO and

Chairman of the Board

(Deceased)

"Wow ! That Smells" ...

Large Dairy Coops that we know today were not always the way Hy-Vee's Customers got their Fresh Milk, Eggs and Dairy Products. Those small 'Supply Stores' of Southern Iowa and Northern Missouri towns of the 1930's each had a 'Supplier' that had a herd of Dairy Cows and those Suppliers had a small little Dairy Barn from which they provided Milk, Cottage Cheese, and Cream to the Stores. It was 'the way it was done' in those days.

Eggs were locally purchased from Egg Suppliers that bought the eggs from local 'Chicken Farmers' and then the eggs were 'candled' which is the process of going into a dark room and holding an egg up to a light and checking for blood spots inside. All of this 'gathering and sorting' was done by hand and it was a 'small-town' network from 'Farm to the store'.

I even remember in the mid-1960's we bought eggs at Hy-Vee from Gloyer Hatchery and Ramseyer Hatchery both in Washington, IA. We also bought eggs from some individual 'Chicken Farmers' who had proven to be good suppliers too. Cartons were always 're-used' and we might even have to rinse-off the eggs occasionally to remove the 'spots of Chicken Poop' from them, but that was part of 'doing business in small towns of the Midwest' in those long-ago times of Hy-Vee's beginnings.

If some of Hy-Vee's towns were close enough together in those days, the stores in the area would buy from one Supplier who was large enough to handle all of their business and make the deliveries as the stores needed the items. If a store had no other Hy-Vee relatively close to it, a 'deal was struck' with someone locally for them and they had 'Milk, Dairy Products and Eggs' from someone close-by. It worked for the times and the quality of the products was 'adequate'.

Well, sort of...

As the decades rolled along, the 'large mechanized farms' came into existence and sanitation improved along with quality and delivery to the stores. Those old 'connections' gave away to the 'Big Operations' and those 'Bigger Suppliers' of the 21st Century are now 'Huge' and handle 'hundreds of stores' all over the Midwest.

My earliest recollections of Dairy Products and Eggs only go back to the mid 1960's and it was 'primitive' by today's standards. Things happened then that will never happen again and those 'things that happened' produced a lot of fun stories that need to be told and kept alive in Hy-Vee's History.

One such event was relayed on to me by my good friend and respected mentor, Don. Don was the Store Manager I worked for at the Iowa City, IA #2 Hy-Vee Store from 1975 until early 1977. I was Don's Assistant Store Manager and I learned 'a ton of stuff'

from Don. We talked a lot about Hy-Vee and I always listened intently to his 'stories of Yester-Year' in Hy-Vee. Don is 12 years older than me and 'he too' had come up through Hy-Vee's 'Ranks'. One of his 'stops along the way' was to be the Store Manager at the Albany, MO Hy-Vee Store from 1966 until 1972. Don and his wife, Phyllis, became a big part of the town of Albany while they were there. They made many 'lifelong friends' there.

Don's 'Dairy Story' got 'Hatched' like this....

In 1966, the Hy-Vee in Albany, MO was in a building of 1200 Square Feet. It was a 20' X 60' building with two aisles and a small Meat Department at the back of the Store. It had a small 'Produce Section' in one of the aisles and virtually no Frozen Foods due to such limited space. Excess Stock was kept in the basement of the Store. There were two Checkout Counters at the store's Front End and the Sales Volume was about $4,000 per week. Home Delivery accounted for about 40% of Don's Business in Albany in 1966.

So, you can easily see that Hy-Vee had actually 'grown roots' in these smaller towns and even though the decades of the 1950's and 1960's were producing Hy-Vee Stores of much larger size and in much larger towns, 'lots' of business was still 'in the Roots of the Company' in towns like Albany, MO.

The Albany Hy-Vee in this story had a Dairy Supplier that was a 'very small operation'. The store did get

enough Milk and Butter from them, but the supplier could not supply much more than that and still have been able to handle it.

It was a good relationship for Hy-Vee, however and it was a source for a big staple item.

One day, Don's Customers started coming in with Milk that they said "Didn't taste good" and they complained to Don that "It didn't smell right" either. The number of Customers coming in with 'Milk Returns' started to increase even more over the next day or two. The Customers each got a replacement or a refund, but their descriptions of the Milk and the 'Taste' and 'Smell' sounded very strange. Don called his supplier and asked to meet with him about the Milk. The supplier agreed and they decided on meeting at the store the next morning.

So, when the next morning came, the supplier came to Hy-Vee and met with Don about the 'Smelly Milk'. There had to be an answer, 'But what was it?' Don was eager to know since he didn't want his Customers to buy Milk somewhere else in Albany. Hy-Vee had a competitor there in town and Don certainly didn't want to let his business go to them. He had to find out.

The 'answer' was about to come...

And what an 'answer' it was.

Don's Dairy supplier explained to Don that "What a Dairy Cow eats can sometimes affect the taste of the

Milk that the Cow will then produce." And sometimes that's not good for the taste... Don's supplier went on to admit to Don that "He'd known of his Cows eating some odd stuff that week', but he had hoped it wasn't so much that it would get into the taste."

But it had...

Don's supplier said "The Cows had gotten into the garden and they ate the tops off the Garlic planted in the garden."

And 'Voila'! ... Garlic flavored Milk!

They laughed about it and the supplier assured Don that it wouldn't happen again in the future. He remained a good supplier for many years and the story is remembered fondly by Don.

I love to hear him tell it.

It was the Time...The Cows

'Spiced Things Up' In Missouri !

"Don't just say you care...
Show them."

Ronald D. Pearson

President, CEO and

Chairman of the Board

(Retired)

Bury It Deep...

Hy-Vee's History with alcohol has been a very 'long and complicated journey' over many decades.

Hy-Vee got its start in 'The Bible Belt' of the Midwest and in that area of America and many things were considered 'taboo'. Alcohol was right there at the 'top of the list' alongside of Gambling and that too, would change forever in the late 1900's.

Those early "Supply Stores' of Charles Hyde and David Vredenburg's had emerged in 1930 in Southern Iowa and Northern Missouri during a time near the end of 'Prohibition' of the 1920's and early 1930's. The strong resistance of alcohol by many people in America's Heartland took a long time to overcome after that period. The 'acceptance' of alcohol came 'hand in hand' with opening the stores on Sundays too. Religious Beliefs lived strong in the Midwest.

The 'Midwest Bible-Belt' and other parts of America were still closing their stores on Sundays then and when that started changing, Hy-Vee felt the pressure' from its Customers to open on Sundays. Hy-Vee wanted to look 'reluctant', so the Store Managers asked for 'volunteers' to work Sundays. Of course, they were paid and even paid 'time and a half' wages as a 'Premium Pay' for the work. Eventually, being 'open' and working on Sundays became 'The Norm'.

Beer sales in the Retail Stores of the Midwest proved to be even a bigger problem yet, however. At that

time, mostly Taverns sold Beer in Iowa and Missouri. The Taverns' existence pretty much 'mirrored' America in that they were separated from those who didn't want to be anywhere near alcohol. Tavern locations were generally approved by a 'Town Council' and Taverns were only allowed in 'certain areas' that were not near the 'Business District'. The intent was to separate them from 'Family Activity' whenever possible. It worked, but it did give a 'seedy' atmosphere around them and it was a 'stigma' for the townspeople to have an area like that in their town.

As the 1950's and 1960's rolled along, the 'acceptance' of Grocery Stores selling Beer had started in the Midwest. That 'acceptance' was very slow by Customers in those early years due to the 'stigma' of someone 'consuming alcohol'. The Taverns had sold Beer for a few decades by then, but near the end of the decade of the 1960's Hy-Vee was ready for the move and they 'applied for' and was 'granted' Beer Permits for the sale of Beer in many of its Stores. It was a 'big milestone' for Grocery Stores all over the Midwest, but especially for Hy-Vee.

It was still an 'uphill battle' for sure, however.

Beer Permits and Beer Sales were very slow to start in Hy-Vee because people were 'embarrassed' to be seen buying Beer in the stores...Especially women who felt it 'cheapened' them to be seen with Beer in their grocery cart. Hy-Vee solved some of that

feeling by putting stacks of paper bags on the shelves where the Beer was at. Most people who had been 'embarrassed' then just quietly slipped the Beer into a bag and it went into their cart with other people 'none the wiser'...Although everyone knew what was in the paper bags.

Many States still forbade the sale of Beer on Sundays and that made it a bit more complicated too. To get caught selling Beer on a Sunday was a bad deal and the stores were always on guard to cover it up in the store with white paper or with white sheets draped over it to make sure even the Customers knew it was 'off–limits' for the day. Iowa later passed legislation that made selling Beer on Sundays 'after 12:00 noon' legal.

So, 'inch by inch', Iowa and the surrounding States Hy-Vee serves started allowing more and more types of alcohol to be sold by retailers. By the late 1980's all kinds of Beer, Wine and Hard Liquors were being sold. The 'Old Days' were gone, but not the stories.

There were some 'GREAT ONES' too.

One story that I remember happened at the Kirksville, MO Hy-Vee Store in 1972 and I happened to be working when it happened. It was funny then and it's even funnier today, almost 45 years later...'how' it happened, will make you laugh and shake your head...

It went like this...

I was working as a Full-time 'Front-End Manager' at the Kirksville Store at the time of this story. My job was to keep plenty of help up to the Front-End of the store and to approve checks and delegate duties and Breaks for the crew. If there were Customer problems or questions, I was the 'go-to guy' and we dealt with the issue. There were three of us in the position of 'Front–End Manager' at the time and we rotated shifts around our college schedules.

On this particular day, I was standing on the Front-End near the Cash Registers and I saw a 'very old' and 'rather decrepit' woman coming across the front carrying something. As she got closer, I could tell she was looking for someone in charge and she asked me "Are you in Charge?" I said "Yes" and she proceeded to tell me the following story.

She had shopped the week before and bought her needs for the week. She said she always shopped on the same day of the week and that she waited until today to come back because, she said "It was her 'normal day' to shop again".

It seems that she'd gotten home that previous week and she was putting everything away in her cupboards when she came across "the item in the sack" ... And she wasn't even going to call it by name. She said "It was so embarrassing" that she hardly knew what to do or what to say.

She was mortified.

Now, I could tell that the paper sack was 'filthy dirty' and it had been through the dirt pretty good... Little did I know then, it had 'literally' been through the dirt.

I peeked into the bag and I said nothing as I looked up at her face...Then she told me 'The Rest of the Story'...

It seems that when she arrived home the week before, this bag was 'an extra' and it was not hers, but she had gotten it at home by mistake. She knew she'd be coming back this week and she'd return it then... but "Oh, the embarrassment of it all" she said as she looked away and down.

The 'filthy dirty' crumpled paper sack contained a six-pack of canned Beer and she told me that she'd never had Beer in her house "In all her years" and she said "It really started eating away at her morals" about having Beer in the house...So, she took it out after dark and buried it in the backyard. That's why the bag was so filthy. She went on to say "I couldn't stand the thought of anyone finding out I had Beer In my house."

By this point, I was laughing so hard inside because I could hardly wait to tell her story to the rest of the Gang there at the store. On the outside, however, I had to stay 'cool' and assure her that she'd done the right thing by returning it. I continued to be re-assuring and I even told her "Your secret is safe with us... No one will find out you had it."

She 'Thanked' me and then she was off with a shopping cart to do her shopping for the week. She 'floated away' like a weight had just been removed from around her neck... And perhaps it had been.

I still laugh about her telling about

"Burying it in the backyard" ...

It was the time

The 'Old Bag' Buried The Bag ! ...

"As Long As That Happens By..."

Even way back in 1930, Charles Hyde and David Vredenburg had it figured out that 'the image' they wanted to give was an image of being 'Good Upstanding Members' of their small community. Those small towns of Southern Iowa and Northern Missouri were a bit like 'fishbowls' and they knew they didn't want to look like they were the least bit 'awry' of the law. They were right.

When you work for a company like Hy-Vee, you realize over a period of time that you almost live in that 'fishbowl' and more people know who you are than the other way around. People shop with Hy-Vee at least once per week and many people shop even more than that. It's not uncommon for a Customer to see the same faces on most trips into the store and that's where the 'everybody knows each other' atmosphere developed.

In those towns of smaller population, things happen around town and the local Police Department Officers know immediately 'whose car it is' or 'whose house' it may be. In many cases, they even know where that person works.

This story involves an incident in the Kirksville, MO Store in the Winter of 1972-1973. I soon learned that 'I was known around town'.

This is what happened...

I was in my final year of college at now Truman State University there in Kirksville and I was looking ahead to Summer when I would graduate and then we could move on with Hy-Vee to a different store and 'hopefully', a higher position and more money.

As college kids are most times, my wife and I were Newlyweds and we had 'very-little' money. During that last year of school, we stretched to 'make ends meet' on everything and we 'scrimped' to have enough to do a little 'extra something' every few weeks. It was usually a movie or a simple restaurant meal out. Our budget left nothing for anything 'unexpected'.

We both made just enough money to keep my tuition and books up, the rent on our duplex and gas for the old '63 Comet convertible I drove back and forth everywhere. To say we were 'poor' wouldn't have been right, but we could sure see it and feel it from where we were. Between the two of us, we were making $4.62 per hour. By then, I was making $2.52 per hour and my Spouse was making $2.10 per hour at her College Business Office job.

So, in the late Winter of 1973, we got one of those 'April Snows' that come along every few years and the snow just 'buried' Kirksville. The snow piled up everywhere, the roads got shut down and almost everything came to a 'screeching halt'...Including my old '63 Comet.

I was trying to get the Comet home to our rented duplex that afternoon and it just wasn't going well. With no extra money, the tires on the old Comet were just about 'bald' and they got no traction or decent steering for the car on the snow. As I went around a curve near our place, I spun around in a big circle and then landed 'squarely' in the ditch.

With the snow piling up deep and with my 'bald tires', there was no hope of getting it out on its own so I just gathered my stuff, locked the doors and walked to our place which was less than a block away. As the snow continued to fall overnight, the old Comet was 'totally covered' with only a white 'square' of the convertible top sticking out above the snow. That's all you could see of it.

The predicament the old Comet was in must have caught a lot of attention, because that afternoon, it was pictured in the Kirksville Daily Express with a caption about "The Snowfall Causing Area Traffic Problems". We didn't take the local newspaper, but I had lots of people who knew I'd landed in the ditch tell me about it, so I knew it was in there. I 'mustered-up' the 10 cents to buy a copy of the paper for the fun of it. I still have it.

Now, as it happened, I was the Store Employee who lived closest to the store and I could walk to the store easily. It was less than half a mile, so I was asked to 'Open' and 'Close' the Store for the next two days until everyone could get dug out. College

Classes had been cancelled and I was happy to have the extra hours and extra pay. So, for two days, I 'trudged' over and got things going by 9 AM. More of the crew made it in by noon and I'd go home. Then, I would 'trudge' back to the store before 6 PM and close things down only to 'trudge' home afterward

As those two days rolled along, the town got dug out and things started to loosen up and almost everything opened back up as well. People were back to driving around again... Except me. 'no money' meant I'd just have to wait a few days and as the snow melted, maybe I could just 'drive the old Comet out of the ditch' and I'd save some money I didn't have.

It was a 'Good Plan'.

Later, on the third day after the Big Snow, Officer Davey from the Kirksville Police Department came to the store and he asked for me. I came to where he was in the store and we exchanged nice comments and then he said "Rick, isn't that your car in the ditch over there off Shannon Lane?"

Now, I knew Officer Davey pretty well as I rode to and from the Bank with him in the Squad Car many nights each week. Because of that, I was trying hard in my mind to figure out how to make the best explanation as to why the old Comet was still in the ditch. It was at that moment, I thought I'd be 'cute' and see if I could get out of it easily, so I said "Yes, Davey, that's

my old Comet over there." And I waited for his response.

Officer Davey said "So, when are you going to get it out of the Ditch?" And me, trying to be cute and give him a bit of a 'Snow Job' of my own, I quickly replied "Well, you know, Davey, the Good Lord put all that snow around that car and I figure that when he takes all that snow away from around it, I'll just drive it out."

Hmmmm... I was rather proud of my answer.

I wasn't at all prepared for his 'PRICELESS' answer though...

Officer Davey looked at me and he smiled and he said "Sounds good to me and as long as that all happens by 5:00 tonight, we'll be okay."

At that point, I knew I was 'HAD'. I had to go to a few of my friends and borrow a couple of bucks from each to get the $10 for the Tow-Job I knew it was going to take to get it out. Later, and just before 5:00, I watched the old Comet be pulled from the ditch and I drove it one block home.

It was the

Great 'Snow Job' of '73...

(Well, Almost...)

“There is no substitute for Quality.”

Ronald D. Pearson

President, CEO and

Chairman of the Board

(Retired)

"Coffee and...Bank Money ??"

Safes and 'Burglar Alarms' were way too expensive for the Founders of 'The Supply Stores' to afford in the 1930's. They were generally within close enough 'walking distance' to their Bank to just take the cash over 'on foot' when they needed to. Sometimes, cash was "hidden' in a safe place within the store too for overnight security and it was even taken home with Charles or David for the night occasionally. Any way you study it, the issue of 'How to protect the cash' got more sophisticated over the years and during that time, many circumstances played a role in that.

In those years before Hy-Vee used Armored Car Services and before they had 'Electronic Alarms' on the Safes in the Stores, the Store's money and Daily Receipts had to be driven to the Bank by one of the members of management after the Store closed each night. In most cases, the person taking the money bags to the Bank's 'Night Deposit Drawer' would do it on his way home from the store. Sometimes, this routine got pretty funny in the process.

Now, I'm not saying that the 'closing-up guys' at any Hy-Vee liked to have a 'Beer or two' after work, but that's the way it seemed to shape up lots of times while that person was driving the Bank Bags to the Bank. In most cases, a 'cold 6-pack' or even a 12 pack of Beer was 'cracked open' to enjoy on the way home. Obviously, this was not legal and sometimes it was a pretty close call for the driver.

That's what happened here in this story...

One night in the late 1960's, Tommy, one of Hy-Vee's management people at one the Des Moines, IA Stores, was closing up the store and the routine would take him to the Bank on the way home for the money to be deposited. Before Tommy left the store, he bought some cold Beer, some donuts and a few other things he needed at home. He carried all the stuff out to his car in Hy-Vee paper sacks and set them on the front seat next to him.

Upon getting into the car to go to the Bank and home, Tommy 'cracked open' a cold Beer and began to enjoy it as he drove slowly to the Bank. It wasn't a long drive to the Bank for the guys from the Store, but it was a long enough drive that the Des Moines Police would occasionally 'tail them' for a bit of added protection while they took the money to the Night Deposit Drawer at the Bank.

So, as Tommy drove slowly and sipped on his cold Beer, he didn't notice for a few minutes that he was being followed by a Police Squad Car. When he did notice the Squad Car, Tommy almost went into a panic. There he was with 'thousands of dollars' of Hy-Vee money, some groceries in a bag and a six pack (well, now almost a 5-pack) of cold Beer. What would he do if he got stopped...?? It would surely result in his arrest for consuming beer in a vehicle and then ... 'What about his job?'... 'worry' was really setting in now.

Tommy decided he'd 'zig-zag' a little on the way to the Bank to see if the Squad Car would turn off and go another direction. So, as he made a 'turn here' and a 'turn there' on a little longer route to the Bank, the Squad Car kept right on following him. It didn't look like the Squad Car was going to turn, so Tommy had no choice, but to go to the Bank and deposit the Money Bags in the Night Deposit Drawer.

He was almost shaking by now.

As Tommy turned into the Bank, the Squad Car turned in too and it was becoming obvious that the Police were making sure he got the money there safely. This might even mean a few words between Tommy and the Officers at the end of the 'Escort'.

Tommy's mind raced.

What was he going to say...?? Would he act suspicious...?? Would they guess he was 'sipping' an open can of Beer ...?? He was really worked up and in a full-blown state of 'WORRIED'... He had no choice, but to get out and put the Bank Bags in the Deposit Drawer. So, he left the car idling and he grabbed the paper sack of Bank Bags and walked up to the Bank's Night Deposit Drawer. As he did, one of the Officers stepped out of the Squad Car and made some 'small talk' with him. Tommy quickly opened the Bank Drawer and stuffed the paper sack with the Bank Bags (so he thought) down the drawer and then locked it back up.

A few 'appreciation comments' were made by Tommy to the Officers for the 'Escort' and then they each went their separate ways. "Holy Cow" Terry thought to himself as he drove home. "I just dodged a pretty big bullet here". He could have been arrested and the night could have ended far different than it did. He was relieved for sure.

It wasn't until he arrived at home and carried the grocery bags into the house and set them down that he realized he had the Bank Bags there in his kitchen...In his fear of being caught 'sipping' the Beer in his car, he'd gotten flustered and put the paper bag with the donuts and other items in it into the Night Depository Drawer...So, he had to go back out and 'visit' the Bank one more time to get the Money Bags where they needed to be.

It was now that he had a little bit of 'explaining' to do the next morning as to 'why' the bag of donuts and groceries were in the Night Deposit Drawer.

It was the day that Tommy had to tell

'The 'Hole' Story About The Bank !

“Mom…Did You Hear That ??” …

Since the days of ‘The Supply Stores’ in the 1930’s, the people of Hy-Vee have always found ways to make their work fun and to have some Laughs whenever they could. You know the old saying… “Laughter is the Best Medicine.” and the ‘Medicine’ here is to ‘Treat the Monotony’ of routine days.

Working with a lot of people all under one roof is a ‘Blast’. The friends we made and the times we enjoyed together have lived as ‘Wonderful Memories’ for all of our lives. Hy-Vee just simply provides more to an Associate than a paycheck. For most of the people who ever worked in a Hy-Vee Store, it became a ‘way of life’ and they took part of it everywhere they went over the remaining years of their lifetime.

The ‘personalities’ of the people in the stores is a great mix of all types, Quiet, A Bit Shy, Extraverted, Bubbly and lots of ‘Fun-Lovers’. It does take all kinds to work in an atmosphere of 300 or 400 people working together to serve the ‘tens of thousands of Customers’ coming through the door every week of the year. It is those ‘personality differences’ that make Hy-Vee so popular in the Midwest.

It is no accident that the History of Hy-Vee, started all those years ago in those “Supply Stores’ of 1930 with two men who could have not been much farther apart on their ‘Demeanor and Personality’.

Charles Hyde (Hy) was a very serious and detail oriented man who was pretty much 'The Bean-Counter' of the partnership. He excelled in knowing all the numbers and keeping track of the 'Money In' and 'Money Out'. He took care of lots of the 'little stuff' too.

Now, David Vredenburg (Vee), on the other hand, was the outgoing and personable one of the two. He loved being in the store with the crew and the Customers because his biggest attribute was dealing with the people in those Southern Iowa and Northern Missouri Towns. He was the 'Personality' of the Partnership.

It was a perfect 'partnership'...

Over the decades since those early years, the blend of people who have passed through Hy-Vee's doors as Associates and part of 'The Hy-Vee Family', has been just plain 'Phenomenal'. In every town and store, there are people whose lives are 'happy and productive' because of Hy-Vee. They are this way because they are enjoying a life with exposure to lots and lots of people around them and fun times every day.

It has made for some fun memories for all of us over the years.

One 'fun memory' for me happened in the Kirksville, MO Hy-Vee Store that I worked at while I was attending college at now Truman State University. I worked there alongside many longtime residents of

Kirksville as well as many College Students from all over 'Hy-Vee's Territory'. There were lots of Kirksville High School kids working there too.

The story I am about to tell you about involved a young man that I'd gone to high school with in Washington, IA. We were classmates together and coincidentally, we both ended up at college and Hy-Vee in Kirksville at the same time. His name was Ed and the years were 1971 and 1972. Ed sure was lots of fun...both 'socially' and 'at the store'.

His story is told like this.

All of the various jobs in the Grocery Stores require putting the right people in the right places and then making sure they understand the task you want them to do. In nearly 100% of the cases that could be used as examples, Hy-Vee People will 'work their hearts out' to do what they are assigned to do...And they'll even go 'above and beyond' in many cases. So, it was with Ed. He went to the extra lengths to make it fun for everyone.

Now, Ed had been trained to work in the Dairy Department and that was a lot of work in a 'High Sales Volume' store like the Kirksville Store. He was taught the 'important stuff' like... 'watching for code dates', 'rotating the products for freshness' and also making sure that the very fragile Dairy Items were 'handled gently' and 'kept cold'. It was a big assignment and it was not given to just anyone.

It had to be someone who 'cared'.

So, Ed would do all the important things in the Dairy Department and he'd stock the Milk Case from inside the Cooler pushing the products forward on the shelves by way of the sliding doors at the back of the case. Stocking from the 'backside' of the case served a couple of purposes that were 'must do's' and Ed knew all that, but the one thing Ed did 'above and beyond' was to add some 'Personality' to this 'backside' of his department.

'Personality' was on Ed's 'Must Do List' for his life.

Most times, Ed would go out front of his Milk Case to survey the needs of the 're-stocking' he had to do. He'd pull the products forward and organize them in their rows on the shelves, but the whole time he was out there, he was talking to the Customers and 'scouting out' his next 'Happening'. Generally, it didn't take long and then he was back inside the cooler on the 'backside' of the Milk Case... 'ready to go into action'...

You see, it wasn't the 'Adult Customers' he was looking for. Ed was waiting for the 'Little Ones' to come by with their Moms. Ed wanted to get them involved and have some fun with them because Ed knew doing that would get their Moms involved too. He knew that if the kids were 'stirred-up' a little, then he could have some fun watching the Moms talk their way out of it with the kids...Or try to.

Once he was 'back' inside the Cooler and on the 'backside' of the Milk Case, he'd wait for a Mom and Child he'd spotted to come in front of where he was. Then, at just the right time, he'd let out with the 'biggest and loudest' "MOOOOOOOO !" you have ever heard. And it was a 'Bellar-MOOOOOOOO' he'd worked on and perfected over time. It was so convincing that the looks on the kids' faces and the 'immediate reaction' by the Moms to those sounds were the best part of his day. The kids 'knew' it was a Cow and the Moms didn't know 'how' to explain that it couldn't be a Cow... 'Not in a Grocery Store !'

As the day would wear along at Hy-Vee, Ed would repeat his "MOOOOOOO!" many times. His perfected 'Bellar' could be heard all over the Store and everyone laughed when it happened. He was the 'center of attention' and he loved that too. He was a real 'Showman' and after being at Hy-Vee for a couple of years, he went off to play his banjo in an Ozark Music Show. We missed him greatly at Hy-Vee and the kids probably missed him as much as we did.

Ed kept things organized in the cooler and made his Dairy Department into 'The Place to Be' at the Kirksville Hy-Vee...

You see...Ed took care of the herd...

'In The Dairy Barn'...

"Sell the 'Sizzle' not the Steak."

Ronald D. Pearson

President, CEO and

Chairman of the Board

(Retired)

“HOLY COW! ... What Did He Say??”

Over the nearly nine decades of Hy-Vee’s Heritage from ‘The Supply Stores’ of Southern Iowa and Northern Missouri, there have always times in The Stores when the words that come out of someone’s mouth not only take you back a bit, but they almost knock you over. Those comments can be ‘Funny’, they can be ‘Mean’ and in rare occasions, they can be ‘Pretty Off-Limits’ on being appropriate.

One such story left me in total amazement that it was said and I still remember it well today, after 45 years.

Here’s how it came out... ‘Of Jim’s Mouth’....

While I worked at the Kirksville Hy-Vee through college in the early 1970’s, I was a Full-timer at the store and my job as ‘Front-End Manager’ was to ‘Open and Close’ the Store, be in charge of the work duties for the crew and report to “Mitch”, the Store Manager, about the details of the operations of the store while I was in charge.

As a ‘Front-End Manager’, (the term for the position as used by lots of Hy-Vee Stores of the day), I worked a rotating shift that ‘rotated hours’ with two or three other ‘Front-End Managers’ to cover all the hours that the store was open during the seven days each week.

It was a fun job. We ‘interacted’ with lots of people.

One of the duties the ‘Front-End Manager’ was to deal with Customer Complaints, Refunds and

Replacements when necessary. This wasn't really difficult, but once in a while we ran into someone who 'tested our patience' by the attitude with which they approached us on their complaint. Mostly, the Customers were polite and honestly deserving of a 'credit', but the others could be 'difficult'.

One afternoon, a Customer came in and he was carrying a 90% eaten plate lunch from the Deli/Kitchen and he wanted his money back. He said the meal "Didn't taste right." So, I talked with him for a moment or two and then I 'Cheerfully' refunded his money. It was about $3 and he went on his way.

The next afternoon, he returned about the same time of the day with another 90% eaten plate lunch and said he wanted his money back. Again, he said "It didn't taste right", So, I talked with him about it for a few minutes and then I 'Cheerfully' refunded his money...Again.

As the week went along, this same man came back at least three more times and used the same request to get his money back. All totaled, he had now asked for a refund for about five or six days in a row.

At this point, I figured that the best thing to do was to get the Deli Manager, Jim, out from behind the Deli Counter and let him deal with it. I knew Jim would get to the bottom of it for the 'taste issues' and it would be resolved.

What I didn't know was 'how' Jim was going to do it and the way he handled it really sent the whole issue 'over the edge'...

As I went to get Jim, I left the Customer standing alone about 15' from the Deli/Kitchen Counter. I approached the Deli Counter and hollered at Jim to come out to talk to the Customer. Then, I walked back over to where the Customer was and we waited for Jim to come out and help us resolve the refund request.

Jim had been cutting Fresh Chickens to prepare the pieces for frying in the big fryer and when he came out from behind the counter, he carried the sharp pointed 'Chicken Boning Knife' with him. As he approached the two of us standing there, he was wiping the knife on his apron to clean the blade.

So, I explained to Jim (in front of the Customer) that this man was requesting a refund for his meal and that this was the 5th or 6th day in a row that he had been back for a refund with the same reason... He said "It didn't taste right".

As I talked, Jim stood there wiping the knife blade back and forth on his apron in a rather nervous fashion. Then, it happened. Jim shifted the entire situation into a really morbid direction and he said "You know, you S.O.B., I ought to stick this knife in you and walk around you a couple of times."

WOW!

I just about fell over...

I didn't see that one coming at all and I could tell it frightened the Customer as he quickly backed away from Jim and me and he headed for the door.

Jim turned and walked back to the Deli laughing to himself. I quickly walked to the Office and relayed the story to our Store Manager, Mitch. We were both absolutely appalled at how Jim had handled it and when Jim was asked by Mitch "Why did you do that?" Jim's response was "I figured it was the quickest way to scare him off." And then he laughed.

I didn't think it was funny, Mitch didn't think it was funny and I can assure you that the Customer didn't think it was funny. I still shake my head about it today. Somehow, Jim's message must have reached its target because we never saw the Customer again after that...Mitch and Jim had a 'long and private' conversation and we heard nothing more about it.

Mitch did instruct us not to involve Jim in any more Customer refund requests...

It was the day we were glad

Jim 'Didn't Make The Cut' ...

Awww...You Shouldn't Have...

Hy-Vee's 'Down-Home Friendly Spirit' came along as part of the Company's Heritage because the 'roots' were started by the Founders, Charles Hyde and David Vredenburg in very small Southern Iowa and Northern Missouri towns where everyone knew everyone else. Knowing everyone was a real Blessing in a small town, but it lent itself to 'everyone knowing your business' too. Sometimes, when something you did 'got all around town', it could make for embarrassing times.

As the years went along, this 'Down-Home Friendly Spirit' grew along with the Company and when Hy-Vee began to enter the larger towns in the 1950's, it was important to the success of the Company that everyone still try to 'know the customers' and to also try to learn as much of the background on people as they could to keep in touch with their Customers. So, 'Nametags' were issued to the crews and the Customers then began to know their names and they were then able to pass on a 'good' or 'not-so-good' comment on to the Store Management when necessary. It was a 'winner' in the 'long-list' of 'good decisions' that were made early-on that would set Hy-Vee apart from the other stores in a Market area.

Around 1960, when Hy-Vee entered the Des Moines, IA Area with its first Store in the Market, W. T. Dahl, the Founder of the 'now defunct' Dahl Foods, said "Hy-Vee won't make it in the City...They're nothing

but a bunch of Cornmeal Merchants from Southern Iowa." Dahl went on to say that "People in the cities don't want all that Friendliness and Customer Interaction" ... Both were statements that I'm pretty sure W. T. Dahl would go on to regret in later years.

With this 'great asset' of Friendliness, Hy-Vee has gone on to conquer every town it has opened a store in for almost 90 years now. When a store was placed in a new town, the crew hired there was heavily 'trained' to the Philosophy of the 'The Customer Comes First' and that we 'Run These Stores for Our Customers' belief in Customer Satisfaction.

Now, as we have talked about already, 'Fun and Pranks' seem to go along with working in a Grocery Store and sometimes those became a sort of 'Rite of Passage' as the new crew-members come on-board in a store. It's the 'Down-Home Friendly Pranks' that are played that make stories like this one fun to remember.

It's a 'GREAT STORY' and it happened to me. It's still fun to tell this story today...Almost 45 years later.

In August of 1973, I graduated from College at Kirksville, MO and I immediately transferred to the Muscatine, IA Store. I hired on Full-time for $3 per hour...fresh from College. I knew the Store Manager, Lynn, but I didn't know the others in the store. I knew I'd soon learn the names and the personalities of the Department Managers and the Full-timers. I also knew I'd get to work with the Part-timers too and I'd

get to know them as well. Again, there were lots of new faces and names and that's a fun thing too.

I hadn't been in the store, but a day or two when the Bakery Manager, Larry, cornered me early one morning and said "Hey, Rick, we're really happy to have you here in the store and we're going to get a few of the Department Managers together in the Breakroom at 9:30 and treat you to some donuts and coffee."

Now, I thought to myself, how nice that was and I looked forward to 9:30 coming so I could have donuts and coffee with 'The Gang'.

Larry was a rather large man...He was pretty 'Roly-Poly' in his appearance and he always dressed in 'Bakers Whites' clothing. He always wore a black 'clip-on' necktie and a white paper hat too. He was one of those guys that smiled a lot and he was 'Loved by Everyone'.

I was about to see the 'fun side' of Larry the Baker...

As 9:30 approached, I could see some of the crew heading for the Backroom where the Breakroom was and I started to get anxious to get back there and join them. So, I finished the task I was doing and I headed to the Breakroom too.

As I got to the Breakroom, there were about a dozen people in there waiting for me and I recognized several as Department Managers I had met the day before. I saw Jim from the Meat Department, Jim

from the Produce Department, Don from the Deli, Ray the Assistant Store Manager, Lynn, the Store Manager, Larry the Baker and Ric Jurgens who would later go on in his Hy-Vee career to become Hy-Vee's President, CEO and Chairman of the Board. Some of the Full-time Meatcutters and a few others were there too. The Breakroom seemed full. It was a fun group.

As I started to settle in, I poured myself a cup of coffee from the big silver coffee pot that always adorns a Hy-Vee Breakroom, I pulled a couple of paper towels from the holder on the wall by the sink and I sat down across from Larry in the empty spot I knew he was saving for me. Everyone said "Hi' and "Welcome to Muscatine" and everyone was really friendly. It made me feel very good. It was an example of the 'Down-Home Friendly Spirit' that we'd always been taught...

So, I thought.

It was then that Larry the Baker pointed to the large tray of Jelly Bismarks on the table and he said. "Have one—Our Treat" ... So, I picked up the one closest to me and I said "Thanks" to everyone. I sort of waved the Bismark like a 'toast' and then I took the first bite....

OH, MY GOD!... Being the Prankster that he was, Larry had pumped yellow mustard into the Bismarks (at least a few) and the ones closest to me were full

of mustard and not the normal sweet tasting 'Jelly Filling'.

The taste was AWFUL!

So, now, I knew I'd been 'Had' and everyone else knew too...The 'Laughing' and 'Hooting' was so loud that I was sure it could be heard clear out on the Sales Floor. It really was funny! Larry sat there 'smiling' and 'chuckling' the whole time. He was 'proud' of another successful prank on 'The New Kid'.

When the laughing calmed down, they explained that I had just been "initiated" Into the Muscatine Hy-Vee and that it was like a "Brotherhood" and 'Nobody' was to be told about it so the prank could live on by doing it again as others came on-board."

I was 'sworn to secrecy'.

I was at the Muscatine Store for just about a year and I remember 'Having Donuts' to welcome several others during that year...Every time, it got the same reaction...

"Awww...

"You shouldn't have...OH, YUK !"

“Treat people the way you’d like to be treated.”

Dwight C. Vredenburg

President, CEO and

Chairman of the Board

(Deceased)

The Big Getaway...

Bonnie and Clyde were roaming all over the Midwest of America in the early 1930's when the 'fledgling company' known as 'The Hyde and Vredenburg Supply Stores' were getting their 'start'. Things in America were pretty primitive by today's standards. The Customers in the stores were well-known by those early Store Crews and because of that, when 'something went wrong', it was pretty obvious pretty quickly.

Banking over the years has taken many 'twists and turns' to get where the 'Electronic Age' is at now as well. The Banks didn't foresee the 'fraud' that would come in the 1960's and beyond...Policies regarding Personal Checks and the way they are handled would change dramatically. Checks became a real 'source of loss' for the stores and the Banks in the 1960's and beyond.

In those early years of Hy-Vee and Banks, 'Counter Checks' were on each Cash Register on a 'Check-Writing Stand' and many people wrote checks from their Banks by finding the 'Counter Check' from their particular Bank and writing a check on their account at the Bank. These 'Counter Checks' were 'pretty generic' and only contained the name and logo of the Bank, the 'To' and 'Signature' lines as well as the line for the amount of the check being written. There was a small box for the Customer to write in their account number and then it was accepted by the store for

payment. No 'pre-printed" information like today's checks.

In some of Hy-Vee's smaller towns, the account number wasn't even necessary because everyone knew everyone else and it was immaterial. The Bank knew who they were and routed the check to their account. Pretty simple and 'very naïve' for what we know today.

By 1973, Hy-Vee had gotten big enough and there were enough employees in the Company that it was time to put together a 'Safety and Security Department' to oversee Safety issues and Security problems as they arose for Hy-Vee. Employee Theft was growing and Customer Fraud was becoming a big issue in the way of Bad Checks and Shoplifting. Losses were getting larger every year for Hy-Vee. Something needed to be addressed...And Soon...

So, a Private Investigator named Joe Smith (His Real Name) was hired out of Kansas City, MO to head it all up. Joe had also been a Private Investigator in Detroit, MI and in Law Enforcement before that. Joe was an 'Ordained Minister' as well and he actually preached in a rural Church on Sundays. He was truly 'The Man for The Job'!

By Fall of 1973, I was fresh out of college and I was still rather new to the Muscatine Store. It was a large store and its Sales Volume was comparable to the Store in Kirksville I had transferred from. There were lots of Customers and employees. In this story, an

employee would be the subject of the solution to a problem and Joe Smith 'Cracked It Wide Open'.

The 'Big Case' came down like this.

At Hy-Vee in Muscatine, we had been getting checks returned from the Bank as 'bogus' and they were all in the same handwriting on Counter Checks. They were on different Banks and it was obvious that the person scamming the store 'knew the system' and this person also knew they could steal money by way of the Counter Checks.

But 'who' was doing it?

Our Store Manager, Lynn, called the newly hired Joe Smith and asked if he'd come over from the Headquarters in Chariton, IA and help 'Crack the Case'. Joe and Lynn made the arrangements for the 'day and time' he'd come to Muscatine and then we sat back and waited for that day to arrive.

On the day of Joe's initial visit, Lynn and Joe met for quite a while in the Office and I'm sure they discussed the 'who' and the 'what ifs' about the 'bogus checks' and then it came time to visit a couple of the Banks to see if they had seen a pattern in it all. After learning that they hadn't seen much of a pattern, Joe headed back to the store to talk to some of us in the crew about it. He looked at the people who were in the 'Front-End Manager' (or Swingman) position, like me, to help him give some organization to the situation and then after that, he started talking

to others...Cashiers mostly. You see, Joe had a hunch that it was 'an inside job' and someone on our crew was writing the checks and pocketing the money. Joe's sense of direction on the Security Training he had told him to start there because he didn't think a Customer would be so bold as to present themselves 'time after time' to cash the checks that now numbered a couple of dozen checks.

A 'Brilliant' observation by Joe.

So, Joe went through the crew interviewing people and trying to sort out who he thought might be the person doing it and after a couple of days and evenings of all the talking and note taking he'd done, he again met with Lynn and the decision was made to 'put the gentle squeeze' on a couple of people that seemed to stand out in the group.

Joe's 'Sunday Preaching' and dealing with people in his church work had given him the ability to get answers from people in a 'spiritual way' as well as the conventional 'Hot-Seat' approach'. He was good at both. So, they made arrangements to meet outside the store with a couple of people and when they met, he started in with using the softer approach and hoping not to have to use his 'Hot-Seat' approach.

Joe hit the Jackpot. The caper was solved.

A young man that Joe talked to first proved to be the likely candidate in his 'gut hunch'. It was a young

man who was sometimes trusted to take over on the Front-end of the store while the Front-End Manager was 'on break' for a few minutes. When Joe's meeting with the young man was over, the young man confessed to being the 'Bogus Check Writer'.

Joe's approach to it had been to let him know that "It's okay to make mistakes, but it's always better to admit it and come clean with God and One's Inner Guilt". It was an approach that had worked for Joe many times over the years.

By the time the conversation was over and the young man's written confession was taken, the young man led Lynn and Joe to a local bank to get the $1700 amount of money he'd taken by writing the 'bogus checks'. He'd been stealing the money with the idea that he was miserable at home and he was going to run away from home and his plan was use it as his 'Get-Away Money'... It was all returned to the store...Every dime of it.

It was the first of many times I saw Joe Smith 'Crack' a big case at Hy-Vee...

It was a day I saw Joe use

'The Power of The Pulpit' ...

“Our Fresh Flowers, Decorated Cakes and Specialty Fruit Baskets are saying “I Love You” to the recipient. The sender needs to know Hy-Vee sent the message just like they wanted it sent.”

Ronald D. Pearson

President, CEO and

Chairman of the Board

(Retired)

"Send What...??" ...

Even as far back as 1930 in 'The Supply Stores', the people of the future company named 'Hy-Vee' were busy with daily duties and trying to get things done 'on-time' so as to be efficient in the stuff needing done to keep the store running smoothly. Along-side of being busy, 'Humor' was on the scene too and those days produced lots of 'funny stuff' too. Now, after nearly 90 years, we know it's true that the 'Humor' is what keeps the stress down in such an 'unpredictable' type of business.

The Backrooms of the stores were the places that lots of 'behind the scenes' things took place. The re-organizing of merchandise, unloading of trucks and lots of inter-departmental contact between the employees took place in the Backrooms and it's all of this 'interaction' that mixed with the 'Humor' and 'Practical Jokes' along the way.

Wednesdays seemed to be a day when 'lots' of this seemed to occur. That was mostly because 'The Boss' was gone every Wednesday to Headquarters and there was a 'playful atmosphere' while he was gone. Everything got done, but with 'Humor' added to it all.

One such Wednesday in late 1973 at our store in Muscatine, 'The Boss' was at Headquarters in Chariton, IA and we were busy working away at the duties in the store to prepare for the busy weekend

that would be coming up. A story for 'The Ages' crept right in and 'grabbed us'.

Here's the scoop...

The Frozen Foods/Produce Truck had arrived from Hy-Vee's Warehouse in Chariton, IA earlier in the morning and the crews from those departments were busy sorting the new merchandise that had arrived. As it was sorted, it was moved to the proper cooler for stocking later.

The Meat Deliveries had also arrived from the Meat Packers and the 'sides of beef' were swinging on hooks in the Backroom after being weighed and checked-in. The Cheese items were neatly separated from the rest of the merchandise from Chariton and they were ready to be stocked to the Sales Floor. The Grocery Department (Dry Goods) Crew was busy sorting and stocking the newly arrived cases in their department onto the shelves or displays.

During all of this activity, the 'catcalls', 'snide remarks' and 'laughter' abounded. Sometimes, an occasional 'missile' would be launched and someone might get a tomato stain or a grape to the side of the head.

There was a lot going on.

It was at this point that the Hometown Dairy Milk truck arrived and we scrambled to get it unloaded. Milk is the one of the store's most Perishable items

and nearly all effort was made to get it in the cooler right away after it arrived. The Muscatine Store was a 'High Sales Volume' store and we received lots of Milk and Dairy products on these deliveries. It was 'high priority' to get it in quickly.

The Hometown Dairy trucks of that time used a system of 'Milk Dollies' that held four stacks (five high) of wire crates. Each crate held four gallon jugs of milk or an equal amount of half gallons and other dairy products like Cottage Cheese and Dips. The trucks had a 'lift-system' that would allow an entire 'Dolly' of Milk to be lifted out of the truck and lowered to the ground so that it could be pushed on its wheels across the backroom and into the cooler. It made unloading the truck and then the stocking of the dairy cases so much easier to have the Dollies on wheels.

So, the driver of the Hometown truck was busy lowering the Dollies down to the ground and we were busy pushing them into the cooler to keep them properly chilled.

Then it happened...

A Dolly of half-gallon cartons of Milk had been lowered to the ground from the truck. Just after it was pushed into the building, something went wrong and it tipped completely on its side and 'splattered' to the floor of the backroom. The paper cartons burst open from pressure at the tops and most of the 80 gallons of the milk on the Dolly was 'instantly' flooding the floor. We nearly panicked...

It was at this point, that the Humor of the whole thing was captured... Forever.

The Meat Department Manager, Jim, calmly walked over to the wall where the store intercom microphone hung on its hook. He took the microphone off its hook and then made an announcement to everyone in the store. In a very calm voice, he said "Would someone please send a large cat to the Backroom?"

It was 'PRICELESS'...

Our laughter could be heard all over the store and from that moment on, the "Send a large cat to the Backroom story" would live on forever.

It was the day...

We Were 'Crying With Laughter'

Over Spilled Milk...

“Hey---Bring That Back !” ...

When the Founders of those primitive Supply Stores of the 1930’s set the whole Company in motion, they instilled a feeling of Loyalty in their crews that has radiated for nearly 90 years. The feeling of being ‘Part of Something Great’ and the idea of ‘The Pride of Ownership’.

They are each a ‘powerful force’ and together, they are ‘unstoppable’.

Now, a young energetic male in charge of a store can sometimes get themselves into a ‘big bind’ and that person can be ‘up to their ears’ in that ‘big bind’ before they know they should have just left well enough alone...All too quickly, that ‘invincible’ attitude gets lost in the ‘Holy Cow!’ of the situation.

I was involved in a situation that left me thankful for my ‘Safety and Well-Being’ after it all calmed down.

Here’s what happened.

One evening in the late Fall of 1973, I was in charge of the store at the Muscatine, IA Hy-Vee and an incident got clear out of hand before I realized I should have ‘stayed on the porch’. At 22 years-old, I had a lesson to learn and ‘Little did I know’ it was coming that night.

Our first store at Muscatine sat in the Muscatine Mall and we had two entrances. One opened out to the side of the building and into the parking lot. People

drove their cars up to this entrance to pick-up their groceries after they paid for them. The other entrance led right off the Checkout Area and opened up to a corridor down to the inside of the main area of The Muscatine Mall. The Mall entrance got some use, but not a lot.

In the very first aisle of the Store were the Bakery and the Deli/Kitchen and they both did lots of Sales Volume. It happened, occasionally, that the Deli/Kitchen would get backed up and need help. In that instance, the person in charge of the store would go over and guide traffic to keep the aisle open. It was easy to keep up with the store traffic and still help the Deli keep their 'quality service' intact.

We kept it 'organized' for them.

So, as it happened sometimes, the Deli got backed up and I went over to see about directing the Customers into an orderly fashion of 'waiting their turn' to be served. A young man stepped up to the Deli Counter and asked for a '21-piece Bucket of Fried Chicken'. He was soon served and as he left, I couldn't help noticing that he didn't go through the Cash Registers, but rather he 'exited' the store through the doors going down into the Mall itself. He hadn't paid for the Fried Chicken.

So, I took off after him and I hollered at him to stop and he took off in a 'dead run' with the Fried Chicken under his arm. It was about 150'-200' down to the

main Mall Corridor and I chased him down to there and around the corner.

That's when I got the 'Surprise of My Life'.

There he was, standing behind six other guys and they were going to protect him at all cost. I stopped abruptly and the six guys came after me shoving me, cussing at me, tearing my shirt, tearing my tie, hitting me, kicking at me and doing everything they could to 'deter' me. Well, it was working because I just couldn't get away from them and it was getting worse by the second.

Suddenly, someone (a Mall patron or employee) yelled at them and they left me and they all ran down the Mall and out the rear entrance corridor to the backside of the Mall taking the Bucket of Chicken with them.

So, there I was. I had been 'roughed-up' pretty well and my clothes were tattered, but I wasn't really hurt or injured in any way. I was minus my Feather Duster and I found my Price Stamper on the floor. I was feeling pretty lucky and I knew I should get back to the store. I had been gone for about three to five minutes and I knew I needed to get back in case anything was going awry there.

Later, I reflected on what really happened and I came to a couple of conclusions. 1. 'With age comes Wisdom'. 2. 'With Wisdom, you realize that one

person stealing a 21-piece Bucket of Chicken isn't going to eat all that Fried Chicken by himself'.

So, Lucky me...Lesson Learned.

After that, it was easier to tell myself ...

"Down Boy... Down" ...

"It Better Not Be Here Tomorrow" ...

Since 1930 and the inception of those primitive 'Supply Stores' of Charles Hyde and David Vredenburg's, space for storing items in a Grocery Store has been 'a premium'. So-called 'good buys' on items were only a 'good buy' if they could be bought and sold and not have to be moved around a lot before they sold. You know... 'It Costs Money to Move It Around'.

It added up quickly...

Excess Stock in a store's Backroom is called 'Backstock' and it was often a source of irritation for lots of the crew in a store. The person who ordered it, the person who stocked it and the person whose final decision of how to get rid of it were generally under stress about it at one point or another. 'Backstock' was not popular.

An interesting and stressful 'Backstock' situation happened to me while I was working at the Muscatine Hy-Vee in early 1974. It turned out to be a really 'close call' for me and it certainly got talked about for years to come.

Here's how it all 'Stacked Up'...

Our Store Manager, Lynn, was great. He was a 'Highly Successful' Store Manager, but he was very temperamental and he was 'feisty' to say the least. His displays of temper usually produced a pretty

good 'tirade' and in my case, 'finger-pokes' to my chest that actually left bruises the next day. Lynn was one of the Store Managers I learned the most from in my Hy-Vee Career and 'Perseverance' was perhaps the most important thing I learned from him. I learned how to be 'Tough' at every turn and have 'Nerves of Steel' when they were needed. It served me well over the years, but this trait has a way of coming around to bite you sometimes too...Yes 'Bite You'!

This is the Story.

The Muscatine Store had grown so quickly in Sales Volume that we were really scrambling. In fact, The Muscatine Store was (and may still be) the only Hy-Vee that Grand-Opening Week was the 'smallest' sales week the store ever had. It opened in June of 1971 and it 'Never Looked Back'. There were lots of 'growing pains' in Muscatine and it was fun to say the least.

The Hy-Vee Warehouse in Chariton, IA would only give us three 'dry goods' Grocery Trucks per week that we ordered ourselves. The fourth truck was a 'computer generated' order that sent the 'same items' in the 'same quantities' each Monday. The warehouse didn't load trucks on Sundays and this load could be loaded Friday night or Saturday to be delivered early on Monday. The items in the order were based entirely on previous weekly movement records kept at the warehouse level. We could 'add

or subtract' individual items, but the rest of the order stood. It was called 'A Standing Order' for that reason and it was a full semi-trailer load of dry groceries.

Now, Lynn always liked to go through the Backroom with the person in charge of closing the store that night. They would walk through the Backroom and Lynn would generally give a 'good lecture' and he would somewhat 'brow-beat' the man closing the store that week of 7 straight nights. We would walk up and down the rows of merchandise in the area of 'leftover Backstock' and that's where things got 'dicey' sometimes. Lynn would usually stress that "Every item that was back there needed to get out and worked to the shelf." thus, emptying the Backroom for more efficiency.

It wasn't all going to fit on the shelves and Lynn knew it. We knew it too, but the pressure to get it out of the Backroom was upon us and we knew that 'for sure'. Lynn always knew I would do my best to follow his instructions, but he would 'brow beat' me anyway.

It was sort of a 'mind game' he liked playing to 'toughen us up'.

So, one evening, Lynn and I were going through the Backroom and he was busy giving instructions about this item and that item. When we came to Backstock area, Lynn just 'went into orbit' over the amount of Wishbone Italian Dressing in the Backstock. This Wishbone Dressing was part of the 'Standing Order'

every Monday and the guy who ordered that aisle (not me) was not stopping it from arriving on the 'Standing Order'. The 'pile' of it was just getting bigger and bigger each week...There were about 25 cases of it with 24 bottles in each case. It was a big stack.

In his usual way, Lynn 'squared-off' with me and he started raving about the Wishbone Dressing and as he repeatedly poked me hard on the chest, he finally said "And I don't give a Damn what you do with it, but it better not be here tomorrow."

So, it was clear he was mad and I knew better than to say anything. I just simply wrote on my list of duties "Salad Dressing". I knew it had to go, but 'Where?' was the question I was going over in my mind. We finished going through the Backroom and about 30 minutes later, Lynn left to go home for the evening.

By this time, it was around 5:30 PM and I took action. I 'stationed' a young girl Cashier at the front entry area of the store. We put a couple of stacks of the Wishbone Dressing by her and I instructed her to tell every customer that it was "Free with a $5 Order" ...

Yes, 'Free'!

So, the evening went along and the work got done and the Wishbone Dressing was 'GONE' ! I held my breath and went home for the night. I hardly slept that night wondering about the outcome of my

decision. I was unsure if I had made a smart decision or not.

I was working nights the entire week, so at 3:30 PM the next afternoon, I reported for work a little early as I always did. I arrived there and as I walked through the front door of the store, Lynn spotted me from his Office over-looking the 'Front-End' of the store. He picked up his microphone and announced over the intercom loudspeaker... "Rick Lampkin Office Please".

I could tell by his voice. 'This was it!'

So, I walked across the Front-End and bounded up the Office stairs to a waiting Lynn and our Assistant Store Manager, Ray. It was a somber moment and I knew something was about to happen. I said "Hi Guys".

Then Lynn said "What did you do with the Wishbone Dressing?" He stared at me and waited for an answer. I swallowed and then I said "I gave it away." Immediately, I wanted to be just about anywhere else instead of where I was standing, but I had to stand there under fire and just 'take it'.

Very quietly and calmly, Lynn said "You gave it away? Why in Hell would you give it away?" As I stood there, I could see my entire 'Hy-Vee Life' flash before my eyes and I knew this could be the end. Then, as I mocked him by pounding on my own chest with my finger, I said "Well, you said 'I don't give a

Damn what you do with it, but it better not be here tomorrow', so I put a part-timer at the front door and I gave it away free with a $5 order."

Then, I shut-up and just looked at him.

Lynn shook his head as he said "What would possess you to do that?" I then replied "Lynn, you have a bad habit of telling people to do things you really don't want them to do. I was just following your orders."

It was then I decided I better not say one more word. And I didn't. Lynn said "Go punch in and get to work."

I wasted no time going down the Office stairs to go to work. I felt lucky to be alive. Never again did I get any instructions from Lynn that were as 'open-ended' as the 'Wishbone Dressing Instructions' were.

I know Lynn hasn't forgotten it and I'm sure I will never forget it...

And For a few minutes that day,

I Was 'Wishin' I Was

Somewhere Else ! ...

Pfooooooosh ! ... "Oh, Dear Lord !"

Much has been said in this book and over the years about Hy-Vee's beginning all those years ago in the 1930's in Southern Iowa and Northern Missouri. What hasn't been covered yet is Hy-Vee's entry into 'The 21st Century and Beyond'...

We've heard it said in our lives that "For every successful company, someone gave their life for it". In Hy-Vee's example of that, there have been 'lots of someones' and at the top of that list is retired President and CEO, Ron Pearson. Ron is responsible for taking Hy-Vee from 'Mid-Size Midwest Company' and building it into 'A Complete and Awesome Powerhouse' in the Grocery Industry. It is one of America's largest grocery chains. Hy-Vee is respected and envied 'world-wide'.

Ron guided an already great company to be a 'Legendary' company in America.

The vision and confidence with which Ron took the 'helm' of Hy-Vee in the mid-1970's is evidenced in the results achieved with 'His Team'. That 'Team' saw growth in Hy-Vee's store numbers over the years from the 100+ stores at his elevation to the President and CEO spot to 'over 200 stores' at his retirement. Sales Volume in Hy-Vee went from just under $1 Billion annually to over $7 Billion annually. And in each of the years Ron was in charge, 'sales were up' and the company was 'highly profitable'... Every Year.

Results like that don't happen by accident. It requires the 'right planning' and 'the right people'...It also takes a 'ramrod' like Ron to make it all work. Ron's quest to 'excel at every corner' came from a 'vision' he had of where Hy-Vee could go 'if'... Yes, 'if' the company was allowed to 'Spread its Wings and Fly'.

And 'Fly' it has done...It has 'SOARED'...

I was lucky enough in my career to work with Dwight Vredenburg for over 12 Years while I was a Store Manager. I was even luckier to get to work with Ron for almost 25 years. I served an 'elected term' on the Hy-Vee Board of Directors with both of them for a year and it was an 'Honor'. It is impossible to tell you what an experience that was.

'What I am' and 'What I have' is directly attributable to Hy-Vee and largely to those two men.

Dwight taught me the 'Philosophy' side of things and Ron taught me more Philosophy plus 'the get it done' side of things. They are both 'extremely essential' for 'Success' to show up at the party when celebrating the accomplishments of a company.

Now, I worked with those two men close enough to feel comfortable around them and know them as 'mentors, bosses and friends'. For that, I feel very fortunate. But at one time in my Hy-Vee career, I was not so close to them and there was still an 'awe' and 'admiration' that was part of coming up through the

ranks. Sometimes, humorous things happen when people are still 'relative strangers' in a setting where one is already 'at the top' and one is still 'trying to climb closer to the top'.

Something happened in 1976 that Ron Pearson and I were involved in...And boy, was I 'involved'...

This is the story.

I was Assistant Store Manager at the Iowa City, IA #2 Hy-Vee from 1975 until early 1977. I had a Great Store Manager in Don and he was teaching me everything I needed to know to 'get started' as a Store Manager in a Hy-Vee store of my own somewhere. Don invited me to go to Headquarters on a Wednesday to the weekly Managers Meeting as a 'guest'. He was 'grooming me' for my next step and he wanted me to go in and see how the weekly Managers Meetings were conducted. Hopefully, I'd get a little more exposure to the Executives who made up 'The Selection Committee' of Hy-Vee. That 'Selection Committee', is the group of five people in Hy-Vee who chose the new Store Manager/Directors as they were needed.

I was excited and nervous at the same time. A 'big day' was coming for me ...

Now, this 'day coming' was a chance to broaden my experiences, hear some 'words of wisdom' and 'grow' in my job as I wanted so desperately to do. At 25 years-old, I was anxious and excited.

While at the Manager's Meeting on that Wednesday, it was announced early in the agenda, that the meeting would be 'adjourning early' to move to an area behind the Grocery Warehouse for some training. It had been decided that the Store Managers should each go home and 'train' their key people on the proper ways to put out a fire with a fire extinguisher. The new cardboard balers were now in the stores and the bales of cardboard were a fire hazard of a large proportion. That whole idea seemed pretty logical and I knew I'd get in on sharing that training back in Iowa City because I was there to learn it all 'firsthand'.

So, the meeting went along and we did adjourn at around 2 PM instead of the usual 4 PM. At that point, we were all asked to meet behind the Grocery Warehouse and further instructions would be given when we arrived there.

When we arrived at the location, personnel from Hy-Vee's Safety and Security Department were on hand to 'start fires' on piles of cardboard that were already built. Then, for the training, they would 'instruct' everyone on how to quickly and effectively extinguish the fires. So, for the next hour or so, fires were started and each person would step up to the 'head of their line', take instruction and then, douse the fire with a large fire extinguisher.

It looked 'SOOOO Simple'....

Uh huh!

Well, I watched everyone ahead of me in my line and when it came to be my turn, I was told where to aim the extinguisher and how to 'go after' the fire. Suddenly, I was 'turned loose' and frankly, I did pretty well.

Until…

I had 'doused' the fire very quickly by aiming at the base of the fire, but as I turned around to be done, the trigger on the extinguisher sort of stuck and I swung right around into Ron who had walked over to be closer to where I was. The trigger stayed on long enough to "PFOOOOOOSH" the spray from the fire extinguisher directly onto Ron from about the 'knees down. His shoes got the worst of it.

Oh, Dear Lord… What Had I Done?

The man whose support I would need to gain the most, was now standing there and looking at me. A man whose appearance was always 'absolutely impeccable' and whose wardrobe was 'stylish and fresh', was now covered in 'extinguisher spray' from the knees down. I am pretty sure I looked like 'a Deer in the headlights' to everyone. I couldn't say my apologies quick enough. I hurried over and helped him wipe his shoes off and then surprisingly enough…He chuckled and it became more humorous.

I acted like I was a bit amused, but I wasn't crazy…What person in their 'right mind' would want to be in that spot? …

Nobody that I could ever imagine.

I laugh about it now, but I sure didn't laugh about it that day. It was a perfect example of Ron 'The Great Leader' having some Humility and Patience. He would show me that side of himself 'many times' over the years since.

What a 'GREAT GIFT' Ron Pearson was to Hy-Vee...

It was the day...

I Thought I Had 'Extinguished' My Whole Career...

"Can We Borrow Some Pop…??"

In those very early years of Hy-Vee, 'The 'Hyde and Vredenburg Supply Stores' of the 1930's would have only one store to serve the town it was in. As the decades went along, however, it was decided that some towns could easily support two or more Stores and that 'The Company' could benefit from many things. Shared costs on advertising and other things that were involved with having a store in a town were minimized in cost because of that sharing.

So, the numbers of 'multi-store' towns that Hy-Vee is represented in are a unique and sometimes a great source of stories about the 'partnering' or 'lack of', that took place between the Stores.

While I was the Assistant Store Manager at the Iowa City, IA #2 Hy-Vee, a story of the 'partnering' took place and it will be remembered for many years to come.

It went like this.

Since 1965, Hy-Vee had two stores in Iowa City, IA and one in Coralville, IA after 1974. The Stores were 'notorious' for having a 'Pop item' and a 'Beer item' featured each week in the Ad so as to please the needs of the University of Iowa crowd that made up a large part of our business. Those three stores did 'lots' of business and the 'Pop and Beer' items were big Sales Volume items. They were generally a 'hot price' to get the Customers in.

The Iowa City #2 store was a 14, 500 square foot store that was much smaller physically than the business warranted. The sales per square foot were extremely high and it was necessary to be strategic with ordering our 'Ad Specials' so that they were nestled 'out of the way' in the Backroom and could leave the Backroom 'open' enough to handle the normal everyday merchandise coming through for the shelves as needed.

As Assistant Store Manager, one of my duties was to order the Ad Specials that would be needed for the weekly ads and I always tried to be as precise as I could because we just simply had no space to allow for excess cases if we had extra left over. I had been in the habit of keeping good records for future ordering and I knew that the amount of 1500 cases was about the right number to order for the 'Pop Special' when it was the Hy-Vee Canned Pop in the Weekly Ad. There were about 12 or 14 flavors and the Ad coming on this next Wednesday morning featured Hy-Vee Canned Pop at 10 cents per can. It would 'fly off the shelves' at that price. The 'Beer Special' for the week would usually sell a similar amount, but the Beer suppliers would bring it in as it was needed each day. The Pop was our big issue for space because it had to come on the Hy-Vee Truck.

Since our new Ad started on Wednesday each week, I had also decided that we could order all the 'Specials' to come in from Hy-Vee's Warehouse on Tuesday and that would give us room to 'nestle' it

into the Backroom in places we wanted it and still allow plenty of room for the other merchandise that would come daily for normal stock. It was a pretty good system because were able to utilize every square inch of the Backroom at a highly efficient level.

Our 'system' was smooth.

On that Tuesday, the 1500 cases of the 'Hy-Vee Pop Special' came on the Hy-Vee Truck and we were busy unloading the truck. We were interrupted a little when the Store Managers from the Iowa City # 1 and Coralville Hy-Vee Stores came 'sauntering' through our Backroom on their way to the store's Office for a meeting with our Store Manager, Don.

As they came through the Backroom, they both had comments to make to me and like most times, those comments were rather arrogant and a bit 'smart-alec'. Kenny, the Store Manager of The Iowa City #1 Store wanted to know why we had all the pop coming in on one load. He said he thought we should split it up over the three trucks that week. I replied that it worked best for us to get it in for the reasons of space and organization and so forth. Gary, the Store Manager of The Coralville Store, made some similar comments, but he didn't get as 'nasty' or 'smart-mouthed' as Kenny did. It was really all in 'smart humor', but the comments were serious.

In his usual brash and rather arrogant way, Kenny said "That is the dumbest thing I've ever heard of."

and he shook his head in mock disgust. I replied that he could run his store and we'd run ours and that was the end of the conversation...for then.

As the morning rolled along, the Store Managers would come through the backroom for a fresh cup of coffee and to use the Restroom and each time, Kenny would make a rather 'smart' comment. It was easy to see he was going to dig as deep as he could to have some fun with me. He liked to chide me about things. Gary would also 'chime in' with a comment too and it was obvious they were having fun with it.

So, as the day went along and got into the late afternoon, the weather got colder, things outside got worse and by the next morning, the Hy-Vee Warehouse called all the stores that were scheduled for Wednesday delivery and reported to them that the roads were so bad in Central Iowa that they were not letting the trucks leave the Warehouse. We were told it could be a day or so before they did let them go. Iowa City #1 Hy-Vee and Coralville Hy-Vee were scheduled for truck deliveries that morning and neither one had any 'Specials' for the Ad that had started that morning...

All of a sudden, the 'tables got turned' and we (I) had the 'upper hand'. It was great...

About 8:30 or 9:00 AM, the phone rang. I answered and as I picked up the phone. I said... "Hello...This is Rick. May I help you?" The voice on the other end of the call said ... "Rick, this is Kenny. You have no idea

how much it hurts to make this call, but we don't have any 'Ad Specials' and I need to get some... If you'll spare them...?" (A similar call would come within about 20 minutes from Gary at The Coralville Store.) It was all I could do to keep from 'Laughing' them right off the phone. But, I didn't.

Although it was 'Sooooo' tempting to 'gloat' and make fun of Kenny, I very graciously said "Sure, Kenny, you can have what you need to get through until yours comes and we'll order enough to replace it here." Kenny said "Thank-you!" and he indicated they would get over to get some. I contained my secret laughter.

Now, as I said, both stores needed 'Specials' and the two of them decided that the best way to get them from us was to rent a 'U-haul truck' from the dealer near Kenny's store and load up with the pop and other 'Specials' at our store and then transport them that way to Coralville and then back to Kenny's Store. Just a complete circle.

It was a great plan...'UNTIL'...

On the way to Coralville, they popped 2 tires (from the weight) on the U-haul truck and they had to be towed in with the 'Specials' still on the truck. After two brand-new tires were purchased and mounted, the 'Specials' were delivered to each Store and the U-haul truck was returned to the U-haul dealer near Kenny's store.

The cost...?? Well, it was the cost of the 'Truck Rental', the cost of the 'Tow Job', the Cost of 'Two New Tires', the Cost of The Driver of the Truck and... perhaps the most expensive part of all... 'The HUMILIATION' both Kenny and Gary suffered because of the whole thing. Everyone knew what had happened and I didn't have to say one word to know that we'd "scored one'.

Never again did Kenny or Gary ever criticize the way we did things in our store. Their 'smart comments' had 'come back to bite them' pretty hard that cold morning in late 1976.

It was the day the

Tires Were 'Pop-pin' On The U-Haul...

“Darn You” ...

Over the years and all the way back to those early days of ‘The Supply Stores’ of the 1930’s, certain items in Grocery Stores have been really ‘controversial’...Should we sell them?... Should we ‘not’ sell them? Yes, it has been a big decision many times, but most of the time, it’s been a case of ‘let the Customers decide’. You see, it’s because Hy-Vee, from its roots in those small rural towns in Southern Iowa and Northern Missouri, learned quickly that our ‘personal preferences’ or even ‘personal prejudices’, in some cases, should not be the determining factor. It should be ‘What the Customers want to buy, not what we want to sell’. And believe me...Their desires are the ‘driving force’ in the equation.

So, for nearly the past ‘nine decades’, Hy-Vee has focused on that last thought. When the decisions of ‘Product Selection’ came along it has always been ‘The Customers’ that were the reason it was stocked in the stores. If an item did not sell, then that became another matter, ‘shelf space’ would enter that final decision and an item may be discontinued.

Because ‘shelf space’ is a ‘premium’, carrying multiple sizes of an item would also be looked at...Hy-Vee would test a couple of sizes and then add more sizes to the shelf if the sales in those other sizes looked like they might warrant the stocking of them all.

Some of the items that were introduced were certain 'losers' in the market-place because of 'common sense' reasons. One good example was the introduction of '3-Liter Coke Products' in the early to mid-1980's. Most of us Store Managers took one look at it and realized that it wasn't going to be successful for two reasons... 1. The plastic bottle was too tall and too fat to fit on a normal refrigerator shelf'...and 2. A bottle that large wouldn't hold its 'fizz' long enough to drink it all'.

We were right...It lasted only a couple of months and then it was 'GONE'. It hasn't returned since.

One other item that has been 'controversial' over the years is still sold today in many Hy-Vee Stores. It's sold by those who believe as I do...That it's a real 'powerhouse' item in both 'Sales' and 'Profits'.

This story of that item chronicles the decision I made to 'add it'... and what happened to make it a 'Sweet' story for sure.

Here's the 'scoop'...Literally...

In June of 1975, I went to the Iowa City, IA #2 Hy-Vee Store to be the Assistant Store Manager and to work for a great Store Manager named Don. We were working in a very small facility of only 14,500 square feet. Obviously, even for those days, that store was small and it was being 'stretched to its limits' on Sales Volume. Though small in size, that store was

really successful in both 'Sales' and 'Profits' and we all worked hard to keep it that way.

Now, with the physical size of the Iowa City #2 Store being so small, product selection was an 'everyday decision' because of that limited amount of shelf space. Some items I'd been used to seeing in other larger stores just weren't in there and my past experience told me 'we needed some of them'...One in particular...I thought.

The item I refer to is Brach's Pick-A-Mix Candies and they have been a very popular item in the Midwest for many decades. Their popularity got 'overshadowed' by the belief by many that it was an item that 'got gobbled-up' too much by the Customers coming through and eating a few pieces while they shopped. The Pick-A-Mix that they had 'scooped up' into the colorful 'Brach's Paper Bag' would not be weighed until they went through the Cash Registers in the checkout process, so the Customers would eat a few pieces as they shopped. This 'grazing' on the candy infuriated some of the Hy-Vee Store Managers and it was not sold in their stores accordingly. They firmly believed they were not getting paid for a lot of the candy that was being eaten.

Now, we didn't carry the Pick-A-Mix line at Iowa City #2 and when Ron, the Brach's salesman, came in for the first time after I started in the store, he asked me if I'd like to look at the line for the store. Ron and I had known each other a long time and he knew we'd

carried it at some of the other stores I had been at previously. He hoped we'd begin carrying it there too.

Don was at the regular Wednesday Managers Meeting and he was not there that day, but my 'autonomy' allowed me to make the call. I said "Yes" to Ron's question because I knew it to be a good product line and a really good 'Sales and Profit' item in other stores I had worked in.

So, Ron and I talked a little more and then, I asked him to figure up an order of about 2500 pounds with a good mix to the candy. We also looked through his 'display pieces' in the catalog he had and we picked one out that would fit our store's size needs. Then, we ordered it all.

I was pleased with the decision.

Now, it never crossed my mind that there 'may be a reason' that Brach's Pick-A-Mix Candy was not already in the Iowa City #2 Store.

There sure was a reason, as I would soon find out.

The candy arrived late one Tuesday and I called Ron to tell him it had arrived. He said he'd be in the next day to set it all up and get it going for us. That next day happened to also be a Wednesday and Store Manager Don was at Headquarters for the normal weekly Managers Meeting.

When Don arrived back at the Store for work the next day on Thursday morning, he immediately 'pinned me down' on the Pick-A-Mix... He was 'not mad', but he was sure 'not happy' with my decision to add the Brach's candy.

Over the next 20 minutes, we discussed it at length and he conveyed his feelings about the 'grazing losses' he'd incurred in his previous store with Hy-Vee and in return, I told him that Ron suggested we just simply add 10 cents per pound to the 'suggested price' and that extra amount would cover the 'grazing'...and it probably did.

When our conversation was over, we had decided we'd 'sell-through' on the order and then we'd review the results. If we didn't think we saw too many people 'grazing' on it, then 'maybe' it could stay. Otherwise, it was going to be a 'one-time' item for us at the store.

Then came the fun part of this story...

The 'real clincher' to the whole thing, however, came the day after our conversation when Don came in and he laughingly said, "Darn you, Lampkin, I went home last night and there on the table was about a four-pound bag of Pick-A-Mix and when I commented on it, Phyllis (his wife) said 'Oh Don, I'm so glad you're carrying that now. I always liked that stuff."

Then, with a grin on his face, he said to me

"So, now, we have to keep it!"

We laughed about it for a minute or two and then went to work doing other things. As the next few months wore along, the Brach salesman, Ron, was in regularly and we re-ordered Pick-A-Mix several times. It did prove to be a great item and our calculations proved we really had made 'LOTS' of profit on the candy.

I still laugh over 40 years later about the time Phyllis saved me when

We Got 'All Mixed Up' In the Candy !

"Well, When We Are Out" ...

The old saying that "Perception Is Reality" really holds true in the Grocery Industry. For sure, if a Customer believes something is true, in their mind it is true. They see it and they believe it to be something it 'may or may not be'...

This has all been 'Human Nature' since long before the days of 'The Supply Stores' of the 1930's in Southern Iowa and Northern Missouri. Customers in those primitive 1200 square foot stores in those early years 'believed' things to be true and the only way out of it for the stores was to 'give them quality products' and then 'let the Customer choose'. Hy-Vee's Founders, Charles Hyde and David Vredenburg, knew that the sales of the item would 'Tell the Tale'.

It's a fact that 'whether the Meat or the Produce is better' (or not) can't truly be measured or argued successfully by a clerk trying to defend it to a Customer. In most cases, it just doesn't pay to try because it is an argument that you've lost before it started. The Customer already has their view on it and the Founders of 'The Supply Stores' believed that 'The Customer is Always Right'. So, let it be.

It has worked for nearly 90 years now.

There are, however, things that can be argued and those are the prices of one store versus another. If a store is truly less expensive, then the argument can be won. We have seen many examples of the 'price comparisons' over the decades and they can be 'defended' or 'criticized'...depending on how ethical and accurate things were in the example. You know, if Del Monte Peas are what is being compared to, the ethical thing to do is to compare to the competitor's Del Monte Peas. All of us have gone into a store and walked right past full grocery carts 'wrapped-up" in clear plastic wrap with a long Cash Register tape displayed prominently to show that one cart of groceries is cheaper than the other, but it's an 'illusion' if the same items are not compared.

Being '100% Ethical' is the answer...

Sometimes, 'something' will happen or be said in a store, that will do more to promote a store and at the same time, find fault with the other store just by how it's all worded. It becomes a 'Psychology of Merchandising' image.

The following story and 'how it was handled' has been one of the more 'brilliant' things I have heard in all my years...It spoke 'hugely' to the price image of a store. It was verbal, it was quick and it was 'POWERFUL'!

This is the story.

A very close Hy-Vee friend and mentor of mine, Don, conveyed this to me after he successfully managed a very small store in Albany, MO from 1966-1972. Albany was about 1500 in population at the time and it also had some rural trade from the area in

Northwest Missouri. It was a 1200 Square Foot Hy-Vee Store and it had two aisles... One down to the back of the Store and one coming back to the front of the Store where there were two Cash Registers. Sales Volume was $4,000 per week. By today's standards, the Albany Store of the 1960's would be compared to a small Convenience Store, but it was a profitable store and it 'paid its way' for many years in Hy-Vee and it also served as a great 'stepping-stone store' for many great Hy-Vee Store Managers that would later go on to larger and more profitable stores in Hy-Vee. They all had fond memories of Albany.

At the time, the Albany Hy-Vee had one competitor. The competitor's name was "McGinley's" and they had been around for a long time in Albany. McGinley's was located on the City Square in Albany. McGinley's had a larger store and in many ways, it had a more superior facility to do business from than Hy-Vee did. Hy-Vee had done a great job in the areas they could with their building and Don had proven that his 'ingenuity' was winning out. Every Customer and every dollar were extremely important to both of the stores. It was a real 'hotbed of competition'.

So, one day, Don was working in the aisle stocking his shelves with groceries and a lady came up to him and said "Your 39cent price on Miracle Whip is too high. I can buy it at McGinley's for 29 cents." Then she waited for an answer from Don.

Noticing that she had a quart of Miracle Whip in her cart, Don said "Is that so, well, I see that you have a quart of Miracle Whip in your cart. Why are you buying it here if they are cheaper" The reply surprised him when she said "Well, they're out of it and they don't have any coming in for a day or two."

Now, came the 'comeback line' that made the Customer take notice to what was happening. Not to be outdone, Don thought for a second and then he said to her "Gee, that's too bad, when we're out of Miracle Whip, our price is 19 cents."

'ZING'! The message was delivered very proficiently and without 'ruffling any feathers'. Don said that his Customer instantly understood what was happening at McGinley's. No further explanation was needed.

I always remembered the story Don told of the 'competition' in Albany and the 'mind games' that sometimes got played by his 'competitor. I learned so many great 'lessons' like that one from Don and after hearing this particular story of Don's, I'd always wonder as I walked through a competitor's store looking at their 'Out of Stocks'

"Are they really that price or are they

'Playing Games When They're

'Out Of Stock' ?" ...

“Oh My God...It’s Gone !”

As far back as the 1930’s The Supply Stores used cash as part of their ‘operating needs’. It wasn’t as much a part of the operations then because the Customers ‘charged’ a lot of their groceries and then ‘settled-up’ at the end of the month or on a ‘bi-weekly payday’. Over the next few decades, however, that all started changing and the need for more ‘cash and banking’ became necessary in the operations of the stores.

The Hy-Vee Stores of the 1960’s and 1970’s required lots more ‘day-to-day’ cash to operate them. With no ‘ATM’s’ on the scene yet, Customers paid in ‘cash’ more, they wrote more personal checks with ‘cash-back’ and the stores cashed Payroll Checks as a convenience to their Customers. The cashing of Payroll Checks offered a ‘service’ that usually saw part of that cash coming back to the store in grocery purchases. It was a part of the era.

The Armored Car Services had not really begun to prosper in the smaller towns of Hy-Vee either. The ‘daily deposit’ to the Bank of the prior day’s receipts was driven back and forth by a member of the store’s management. It was usually one of the Assistant Store Managers or the Store Manager himself that took the ‘cash and checks’ to the local Bank and dropped them off for deposit. At the Bank, the person making the ‘drop-off’ also picked up large amounts of cash that went back to the store for the cashing of

the checks and cash transactions of the day or weekend ahead. Sometimes, it was "very large amounts" of cash.

Something happened in 1975 at the Iowa City #1 Store that 'ended well', but it really 'rattled the cage' of about every other store around and it is still talked about in some of the 'older circles' of Hy-Vee to this day.

Here's what happened.

From mid-1975 until early 1977, I was the Assistant Store Manager at the Iowa City, IA #2 Hy-Vee Store. There were two other Hy-Vee Stores in our 'market' then. One was also in Iowa City and one was in Coralville, IA. We tried to operate jointly on weekly ads and pricing.

The Iowa City #1 Hy-Vee Assistant Store Manager, Doyle, was really 'fun-loving' and an 'extremely likeable guy' who had lived in Iowa City for decades. He knew everyone there and most everyone knew Doyle. He was the kind of man that always went out of his way to help someone and in this story, that is what 'just about' got real costly.

One morning, Doyle was making 'The Bank Run' and when he came back to the store, he had a couple of large bags of cash that he had picked up at the Bank for the weekend's needs. As he drove onto the parking lot of the Iowa City #1 Store on Kirkwood Avenue there in Iowa City, he noticed a friend of his

with his 'trunk up' and the 'spare tire out' of his car. It was obvious that the friend had a flat tire. The friend was a good Customer and was considerably older than Doyle, so in his usual friendly way, Doyle decided to 'go to the rescue' of his older friend and change the tire for him.

So, Doyle jumped out of his car and set the two large bags of cash on the trunk of another car sitting close by and then he started right in and helped his friend. After about 10 or 15 minutes, the friend's tire was fixed, the trunk was loaded up with the flat tire and the jack and it was all done. All the friend had to do was drive to the tire shop and get his tire repaired and the 'dilemma' would be over. The friend 'thanked' Doyle and the two parted.

At this point, Doyle turned to the car where the two cash bags were and 'Oh, My God'...The car was gone 'AND SO WERE THE TWO BAGS OF CASH!'

In an almost wild panic, Doyle ran into the store and went straight to the Office to get the Store Manager, Kenny. Doyle was a 'white as a sheet' as he blurted out that he'd left the money on a car and now it was gone. A huge sum of money and it was just 'GONE'. He was in a full-blown 'panic mode' and Kenny tried to calm him down to get the full story so he could dig in and help.

The first thing they did was to call the Iowa City Police Department to see if they would help them with the lost Bank Bags of cash. They agreed they'd

get a Squad Car right over for assistance. Then, Kenny got Doyle calmed down to a point where they could go back and 'piece together' any information about the car he'd set the money on. Doyle repeated the story of coming onto the parking lot and seeing the friend with a flat tire. He told Kenny of setting the Bank Bags on the trunk of the other car, but he just couldn't remember anything about the other car.

The situation seemed really bleak.

It was at this point, that Doyle's 'Guardian Angel' was starting to help out. The Police Department called to tell Kenny that the two bags of cash had been found in the gutter of the street a couple of blocks away from the store and they were 'untouched and unopened'. The Police surmised that the bags of cash had stayed on the back of the other Customer's car until the car made a turn and then they rolled off and then they laid in the street.

HOORAY !—HOORAY !—HOORAY !

So, the money was returned to the store and Doyle's Heart Rate came way back down and it was suddenly all in the past. In the past, 'BUT NOT FORGOTTEN'.

The story of 'The Lost Bank Bags' made its way all over Hy-Vee and every store was reminded that the cash was 'sacred' and it could not be 'jeopardized'.

The story was used as a training lesson about 'What Can Happen' when you lose track of the important things at hand.

It was the day The Bank Bags 'Drove Away' With A Flat Tire...

“Our Customers like to think of our stores as their stores.”

Ronald D. Pearson

President, CEO and

Chairman of the Board

(Retired)

“Stand Up Close” ...

Since those early days of the 1930’s in ‘The Supply Stores’ of Southern Iowa and Northern Missouri, people of all ages have come to work at the stores and for all sorts of reasons. Obviously, everyone wants paid, but it’s more than that. The reasons range from ‘keeping busy’ all the way to ‘wanting exercise’ and even to ‘getting out of the house’.

So many reasons are responsible for people wanting to work at Hy-Vee and with the many ages represented in the crews of Grocery Stores, it is fun to see how they all work together and do their ‘individual job’ to complete ‘The Team’. ‘Everyone together’ makes up the ‘personality’ of a store.

The ‘Senior Citizens’ are a great part of the ‘personality’ of any Hy-Vee store. They offer a lot of things and it is fun to see them interact with everyone in the store crew as well as their interaction with the Customers. Great stories come from the Seniors.

This is one of my ‘Favorites of All’...

While I was the Assistant Store Manager at Iowa City, IA #2 Hy-Vee in 1975, we had a ‘Senior Employee’ who was loved by everyone who knew him. Sometimes, we had to re-think ‘why’ we loved him, but we sure did.

His name was Ewald.

Ewald was an 85-year-old German-American whose parents had immigrated to America when he was a little boy. He was a World War I Veteran and he was very proud to be an American. Ewald was about 5'6" tall and he weighed about 100 pounds... 'maybe'. He wore thick glasses that magnified his eyes when you looked at him and he had a thick well-trimmed Silver Mustache. He spoke a little bit of 'German-Accent English'. Ewald had a 'liking for the ladies' and he had a great sense of humor.

Ewald was our Store Janitor and he worked very hard to keep the store up and in top condition. Every morning at 1:00 AM, he would come to the store and start his 'routine' for the day. He would clean the Break Area, the Restrooms and then 'sweep and scrub' the Sales Floor. It was always looking good and he was proud of the way it looked.

He was... 'A Jewel'.

As the Sales in the store grew, it was getting harder and harder for 85-year-old Ewald to keep up and one day, he said to me "Rick, I need help in here on Saturday mornings because I can't get it done by the time the Customers come in." (We opened at 7 AM.)

Now, I could easily understand where he was coming from on it because I could see the flow of Customers growing and Ewald getting a little older. He was in need of someone to help him. More Customers meant more 'cleaning' to keep it all up.

So, I asked him to come in on Monday and we'd look at the issue. When Monday came, I sat down with Ewald and we looked at his work-week and duties each day. Saturday was the 'problem day' and he thought that an extra person at 4 AM would take the pressure off.

I knew just the person for the job.

Since I usually came in at 6 AM on Saturdays, I thought I was 'the guy' for the job. I just simply started coming in at 4 AM and 'I' was 'Ewald's Helper'. It worked great.

Ewald would 'bark the orders' and I would do the jobs needing done. We would finish with the Sales Floor around 6:30 or 6:45 AM and it would then dry and be ready for the Customers at 7 AM.

I thoroughly enjoyed Ewald. He loved to complain to me about the 'problems' in the cleaning of the store. He'd go on and on with "This person makes a mess", "That person doesn't care how his work station looks" and "Everyone needs to work neater and create less of an eyesore in the Store." And on and on.

I loved it.

I was becoming very close friends with him and we seemed to be 'on the same wave-length' about the needs of running a clean store. We were a 'Good Team'.

There was 'one area' of the Store that really got under Ewald's skin. It was the Men's Restroom and the floor below the urinal. Boy, it really made him 'go into orbit' when the urinal had a puddle of urine on the floor under it and nobody seemed to be able to 'hit the target'. Ewald complained 'week after week' about it and I knew it was coming to a 'showdown' between Ewald and the 'army of guys' peeing on the floor (or dribbling) below the urinal. I didn't know what to expect, but I could see 'something' coming' as it was all unfolding.

Something good was about to happen.

So, one Saturday morning, Ewald asked me if he could borrow my black felt-tip marker. I gave it to him and he headed off toward the Backroom. He was gone about ten minutes and when he returned, he gave me back my marker and he said "That should do it." Nothing else was said, but I knew there was a 'Real Gem' waiting in the Backroom somewhere.

As we finished the floors, I headed to the Backroom to use the Restroom and it was then that I found 'The Gem'. There, hanging by a coat-hanger wire on the neck of the flush handle of the urinal in the Men's Restroom, was a very poorly scrawled note to all men and boys who would come to the Restroom and stand there.

The cardboard sign read "All You Men With Short Horns Stand Up Close".

I laughed out loud for a minute or so and then I flushed the urinal, washed my hands and then left the Restroom to get ready for the Customers. As I came to the Sales Floor, Ewald was coming to the Backroom. As we passed each other, I said "I like the sign." We had a quick laugh and it was then that I decided I would leave the sign up for our Store Manager, Don, to see. It was a 'Real Gem' and I wanted Don to see it and have a laugh too.

And he did.

Sometimes, in my mind, I can still see it hanging on the urinal. I always think of Ewald and how much I grew to love that old guy. Then I think to myself

"Never Underestimate The Thought Process Of A Senior Citizen..."

“We believe that Integrity means we are the Customers’ Keeper.”

Ronald D. Pearson

President, CEO and

Chairman of the Board

(Retired)

"We'll Just Wait It Out" ...

Since the beginning of those long ago 'Supply Stores' of the 1930's, Charles Hyde (Hy) and David Vredenburg (Vee) employed 'kids' to do the 'odd jobs' in their stores. The 'long list' of young people, that would be employed to 'fill-in' on the Work Schedules at times of the week when some extra help was necessary, would become 'Astronomical' in the numbers over the nearly 90 years since. Millions of 'Young People' have been part of it all in Hy-Vee.

'Young Kids' put a real 'exclamation point' on the word 'Fun' when you look at the Grocery Business. So many young people in the stores and all of them learning and growing from 'Childhood to Adulthood'. The things they do can sometimes make you 'cry' and sometimes you 'shake your head', but even more often, they make you 'laugh' at all the things they do.

I probably have as much appreciation and respect for the 'Young People' in our Stores as I do any part of our crew. I was a 'Young Person' at Hy-Vee and I remember the thought processes that I used to 'rationalize' ornery behavior or the pranks we pulled. Yes, it's a 'Rite of Passage' to learn from all those experiences.

Now, Shoplifting, by a 'Young Person', is mostly an innocent thing they have 'concocted' out of their belief they 'need' something. They perceive that they 'need' these things and that they can't live without

them. Whether they can't convince their parents to give them the money or they just think they won't get caught, some pretty funny stories come out of the 'need' these 'kids' think they have. 'From Young Minds' have come some 'Great Stories'.

This story took place in 1976...Here's how it happened.

I was the Assistant Store Manager at The Iowa City, IA #2 Hy-Vee Store on the Southeast corner of 1st Avenue and Rochester in Iowa City. It had originally been built on that corner on land purchased from a Farmer and his wife. When the store opened in 1965, Rochester Avenue past our store was not even paved. The store was slow to start, but it would prove to be a wonderful location for Hy-Vee over the years. It was a 'highly successful' location too.

Now, just down the street about two blocks to the West on Rochester Avenue was the Catholic high school named 'Regina High School' and it had a very large student population. Iowa City's public high school, 'City High', was about 6 blocks South of Hy-Vee on 1st Avenue. It also had a very large student population.

At Hy-Vee, we saw 'lots of kids'...Every Day!

In comparison, we probably saw more kids from Regina and we 'definitely' had more problems with the kids from that school. Our young Part-timers at Hy-Vee had the whole situation 'rationalized' as to

'why' it happened that way. As our Part-timers put it... "They're Catholic and they can do anything they want and then just go to Confession." I never knew whether to believe that, but the kids sure talked about it. In their minds, it was real.

One Shoplifting incident happened at the store in 1976 and I will always laugh about it because it fell 'squarely' into the category of 'The Belief of Need' and 'Not Thinking Very Far Ahead' too. It was funny that day and even funnier now. Over 40 years later, I still laugh when I tell the story.

Here's 'The Scoop' on it... Literally!

This small group of 'Young Boys' came into the store one afternoon after school had let out at Regina. They roamed around for a pretty long period of time and we were sure that at least one (if not more) of the Boys had taken an Ice Cream Bar. We were only sure of one, so we 'singled him out' as they left the store. I asked him to come back in and come to the Office. He was hesitant and looked scared, but he came to the Office with us.

I asked him to sit down and I told him the 'problem' and he denied every word of it. So, I got the 'usual information' of his name etc. from him and we sat there looking at each other. Yes, 'looking' because I knew where the Ice Cream Bar was and 'the location' of the Ice Cream Bar was going to be the catalyst for him to 'confess his sin'.

So, we continued to sit there...

As we sat and looked at each other, the Ice Cream Bar that he'd stuck down the front of his pants had started to 'talk to him'. It was 'cold' and it was melting and the longer we sat there, the more it melted and the bigger the mess was in his underwear. I knew I had the 'upper hand' in the ordeal, so I just waited...and waited... Then, 'finally' it happened.

He started squirming pretty good in his chair as he said "Okay, I did take the Ice Cream Bar." and he continued to squirm. I looked at him and I said "Okay, now that you have admitted it, put it out here on the desk." So, he dug down deep into his pants and he pulled out this 'dripping and melting chocolate covered Ice Cream Bar 'mess'. I had him lay it on a nearby piece of newspaper.

He had to be miserable because we had sat there long enough for the ice cream to mostly melt and quite of bit of the chocolate coating on it too. It had made a 'real mess' in his underwear and pants and he was wishing he was 'anywhere else' and with 'clean dry pants'.

So, I called his parents and got a hold of his Mother...She said she'd be right over and get him... The way he acted, he'd rather have faced a Firing Squad than his Mom. He was very 'antsy' and when his Mom came, she was obviously 'not happy' with

him. I told her "Thank-you!" for coming over to get him and I released him to her.

His biggest punishment was yet to come... 'Mom's Wrath'!

With his Mom, he walked out of the Office wearing a 'big wet spot' on the front of his pants and he was also taking with him just about as much 'embarrassment' as he could handle. He had to walk out with his Mom and in 'full view' of the Part-timers in our Store that were 'watching closely'. I'm also sure that the story of his 'Ice Cream Episode' made it to Regina because some of our Part-timers 'made sure it did'...He probably suffered a lot of 'razzing' over it.

I will always believe he should have put a 'candy bar' down his pants...At least it wouldn't have melted so quickly and it wouldn't have made such a mess...I still laugh when I think about the old saying ...

"I Scream, You Scream, We All Scream For Ice Cream"

And 'Boy, Did He Scream' !

“We keep our Inventories as low as possible…It allows us to operate on much lower cash needs.”

Marion M. Coons

Senior Vice-President

and CFO

(Deceased)

"My Job Is To Drive That '*%@#' Truck And Keep My Mouth Shut" ...

In the earlier years of Hy-Vee in the 1960's and 1970's, the 'journey' into the Bakery Business got well under way. It was common for a market area with more than one store to have one Bakery in town and that Bakery would serve the other store (or stores) with fresh Bakery Goods each day of the week. By having it set up that way, Hy-Vee could spread out the modernization of the company with 'The Bakeries' and not have the expense of them creating an imbalance in the expenses for the 'growing company'.

While I was the Assistant Store Manager at the Iowa City, IA #2 Hy-Vee Store, the Iowa City, IA #1 Store had an 'In-store Bakery' and we were on the receiving end of the products they produced. We paid them the retail prices of the products (as marked) and they discounted the total order by 20% so we could make a profit. The added Sales Volume for them was worth it because they could 'mass produce' more items and then the added sales would reduce their Operating Costs. Of course, we could offer the 'Fresh Bakery Goodies' for our Customers and it was a 'Win-Win' for both stores.

It was a good set-up and it worked 'Very Well' for many years.

The Iowa City #1 Store Bakery did the planning and brought to us what they thought we could sell. They knew 'the best items' and it took the 'guess work' out it for us. With that arrangement, they stood the cost of the leftover products. It was a bit of a 'Double-edged Sword', however, because it went both ways as to the benefit of the quantity brought to us. If they 'brought too much', they had to credit us the cost of the overage. If they 'brought too little', then we both lost potential sales. Overall, it worked very well though and we had a pretty good working relationship with the Iowa City #1 Store and its Bakery crew.

Each day, the Bakery Van would roll into our store early and we'd unload the items they were bringing and then we'd stock the shelves. The 'charges and credits' were figured to everyone's agreement and then the Bakery Van would return to their store ready to repeat the process again the next day.

Occasionally, there would be 'other' grocery items that one store needed to get from the other store depending on the 'Ad Specials' that week. We could get extra from each other via the Bakery Van as needed for those Ads. It was sometimes small amounts, but other times, it got into larger items and more cases.

The daily driver from The Iowa City #1 Store to our Store was a 'really great', but wimpy little guy named Joe. Joe was probably about 5'6" tall and weighed

about 125 pounds 'soaking wet'. He wore black rimmed glasses and he always wore white pants and a white Tee-Shirt. He could be a real 'talkative' and sometimes even a borderline 'mouthy guy'. We all liked Joe and as I said, Joe was a great guy, but he had a way of getting himself 'dug into a hole' that quickly reached his neck. Sometimes, it got quite comical to watch.

Now, one day, Joe rolled in with the Bakery Goods and just about the time he was ready to head back to his store, the Iowa City #1 Store Manager, Kenny, called and asked if we had extra Charmin Tissue that was in the weekly newspaper Ad. I told him we did and we could spare 15 cases.

So, I rounded up the 15 cases of Charmin and I approached Joe and said... "Kenny just called. He wants you to bring back 15 cases of Charmin when you go back to the store. I'll load it up for you and here is the 'inter-store transfer slip' for you to take back to Kenny."

At this point, Joe would have been better off to just do it and shut-up, but that wasn't going to happen. Joe wrinkled up his face and said "I wish that 'G#D DA%N' Kenny would just come and get his own 'G#D DA%N' Charmin. I get sick and tired of hauling his stuff back and forth."

They were words that would catch up to him...and quickly.

Joe returned to their store as normal. A little later in the morning, Kenny called about something else and while I had him on the phone, I gave him a bit of the conversation I had with Joe about the hauling of the Charmin. I told Kenny that I just wanted him to be aware of it because it could really be taken badly by an employee that didn't know Joe and his mouth very well.

Kenny 'thanked' me and the rest of the day went along just fine.

The next morning, I wasn't involved in the unloading of the Bakery Goods, but after they were unloaded, Joe looked for me in the store and when he found me, he approached me and said... "Do you have anything that needs to be hauled back to our store this morning?" His tone and words were so much opposite of his attitude the day before, so I said "Joe, yesterday you squawked every step of the way about hauling stuff back... Today, you're almost begging me to have some things to take back. What got into you?"

"Well", Joe said "Yesterday, I had a short conversation with 'Mr. Kenny' about the whole thing and he told me that My job was to drive that '$@&*$%@' truck and that I wasn't to question what was sent back and forth on it. So, I just want you to know that I'll be available to take anything back at any time... And if you ever need anything brought over, you're just supposed to call me before I leave

for your store and I'll have it on with the Bakery Goods."

Then, he looked at me and smiled. And with that, he took off for his store.

Never again, did we have any trouble with Joe taking things back and forth...Kenny had 'explained' the whole thing to him and he understood exactly where it put him...And that was 'Driving the Truck with His Mouth Shut'.

It was the time he opened his mouth and

Bakery Joe

'Got His Buns In Trouble' !

“Don’t be afraid to use someone else’s good idea...No matter whose idea it was, we all win.”

Ronald D. Pearson

President, CEO and

Chairman of the Board

(Retired)

“Lights, Camera...Action !”

When Hy-Vee got its start in the 1930’s, ‘informal meetings’ got started with the Store Managers of the small Southern Iowa and Northern Missouri Stores. Those Store Managers in those original 15 Stores knew that some of the ideas they could share would benefit each other and the whole group would then strengthen and Hy-Vee would grow.

Those first ‘meetings’, of what would go on to formally be called “Managers Meetings”, were primitive. They were generally held in Centerville, IA where a group of 8 or 10 men in the Backroom of a very tiny little store all gathered around drinking coffee and most smoking ‘cigarette after cigarette’. Full cases of Post Toasties Corn Flakes or Wheaties Cereal would serve as a table and they would use pencils and white ‘Butcher Paper’ to draw on as they created a new ‘Weekly Ad’ that could be used in each of the little towns...an Ad used by all or by some of them anyway. Very soon, the ‘meetings’ became a routine...And a ‘great routine’ it has proven to be for now almost 90 Years.

So, as Hy-Vee moved from the 1930’s and on into each decade thereafter, those ‘Managers Meetings’ have been ‘The Life-Blood’ of the Company for the purposes of Unity and Cohesiveness of the Store Managers. Now numbering 240 Men and Women as Store Manager/Directors, those ‘every Wednesday

meetings' are as vital as ever to keep things moving forward and upward. They are 'Invaluable'.

In every one of Hy-Vee's stores, the crew in the store knows that their Store Manager will be out of the building for the entire day on Wednesday. Only the stores very close to Headquarters will see their Store Managers on that day and some stores are far enough away that they even leave on Tuesday evenings...The 'weekly drive' can be very rigorous for the Store Managers.

That 'Wednesday Out' can be a day where things happen in the stores that may not be happening when 'The Boss' is there and can see the activity. You can be certain that sometimes 'Surprises Happen on Wednesdays'. One of those 'Wednesday Surprises' happened in 1976.

This is 'How the Camera Caught it all'...

I was the Assistant Store Manager at the Iowa City, IA #2 Hy-Vee from mid-1975 until late Spring of 1977. Our Store Manager, Don, was gone each Wednesday and that left the Store Crew there as a group just 'TCOB' (Taking Care of Business) while he was away each week. We always worked hard when Don was gone, but while talking about the upcoming Christmas Season one day, we got a 'wild idea' for a gift we could get for Don and Phyllis (his wife), for the annual 'Christmas Gift' we always got them. That 'Christmas Gift' was a way we could show our appreciation for the things they did each day and

year to be a great Boss and make our working conditions the best we could want.

Don and Phyllis were wonderful...

As we tossed around the ideas some of us had, the point was made that Don and Phyllis were so active with the 'sporting events' of their 11 and 13-year-old sons. Everyone knew that they went to all the Boys' baseball games and other events and the idea came up that we'd get them 'An 8mm Movie Camera and A Projector' as a Christmas Gift.

It would be perfect!

And then, someone jokingly said "And we should make a movie for them too. You know...An 'Action Movie' of the store."

BINGO! ... Even 'more perfect' !

So, the idea was born and we calculated the costs and figured what kind of donation each person would have to make and we ordered the Camera and Projector. They would arrive well ahead of the annual Store Christmas Party and we knew the movie was 'within our grasp'. We were excited and 'little did we know' that the Camera and Projector would produce one of the 'fondest memories' any of us ever had at the Iowa City #2 Hy-Vee.

Our Story Goes On...

First, we sat down and figured out on paper just 'how many skits' we'd need to put together and then we delegated the responsibility of a 'skit' for each of the people who had volunteered to help. Their ideas would be put together and refined and a 'Silent Movie' for all-time would be created.

We came up with about 20 funny things that we could film the crew doing that were so 'out of the norm', that watching it would make Don cringe a little, but laugh hard doing it.

Oh, was this going to be fun...

So, for 7 Wednesdays while Don was gone, we 'Scripted and Shot Scenes' for our Movie and when we were all done with our 'Masterpiece', we viewed it and 'Laughed Our Butts Off'.

We had exceeded our own expectations.

The movie had all been done in secret and with nobody willing to talk about it. We had captured so much humor and so many 'shenanigans' on a 25minute silent tape. We could hardly wait to wrap it all up and then just let the video tape 'fall out of the box' as Don and Phyllis opened their gift at the Store Christmas Party coming in a few weeks.

Boy, was this going to be fun...

So, the boxes with the Camera and the Projector in them were all wrapped up for the big party. We had

'slipped' the movie tape into the Projector box. We were ready for the surprise that awaited.

We could hardly contain ourselves.

At the big Christmas Party, we had a large attendance by the crew and when it came time for the presentation of our 'Christmas Gift' to Don and Phyllis, everyone crowded around. With a Projector Screen in hiding in another room, we told them "How much we appreciated them." and we said "Thank-You for the 'Wonderful Ways' they both treated all of us." And then, we gave them the boxes to unwrap.

You could have heard a pin drop.

We had them unwrap the Camera Box first and then came the Projector Box. When that second box was opened, a couple of us 'made a big deal' about what "Just Rolled Out of the Box" ... It was the small canister that the video was in and of course, we said... "Hey, It's a movie, let's see what's on it." ...

So, we did.

We got the Screen from the other room and we strung an extension cord across the room and we put on the video...Holy Cow!

There on video for Don and Phyllis to see was a display of 25-minutes of nearly all the employees doing things that were so creative and so much fun and with 'mischief tossed in'. As it played through, we all laughed and Don and Phyllis laughed the

hardest. With no sound, all the lines were printed on 'cue cards' for the viewers to read and then some of the funniest things ever imagined came off 'all on camera'.

It was 'Great' and we all loved it.

Everyone loved it so much, that 40 years after, we held a 'Reunion' of all of those people who were there. We held it in Iowa City at a Sports Bar and the 'Number One Request' was "Could We Show the Video?".

Universally, that's what everyone wanted to know. So, we got busy and converted 'the old VHS tapes' that had been made from the 'original 8mm tapes' over to the 'modern day DVD format'.

It was 'As alive as ever.'

Wow! Our old 1976 movie had 'outlived' three generations of Video Recording formats.

For the Reunion, we went even farther. We made a DVD copy for anyone who wanted one. It was a 'huge hit'. We made over 35 copies for the now '45 year-older' crew who starred in the movie.

The night of the Reunion, we had the new DVD format of our 1976 'Silent Video' running all evening on some TV's in the Sports Bar. We made the presentation 'a loop' so everyone who came and went to the party could see it. It was a huge hit---40 years later and we 'Laughed All Over Again'.

Several of the people from the Video have passed on and we 'Paid Tribute' to them as we watched the 25 Minute Show 'over and over' that night. It was a memory that had 'Brought us together again four decades later.

One more example of 'The Hy-Vee Family'...

I know Don and Phyllis still cherish the 'Silent Video' all these years later and the entire Store Crew in it wouldn't trade it for the 'Stars'.

It was the time the

'Lights Of Hollywood'

Came To Iowa City !

“Store level autonomy leads to Customer Loyalty and Customer Loyalty is the key to long-term Success.”

Ronald D. Pearson

President, CEO and

Chairman of the Board

(Retired)

"What Goes In" ...

Since its inception in 1930, the partnership between Founders, Charles Hyde (Hy) and David Vredenburg (Vee) included strong beliefs that have followed their company well into the 21st Century now. They knew the importance of some 'Basic Principles' of business that should be built upon as they grew.

In those 'Supply Stores', they believed that the 'Fair and Ethical' treatment of everyone involved in the stores was of the utmost importance. The Founders believed that the way in which Customers were treated was a major part of the 'long-term success' in getting those Customers to make The Supply Stores where they shopped regularly.

Equally important, the Founders believed in 'great employee relations' too. The Loyalty they wanted with their crews in those fledgling stores was important to them to help build the 'Bond' with the Customers. Yes, it was a 'simple philosophy' and it has been a part of the 'Business Relationship' ever since. Most other retailers seem to have forgotten those beliefs and they continue to forget them today.

It has been instilled in Hy-Vee's People for almost 90 years now that it is 'The Customers That Pay The Bills'... Period.

Company Founder, David Vredenburg, used to tell the Crew that "If you have a Customer and a fire at the same time, take care of the Customer first and then

put out the fire." Obviously, it would be hard to do that, but it was Dave's way of getting the message to the crew of just 'how important' the Customers are.

So, as the decade of the 1930's moved into the 1940's and beyond, the 'Hyde and Vredenburg Supply Stores' became known for their 'Happy Customers' and 'Happy Employees'...It has been a 'Win-Win' situation for all the years and it looks like it can go on forever.

In my career as a Store Manager, I always told my crew "We're in the People Business, we just sell groceries on the side". It is a 'belief' I still share with others 50 years after I was hired as a 15-year-old 'Carryout' in the Washington, IA Hy-Vee. This 'Belief' is also shared by thousands of people all over the Midwest. The Company is affectionately referred to as "The Family of Hy-Vee."

As Hy-Vee emerged out of the 1940's and into the 1950's, America's Labor Unions became very strong. It was an affiliation that Hy-Vee wanted to avoid because the feeling of the Founders was that the 'Fair and Ethical' treatment of the Hy-Vee Employees serves as a 'strong bond' between the levels of Management and the crews in the stores. The feeling of needing 'a third party' was viewed as 'not necessary'. After all, the Founders had set the course for 'Good Employee Relations'.

So, Hy-Vee has been able to operate for nearly 90 years without Labor Unions entering the relationship between Management and the crews in the Retail

Stores of Hy-Vee. There was one exception to that and it was in a small Department in a Northern Missouri Store in 1971. In that small department of 1971, the Labor Union represented the 8 members of that department for a year and after a full year, those 8 members decided they had it better before the relationship with the Labor Union, so they voted them back out. There has been no other Union Representation since in the Retail areas of Hy-Vee. It is a Testament to Hy-Vee's ongoing commitment to its employees in every store.

After the purchase of the Chariton Wholesale Grocery in 1945, the Company believed that the Truck Drivers and some Warehouse crew-members were probably 'safer' and more in line with the Trucking Industry in America to be part of the membership of a Labor Union. Safety and the ease of making the 'routes' and the 'connections' for merchandise have been believed to be in the best interest of the Drivers and Dock Workers in the Hy-Vee Warehouse since.

Only one time in Hy-Vee's entire 90 year-history, has there been a Strike by those Drivers and it happened in the Spring of 1977. I was directly involved with that Strike and its effects on Hy-Vee as I was working as the Assistant Store Manager of the Iowa City, IA #2 Store.

This is what happened.

In the Spring of 1977, the Drivers of Hy-Vee and the workers loading the trucks at the Hy-Vee Warehouse

voted to go on Strike upon the advice of the Union they belonged to. What this decision meant to Hy-Vee was that trucks would not be loaded and nobody would deliver the trucks if they were loaded. So, it was a 'quandary' for Management and the stores for sure.

Hy-Vee's Northern Stores were already buying Dry Groceries, Produce and Frozen Foods from a company in La Crosse, WI named Gateway Foods. The Gateway Foods Company had proven to be an excellent Supplier and they stepped forward and said that they'd take on and help any stores that could easily be handled by them. They knew full-well that this was going to disrupt their other stores a bit, but it was believed that it would keep the Hy-Vee Strike to a bare minimum on 'time and hard feelings'. Gateway's help had a few 'bumps in the road', but it worked extremely well.

As the first week or two of the Strike rolled along, our store at Iowa City began to deplete on stock status and it was becoming clear that it may be way down to empty shelves by the time it was all settled. The Store Manager, Don, and I had discussed what to do and we decided that the best thing to do was to send an order to Gateway every morning. The same items would be ordered each morning in hopes that we'd get some groceries and then get even more 'regularly' as Gateway got in the 'full swing' of the added stores. We just needed to 'get in line' and hope for the best.

So, that's what we did.

Each morning, I'd transmit an Electronic Order to Gateway and then we'd 'get busy' for the day and sell what we had, which was getting to be less each day for Dry Groceries, Produce and Frozen Foods. We had great suppliers for our items brought in by Vendor Companies and they kept us stocked-up right along. Those were items like Meats, Milk and Dairy items, Potato Chips, Cookies and Crackers, Soft Drinks, Beer and any other items we could procure locally.

In anticipation of what might happen with a Strike, we had 'stocked up' from our Hy-Vee Warehouse as well as we could for what a 14,500 square-foot store would hold. That 'stocking-up' proved to be very valuable and we looked back on it as being the 'safety valve' that kept us going.

In those first two weeks, however, the shelves did start depleting and we were seeing no signs yet of any deliveries from Gateway Foods. They were 'overwhelmed' with orders and doing the very best job they could. They had agreed to take on enough stores that it would more than 'double' their normal amounts. Things were getting tense for them too.

As the shelves got 'emptier and emptier' we continued to send our Electronic Orders for merchandise into Gateway Foods at La Crosse. We continued to 'hope against hope' for some deliveries and it was looking pretty bleak. And then it all changed directions.

Late one afternoon, with empty store shelves and frustration starting to creep in, we received a phone call from Gateway's Trucking Department that the next day we would be getting the 'the first of many' loads of groceries that would be coming from them...And 'MANY' it turned out to be.

The next morning, we received a 'full load' of Dry Groceries from their warehouse. Boy, were we glad. We called in all of the 'extra help' we could and we had a 'small army' in the store to meet the Gateway Truck and get it on the shelves as quickly as we could...45,000 pounds of Groceries made some improvement, but a fairly 'small dent' in the emptiness of the shelves...Hy-Vee's stores hold a lot of merchandise.

But that was to be 'short-lived'...

Just like 'making sausage in a tube grinder', the more you put in on one end, means that it will all eventually come out on the other end...Yes, it was all about to come our direction and 'The Rest of The Story' is one still told around Iowa City #2 Hy-Vee today.

Each day for the next 14 days, we received an 'identical load' to that first day's delivery. It was 14 loads of 45,000 pounds each and we nearly 'choked ourselves' taking them. We had filled our store's shelves to 'the brim' and we were looking 'pretty safe'. Our Customers were buying 'full orders' again. WHEW!

But that's just the beginning of the "Tale of The Trucks". The Strike had yet to be settled and we were afraid to cancel the loads from Gateway for the fear of then not getting anything. So, we continued to take the loads and keep the store full.

However, we had Dry Groceries 'Nearly Everywhere We Had Extra Space'. We had the entire Backroom filled to the rafters. We had the tops of all Backroom Coolers filled with Cereal, Paper Items and other Lightweight Stuff. We had a stack 'head-high' down the center of every aisle on the Retail Sales Floor. We even had stuff stacked across the windows of the Front-End by the Cash Registers.

But, we were 'So Glad to Have It'.

Next, however, was the problem of knowing 'what' we had in the building. How were we going to do it? After 'Brainstorming' on it, I went down to Radio Shack and I bought a pair of high quality 'Walkie-Talkies' and headed back to the store. We started immediately with our 'Plan of Attack'.

It worked 'GREAT'.

We put one person in the areas of 'excess stock' and one person out in the aisle. The person in the area of excess stock had a black marker and he would ask the person in the aisle about whether an item would fit on the shelf. If it would fit, it was marked with an 'X' with a circle around it. Then the Stock Crew would come behind those two and pull those 'X'

cases. It was really a 'genius idea' and we were again in control.

On Saturday of that first week with all the Groceries in the store and no more deliveries coming, we were paid a 'surprise visit' by Hy-Vee's President and Senior Vice-President, Dwight Vredenburg and Marion Coons respectively. We were glad to see them and they were an 'inspiration' to all of us to "Keep Ahead of It" as they said. They commented that "They were impressed with our use of the 'Walkie-Talkies' and that they were going to pass the idea along to all the other stores." We were proud. We had been creative in the 'face' of tough times.

As the two men walked across the Front-End of the store leaving, I remember saying to them... "Hang in there--we've got it under control out here at Retail".

It was what Senior Vice President, Marion Coons, said next that was 'Worth his weight in Gold'...He turned and looked at me and he said "Great...You know how it goes. It's 'Blood and Guts'...Our Guts and Your Blood". Then, we all laughed so loudly I was sure the Customers wondered what 'the funny' was all about... It was 'Vintage Marion'

I will always remember the Strike Of '77....

We 'Thanked Our 'Lucky Stars'...

And Then We Tried To Stack Merchandise Up There Too !

“I’ll Have A Sandwich.” ...

From the middle of the 1930’s, the Store Managers of ‘The Supply Stores’ started getting together at one of the stores for some ‘almost regular’ meetings to discuss strategy, Ad Layout, Ad Item Selection’ and just plain ‘Problem Solve’. In those early years, the ‘meetings’ were rather informal and the general structure of the meetings was very low key and rather unorganized. Usually, they were in a store’s Backroom with Butcher Paper laid out over some full cases of Wheaties or Post Toasties Cereal and lots of pencils, hot Coffee, donuts and ‘jokes’ told with a ‘thick haze’ of cigarette smoke everywhere. It seemed everyone smoked then. A lot of great ideas came out of those ‘meetings’.

One of the biggest things that got accomplished at those early and primitive ‘Managers Meetings’, however, was that there was an ‘organized direction’ gained for a company whose Philosophy was that each Store Manager ran his own store. That Philosophy of ‘autonomy’ is very much alive today and the Store Managers still run their stores and make almost all of the decisions ‘vital’ to make a company like Hy-Vee succeed in a very tough industry. It is, in large part, the ‘toughness’ and ‘innovative thinking’ of the Store Managers that has gotten the company through its nearly nine decades of being ‘Open for Business’. Those primitive forerunners of today’s Managers Meetings are a big

part of Hy-Vee's heritage. Much success is owed to the 'collective thought' process behind them.

As the late 1940's and early 1950's rolled along, 'The Supply Store' Executives made the decision to hold these Managers Meetings on a regular basis and it was decided that every other week at Headquarters was a good routine. When the 'Monthly Accounting' (now called 'Inventory') of each store to determine final monthly Sales and Profits was held, the Store Managers were required to come into Headquarters again and have the Accountants 'run the numbers' on each store and by that 'Monthly Accounting' the company knew precisely what its Sales and Profits were. That process was perfect to see trends developing in both 'good' and 'not so good' ways. There are sometimes both.

So, the addition of the Manager's Meetings and the Monthly Inventory made a total of three Wednesdays each month that the Store Managers were required to be in Chariton, IA for a meeting of one form or another. Occasionally, a 'special' meeting would be held to include the Meat Managers or the Produce Managers and that meant that the Store Managers would make their way to Chariton...one more time that month. It was 'Every Wednesday' most of the time over the years.

The Store Managers got to know just about 'every crack' in the highway between their town and Chariton, IA. Lots of miles... 'profitable miles' for the

Corporation and for the 'cohesiveness' and 'powerful decisions' that came out of them.

The five Top Executives of Hy-Vee have historically been 'The Selection Committee' and they were the persons who 'selected' Store Managers when one was needed. As the company added stores and had 'attrition" from retirements and other reasons, it got harder and harder for those 'Top Executives' to know all of the Store Managers. It was very common for them, especially Dwight Vredenburg (President and CEO), to make a big effort to spend some time with a new Store Manager. It worked for him to know them better just as it worked for them to know him better.

It was a definite 'win-win' for Communications and Respect.

Now, Dwight, being President and Chairman of the Board (also the namesake of the 'Vee' in Hy-Vee), had made it a special point to 'introduce' the new Store Managers to the entire Manager Group at that new Store Manager's first meeting. Dwight would introduce the new guy by name, give a little background on him and then he would offer the opportunity for the new Store Manager to "Say a few words" ...and we did just that. Perhaps the most important thing said by the new Store Manager was "And I'd like to 'Thank' the Selection Committee". It was like 'bowing down' and 'giving thanks'... Everyone did it and it was pretty much expected. You know, a definite 'Respect Thing'.

At the Weekly Manager's Meetings, lunch was observed and it was usually a 'soup and sandwich' or a 'light meal' of some kind. At these meetings, Dwight would 'always' wait for a new Store Manager to be done shaking hands with every other Store Manager as those veterans went through "The Chow Line" (as it was sometimes called). When everyone had said their 'hellos' to the new Store Manager, Dwight and the new Store Manager would go through the line together and fix their plates for lunch.

Last in line, of course...

This is where my story gets interesting.

At my first Manager's Meeting in early 1977, Dwight and I made our way through the Lunch Line and fixed our plates. Because we were the 'last two' to go through of over 120 people, there was not a large supply of food left, but there was enough for us to each get a sandwich and a bowl of soup along with some with potato chips and a small piece of cake for dessert. It looked good after an early drive to Chariton from my store in Ottumwa, IA and a 'full morning' of Speakers and conversation by a large group in a meeting format...There was so much to absorb.

As I passed through the Lunch Line with Dwight, I took one of the few remaining Roast Beef Sandwiches and I adorned it with some pickle slices, a piece of tomato and a big spoonful of mayonnaise. I put the top back on the bun, grabbed some chips

and a piece of cake and I followed Dwight to a table nearby to enjoy our lunch together.

Wow! Just me and 'The Boss'... Dwight was 'Awesome'... He was a 'Larger Than Life Man' and yet, very humble most times.

Dwight got up and went to a small serving table close-by and brought us each back a glass of Iced Tea and we began to eat. We made 'small-talk' as we started eating and a few chips into the meal, I decided it was time for a bite of the Roast Beef Sandwich, so I bit into it.

I got the surprise of my whole week.

I had put a huge spoonful of Vanilla Pudding all over my Roast Beef Sandwich...So, I swallowed the first bite and then I chuckled and said to Dwight "I just put Vanilla Pudding all over my Roast Beef Sandwich."

Dwight grinned and he said very softly "I saw you do that, but I didn't want to embarrass you by saying anything...I knew you'd find out soon enough." And then he laughed in a friendly way. He had known the whole time, but I'm sure he wanted to see the outcome.

Well, we both got amused by it and before we knew it, we were laughing pretty loudly. Then, a few others around us asked about it and they laughed. It seemed like everyone knew it before the day was over...It really was funny.

It turned out to be something I remembered nearly every time I ever went through the 'Chow Line' at Manager's Meeting. I'd look at that bowl of Vanilla Pudding and remember being a 'Rookie' Store Manager and then I'd chuckle inside about that day all those years before.

Throughout my whole career, as I filled my plate, I'd look for the Roast Beef Sandwiches...

Then I'd laugh to myself and say...

"HOLD THE MAYO" ...

"And That'll Be $25 For" ...

Since the early 1930's, the Stores of 'The Supply Stores' were geographically located close to that Southern Iowa and Northern Missouri area. The Groceries coming to those stores had to be able to get to the Stores quickly and efficiently and it made good sense to have them within easy driving distance. Locations were also looked at that could provide 'Stable Economic Balance' for the year-round success of the stores. It proved to be a 'Winning Strategy' and a 'Growing Strategy' too.

Now, Ottumwa, IA is an 'old' and 'longtime' Hy-Vee town and it is a very unique business climate for the two Stores operating there. Hy-Vee's two stores in Ottumwa (#1 and #2) are separated by the Des Moines River which seems to run almost 'West to East' through a town with a few bridges. The North Side of town had predominantly been the side of town that was always viewed as the 'White Collar' side of town and the South Side of town was predominantly looked at as the 'Blue Collar' side of town. Obviously, it wasn't totally that way, but that's how Ottumwans had viewed it for generations.

The two largest employers, John Deere and John Morrell, Inc were both on the South Side and provided 'several thousand' jobs for the area. Ottumwa had a great clientele good hard-working 'middle class' people living there and 'many' retired Seniors too.

Old Albia Road on the South Side had been the home of 'Ray's Foodland' when Hy-Vee bought Ray Benjamin's Store in 1957 and it became a Hy-Vee Store. Ray stayed on to 'successfully manage' the Store for many years. It became 'Ottumwa Hy-Vee #1" after the 'North Store' (aka Ottumwa #2) was purchased from the owners of Tri-Angle Foods on North Court Street in the early 1960's.

A fire in early July of 1974 had burned the South Store 'clear to the ground' and when the decision to rebuild right on the same spot was made, more land was purchased behind it and the building replaced the 8 houses that had been there. The new building was set to the back of the now larger lot and the old spot became parking. Hy-Vee then owned the entire square block at 1527 Albia Road.

In early 1977, I went to Ottumwa to be the Store Manager on the South Side. Hy-Vee's Store on Old Albia Road was a two-year-old 25,000 square foot 'State of The Art' building that was serving the South Side of Ottumwa. It was an 'AWESOME STORE' to say the least. As I said, "State of The Art' for 1975.

Now, in the History of Hy-Vee, it has always been said that 'Competition is Good'. I am not sure just what angle that statement was being looked at from by the person speaking the words, but they weren't mad at a competitor when they said it. It's also true that 'temper' will take away the positive parts of 'Good Competition' sometimes, especially when the

'Competition' gets so obnoxious it not only bothers your style of operation in a Grocery Store, but it just down-right makes you mad.

One such 'makes you mad' incident developed over a period of two months and it really came to a breaking point on a Friday afternoon while I was the Store Manager of the Ottumwa #1 Hy-Vee.

Here's how it all came about...

Earlier in Ottumwa's History, Albia Road had been the road to Albia, Iowa and when Highway 34 was made new and sort of 'out-skirted' the town, the Ottumwa #1 store 'seemed' to be in a more residential area than before. Just the nature of the traffic flow had given it a more 'neighborhood' feeling.

Lots of older and smaller 1950's –style businesses were on Old Albia Road. There were two small Motels, a couple of Gas Stations, a Dairy Queen, Hy-Vee and Bob's Market. There were a few other businesses too. Bob's Market was the source of this story as it happened in 1979.

In the late Summer and early Fall of 1979, we were beginning to get into 'full swing with the newly enacted 'Iowa Bottle Bill' that required us to redeem cans and bottles for a 5 cent 'deposit return' to the Customers. It was falling into place and we were learning to cope with it just fine. We didn't like it, but we had to live with it, so we were.

Bob, at Bob's Market, was operating his small corner grocery store about 5 blocks down from us on Old Albia Road and he was struggling to keep going. We had started to 'heat things up' to get business and Bob made the decision that he could accept the Hy-Vee label Pop cans for the 5 cent-deposit. By doing that, he thought he could keep his Customers from coming to Hy-Vee.

So, Bob's decision to do that started the cycle of Bob redeeming (at our store) the Hy-Vee Pop Cans he'd accepted at his store and every few weeks, he (or one of his people), would come to our store with 'lots of bags and boxes' of disorganized Hy-Vee Pop cans. It was always on a Friday night about 5:30 or 6:00 PM when our Courtesy Counter was at its busiest point of the week. Bob knew exactly what he was doing to 'clog-up' our operation at the Courtesy Counter while he redeemed all the cans. In the process of that redemption, it brought things to a halt for about 20-30 minutes while our Crew got the cans counted and organized.

Now, I had politely asked Bob to call before they came over and to bring them on a different day so we could make an easier transaction out of it, but Bob wanted to 'clog-up' our operation, so he continued to bring them on Friday nights. It was getting very aggravating and our Crew knew I was getting very upset with it as it went along.

I made up my mind I'd take care of it 'once and for all'.

Since I could see the Courtesy Counter very easily from my Office window, I knew I'd see it develop on a Friday night, so I instructed the Crew at the Courtesy Counter to 'cheerfully' get all the bags and boxes of cans behind the Counter and get them counted like always. I had also told them that when they were done and 'before' they gave the can redemption money to Bob, to call me to the Courtesy Counter. I would give him the money personally.

So, sure enough, Friday came and Bob presented himself at the Courtesy Counter with a large number of bags and boxes full of cans and I watched from the Office window as they were 'counted and organized' by our Crew there. When that was all done, one of our Crew picked up the microphone and paged me to come to the Courtesy Counter. I went down the Office stairs and I walked across the front-end of the store at a medium speed to the Courtesy Counter.

When I arrived at there, I walked through the opening to the backside of the Counter and I took the $55+ from the hand of our Clerk. (at 5 cents each, that's a lot of cans) Then, I turned around to face Bob and the rest of the Customers waiting their turn to be helped. In a loud enough voice for everyone there to hear me, I said "Bob, I have asked you to 'Please' call ahead and we'd agree on a good time to have you bring these cans in so as not to disrupt things here, but you

seem to be insistent on bringing them when it makes a mess here for us and our Customers."

Things were very quiet.

I then held up the $55+ money for the cans and I said "Now the total was $55+ here and I'm keeping $25 of it for our fee to sort these while it messed up our operations here and made these good folks wait. And from now on, Bob, anytime you present yourself here at a busy time, it's going to cost you $25 for that decision." I then handed Bob his $30+ and I handed the $25 back to our Clerk to put in the Cash Register drawer.

Bob started 'squawking and carrying on' about it "Not being fair or even legal" and I calmly looked at several of our good Customers standing there waiting and then I looked directly into Bob's eyes and I said "So, call the Police, Bob."

That was the last time Bob ever came to the store to redeem Hy-Vee Pop cans. After that, he always called and asked about a good time to come in and then he sent one of his employees to redeem the cans.

The whole incident became known

as the day...

We Got 'Canned' By Bob...

Cinderella's Missing Slipper...

Way back in 1930, when Charles Hyde and David Vredenburg formed their partnership and called it 'The Hyde and Vredenburg Supply Stores', little did they know that their Philosophies and early practices would still be 'goin' strong' nearly 90 years later. Those primitive stores with wood floors and single light bulbs hanging from the ceilings were the sites that held the early 'Managers Meetings' and they would eventually make way for the present day 'Managers Meetings'. A gathering of 'The Minds' still get together for 'Idea Sharing' on Wednesdays.

Nowadays, it's more than those early eight or nine Store Managers gathering to draw ads on 'Butcher Paper' for each to use. Such a 'Valuable Tool' these meetings have proven to be.

'In My Day', every Wednesday saw the Store Managers heading to Headquarters in Chariton, IA for 'Managers Meeting'. There really wasn't a good enough excuse to miss the meetings unless it was a death in the family, the birth of a new child or a scheduled vacation. 'Rain or Shine' and 'Snow and Sleet' saw all the Store Managers at Managers Meeting. Tens of thousands of miles were driven on the highways getting to Chariton and back home again.

All in one day...A long day...

It was a day away from the store, but it was a real grueling day. Up at 3AM or 4AM and not home until near

8PM or later, but it was a 'Great Day' and each meeting proved to strengthen Hy-Vee in many ways. All kinds of ideas were shared and it was designed to keep everyone thinking and acting along the same lines in the stores.

Hy-Vee's 'Management Philosophy' was (and still is) that each Store Manager ran their own store and the goal was to grow and make a profit while staying 'legal and ethical' in the day-to-day operations. Each Store Manager 'priced' his own store Merchandise, set their own Wage Structure, planned their own Ads and decided the Store Policies that were good for their own store and area.

It has been a "Winning Combination" for almost 90 years.

Managers Meeting Day was also a great time to physically exchange smaller items that one store had that another store could use. If the items could be carried in a car trunk, they were usually exchanged over the lunch-break and it saved an extra trip somewhere to get the item or items.

Not only was there a serious side to the Managers Meetings', but all these high-powered 'Executive Store Managers' acted like 'Teenage Kids' when it came to the pranks and jokes they played on each other. They were always looking at a way to have some fun. Sometimes, the pranks and jokes border-lined on 'mean'. This story was one of those type of those 'mean pranks'.

Here's the Story...

My older brother, Larry, was the Store Manager at the Urbandale, IA #1 Hy-Vee, and I was in the Ottumwa, IA #1, Store. We had agreed that my store would sell his store some type of a product shipper display and that we could put it in the trunks of our cars and we would make the swap at lunch. So that's what we decided to do.

Lunchtime came and Larry and I ate lunch and then walked to the cars to exchange the shipper display. He opened his trunk and I put the displayer in it. As I started to close his car trunk, I noticed a woman's 'high-heeled shoe' laying on the ground near the corner of his car. I had no idea why it was there, but I did know that the situation was 'ripe' for a good prank.

Now, I knew Larry hadn't seen the shoe, so I waited until he turned to start back to the building and then I grabbed the 'ladies shoe' and I very quickly tossed it into the trunk of his car. I slammed the lid and followed him into the building... I was 'grinning' all the way in.

The meeting got going for the afternoon and I didn't think any more about it until later that night. I was home and had just crawled into bed when the phone rang. It was Larry and he was frantic. "Rick," he said "Did you put a woman's shoe in my trunk today?"

"Who wants to know?" I replied.

Then he blurted out "Cut the crap man, if you put it in there, tell Teresa (his wife). She went to put something

in the trunk tonight and she found the shoe. She won't believe me that I have never seen it before. She thinks I am running around on her."

I had him right where I wanted him.

"Larry, I don't remember seeing a shoe in your trunk. How do you suppose it got there?" I said with a laugh. The desperation in his voice told me he was really on the 'hot seat' over this as he said "Rick, this is serious. If you put it there, tell her or I'll never get outta' this one."

"Put her on the phone." I told him. As she came on the phone, she halfway screamed "You better not be covering for him. I know how you guys are. I want the truth". It was at this point, I realized I had two choices... 1. I could let go of my joke and probably keep it to 'Just A Big Fight' or 2. I could hang on to my joke and cause a divorce for sure. So, I chose to let them 'Just Have a Big Fight'. Generous me.

I am not sure whether his wife was 100% convinced it was the truth, but she listened as I told her the story. She hung up quite angry with Larry and I am sure quite angry with me.

For years after, when we were 'sparring verbally', I would joke with him and tell him...

"Be careful, Cinderella, or I'll put another shoe in your car !" ...

"Cuff Him And Stuff Him" ! ...

Since their inception, the Police Department has been an interesting bunch of people in every community and when you are in the Grocery Business, you see some things that most people don't get to see. These things you get to see are generally the 'inner-workings' of the Department and the personalities of the people in the Department. Sometimes, it can be really funny.

I was the Store Manager at The Ottumwa, IA #1 Store from 1977-1981, I saw these 'inner-workings' of the Ottumwa Police Department on many occasions and I enjoyed the view very much. Some fun things happened and I still enjoy thinking about it today.

One of the most interesting people in the Ottumwa Police Department was a Detective for the Department named Hugh... Now, I think most people who knew Hugh loved him, but most would agree that he was a bit like 'Barney Fife in a Suit'. He was 'Official' all right, but Hugh just always seemed to leave people shaking their heads about 'What' just happened', 'Why' it happened', 'How' it happened' and sometimes with Hugh in on the case... 'Did It Really Happen?'.

Let me fill you in on one of my experiences with Hugh.

In late 1979, we had been having trouble at our Hy-Vee with a guy named Herman. Herman kept coming

in late in the evening and writing 'bogus checks' and we could never 'catch him in the act' to apprehend him. The checks were actually written on an account this man had closed a few years before and of course, his checks matched his identification, so our Clerks at the Customer Service Counter would cash them for him. It all seemed like a legitimate transaction and he was into us for around $800 or $900 before we knew it. It all unfolded as a 'scam' on Herman's part.

I had been to the County Courthouse and to the Police Department for the 'Official Paperwork' parts of us filing charges against Herman for 'Fraudulent Use of a Financial Instrument(s)' and it was put out to the Officers to 'pick him up' when they could. We were told we'd have to wait it out and 'eventually' he'd be apprehended. After that, we'd see him in Wapello County Court. So, a few months went by and I'd sort of forgotten about the possibility of a 'looming arrest' of our culprit, Herman.

After those few months, Herman's arrest finally happened. Hugh was involved and here's how it all happened in Mayberry...I mean Ottumwa.

Sundays were pretty much a 'Day of Rest' for most Store Managers in their Hy-Vee. Oh, we usually attended Church and stopped into the store for an hour or so, but Sundays meant we could sleep in until 8 AM and have a leisurely morning with our families and just basically 're-charge our batteries' a bit. Almost every other day of the week was consumed

with being at the store early and staying late and even then, dragging a project home to finish it at night. The Sunday morning 'R & R' was a bit needed by all of us Store Managers.

So, on the Sunday morning of this story, I was sound asleep when around 4:30 AM, the phone rang... It always scared me to get calls at the odd times of the night because of all the things that could go wrong and me being notified. I answered and of course, I said "Hello". The voice on the other end of the phone said... "Lampkin? ... Hugh, down at the Police Station... We got Herman and you need to come down here to ID him."

With that, I tried to wake up for a moment and I replied "Okay, Hugh, I'll be down around 8 or so." Very quickly, Hugh said "No, you need to come now." With that, I reminded Hugh that it was 4:30 in the morning, but he insisted, so I got dressed, ran the electric razor over my face, combed my hair and brushed my teeth before heading off to the Ottumwa Police Department.

As I entered the front door of 'The Station', I asked the clerk at the desk there where Hugh was and I was directed to a room on the second floor of the building and I made my way up the stairway to where I was told to go. I opened the door and walked into the room where Hugh was.

Now, I have seen lots of television shows and plenty of episodes from 'The Andy Griffith Show' and this 'spectacle' was pretty much 'Vintage Barney Fife'.

Hugh sat in a chair with his suit on and dressed for 'business' and he was smoking a cigarette. Sitting across from Hugh was this 'huge man' that was 'well over' 6' tall and weighed at least 240 pounds. He was handcuffed to the wooden chair he was sitting in and he said nothing. He looked like the 'Incredible Hulk' just after he'd already burst into being 'The Hulk'. His clothes looked disheveled and a bit too small. It was obvious he was really 'put-out' with Hugh.

As I greeted Hugh, he said... "Lampkin, is this Herman? Can you identify him as the man who wrote those checks to you?" I looked over at Herman and 'half-heartedly', I said "Yes that's him."

And I said nothing more.

Just like that, Hugh was out of his chair and standing in front of his prisoner who was still handcuffed to his chair. He leaned over this huge 'Hulk of A Guy', pointed his finger at him and he said "There you go, Herman...We're gonna' send you to the Damn License Plate Factory."

It was just like Barney talking to Otis and I almost laughed as it all unfolded in front of me.

There sat a man about twice Hugh's size and he was being badgered in a scene like we'd all seen dozens of times before. I think Hugh was putting on a show

for me and I stood and watched intently. It occurred to me as I stood there that the small wooden chair Herman was sitting in was so small and so lightweight that the fact of him being handcuffed to it was immaterial in the display by Hugh. Herman could have easily broken that chair in pieces and done anything he wanted to Hugh... and I am not sure I would have blamed him.

So, I went home and Hugh sent Herman off to the jail cell that awaited him. I was pretty sure that even in his situation, Herman had wondered the same thing I did... "What just happened here?"

We did appear in Court against Herman and he was sentenced to serve some time for his Check Writing, but I always felt a bit sorry for him.

Herman had been reduced to being "Otis Campbell of Mayberry" and he'd just been caught-up

in 'Barney playing... 'Cops and Robbers'

(with Andy nowhere around) ...

“The investment of a man’s time and energy should be equal to the investment of the Company’s money.”

David M. Vredenburg

Hy-Vee Co-Founder

(Deceased)

“But We Stopped To Help Someone”

Since those primitive ‘Supply Store’ days of the 1930’s and early 1940’s the weekly Managers Meetings evolved from a gathering of several Store Managers in the Backroom of one of the Stores in Southern Iowa or Northern Missouri. Those ‘Meetings’ would see an exchange of great ideas on every conceivable topic in the Stores.

As the years rolled along it was decided that ’Formal’ Managers Meetings should be held and now almost 90 years later. Wednesday is still ‘Managers Meeting” for the Store Managers.

With Wednesdays being rather ‘sacred’ and with ‘required attendance’ for the Managers Meetings each week, Hy-Vee always felt the need to make sure they knew ‘who’ was there and ‘who’ may have missed a meeting... The need for a ‘system of attendance’ was found as those years rolled along and it proved to be a lot of fun for all.

A permanent ‘Sergeant at Arms’ was designated and each week, the ‘Sergeant at Arms’ would take attendance by simply watching everyone enter and find a seat for the meeting. The Sergeant would check off the names and anyone not accounted for was dealt with at lunch by an ‘out-loud vote’ of the group in attendance.

After lunch was completed and about five minutes before the meeting re-convened, the Sergeant would

get to the podium and announce 'who' was not in attendance and also those who were 'late' for the Managers Meeting that morning. If someone had a legitimate excuse for not being in attendance, they were 'officially excused' and those who had no excuse or were late that morning were 'voted on' to determine their fate.

So, individually the 'Sergeant' would read the name of the 'offender' and the Manager group would cast a vote by a 'Yea' (excuse 'em) or a 'Nay' (fine 'em) and it went like that for each person who were either 'not there' or who were just plain 'late'. Some meetings, there were no offenders and then some meetings had several offenders'. It varied.

The 'guilty offenders' were fined the 'Grand Sum of One Dollar'.

If the person being voted on at the time of the 'Roll Call Vote', was at the meeting (usually the late ones), they were given the opportunity to explain 'what it was' that had made them late and they would 'beg for mercy' from the Humorously Vindictive group voting. There would be a long-winded speech, usually with a lot of 'Puffery' and then a vote.

Pretty much always, however, the final outcome of the vote was 'Nay' and to 'fine 'em'...It was a fun thing and since the fine was the huge sum of 'One Dollar', it was easy to say 'fine 'em' and have everyone laughing for the beginning of the afternoon part of the day. If the person being fined was not there, they

were then subjected later to the 'harassment' by their fellow Store Managers and it was good for a good laugh or two. The 'One Dollar' fine was actually deducted from the monthly paychecks and the money used for flowers to be sent by our group when necessary.

One such incident happened in 1979 and it involved the two Store Managers from the Mason City, IA Hy-Vee Stores. It was great and it was good for many 'repeats' of the story.

It went like this.

I was the Store Manager at The Ottumwa, IA #1 Hy-Vee at the time and I had driven the 47 miles in to Headquarters in Chariton, IA for the weekly Managers Meeting.

On that morning, the Managers Meeting started as 'normal' and within about 20 minutes or so, the 'stragglers' all came in and there were about four that morning. We all knew we'd have fun with them after lunch and we all chided the four and teased them with 'threats' of the vote after lunch. The whole group knew all along 'where' it was all going though and that was going to be a vote to 'fine 'em'...

So, our meeting that day took its normal course and we had the various Speakers from the 'Key' Departments and Company Officers that we heard from each meeting and then we broke for lunch. About 45 minutes was spent on lunch and then it

came time for 'The Vote'...So, the 'Sergeant at Arms' came to the podium and asked for the attention of the 'Rowdy Bunch'. He announced the names of the 'offenders' and as usual, the first two were 'fined a dollar'. Then, he announced that Don and Charlie, the two Store Managers from Mason City, had requested the opportunity to 'plead their case' to the group.

Now, a request to 'plead your case' was always granted and most times, the 'pleading' was really entertaining. Their case was no exception and they both stepped to the podium. First one spoke and then the other.

It seems they had been travelling south down I-35 in Northern Iowa on their way in to the Managers Meeting when they came upon a farmer with a big bag of stuff in the back of his old pickup truck and he was 'broken down' on the Interstate.

As they explained it to the group of Store Managers listening very intently to their story, they went on to say that they felt he was in a "Very Dangerous Spot" on the road and so, they stopped to help him.

They continued on with the story and explained that when they looked at the old pickup, they were sure they could get it started with their 'jumper cables' so, they hooked them to their car to start the pickup. After a little while of working with the carburetor in addition to the low battery power, they were able to get the farmer's pickup going and they followed him into an exit a few miles down the Interstate and then

to a mechanic's garage that was close by. All of this had taken about 30- 45 minutes of their time and they said 'that' was 'why' they were late.

Then came the vote...

As the votes 'usually went', the story had been told to a 'Pretty Skeptical Group' and there were even some 'shouts' ahead of the vote. The vote was taken it was to 'fine 'em' for the mere fact that they stopped to help the old farmer. Then, there were more 'catcalls' yet about their story.

So, the 'Sergeant at Arms' called for a 'second vote' and it was about 120-0 again to 'fine 'em'. That outcome was not unexpected by the two from Mason City and we all laughed hard at their fate...They laughed too. Most of us had been in their shoes a few times and had been fined 'one dollar', so we were just getting our revenge on them for voting to "fine 'em" when it was us.

It was close to the end of the 'podium time' for them when someone in the listening group 'picked-up' on the part of the story where they said they said they stopped to help 'an old farmer with a big bag of stuff in the back of his old pickup truck' and 'The Big Question' was shouted out for everyone to hear...

"What was in the 'Big Bag'?" someone shouted and with that, the door was 'flung right open' for the response of the two Mason City Store Managers. With 'big grins' and a 'laugh', they hollered out "It was

a 'Big Bag' Of 'Bul@S#*t' just like we've been feeding all of you!" ...

The whole room roared with laughter that went on for little while... I think the two laughing the loudest were the two Store Managers from Mason City.

They had gotten their 'revenge' for being fined a dollar.

That Manager Meeting and the 'Big Bag of Stuff' lived on for quite a while in the stories that went around. I always thought about that day as we were voting on others who were late or absent and I'd always chuckle to myself about the day those two "Pled Their Case" and 'Sort Of' lost the vote.

It was, however, the day ...

'The Stuff Got Out Of The Bag'...

And All Over Us ! ...

“Have You Seen The Keys ??” ...

In a ‘Perfect World’, the need for ‘Locks and Keys’ would not be necessary. In the stores of every era of Hy-Vee since the 1930’s, however, ‘Locks and Keys’ have been a ‘Way of Life” for the stores and the Crews.

In a store the size of a large Supermarket, there was a key for everything. There were keys for doors, drawers, cabinets, closets, cash registers, store vans and a hundred other items like these. Anyone with any ‘higher authority’ would have a ‘ring of keys’ and you could always hear that person’s keys ‘jingle’ as they walked or ran around the store. It was sort of a ‘status symbol’ if you had the ‘glob’ of keys ‘jingling’ on your side.

One huge problem, however, was the “Loss of keys’ or the constant dilemma of ‘Who has the keys’ when you need a certain thing opened or unlocked. That dilemma was most apparent in the area of filling the pop machines or any other vending machine that needed filling on a daily basis. Locks on vending machines were very expensive and hard to duplicate. For that reason, there were usually only one or two sets and they were to always be ‘used and then put back’ in the place they were officially stored which was usually ‘The Office’.

It seems simple, but very few things were as complicated as or disrupted things so much as not

knowing where the keys were to the vending machines... Specifically, The Pop Machine'.

Here's how important that can be...

I was the Store Manager at the Southside Ottumwa, IA #1 Hy-Vee Store from 1977-1981 and our Store Manager at the Northside Ottumwa #2 Hy-Vee was a man named Emmett. He was a really great guy with a very soft-spoken personality. We shared Ads and worked Price Changes together and pretty much made sure that Hy-Vee's Customers in Ottumwa could find the same items and the same prices at both locations.

Now, this type of an arrangement made it necessary for Emmett and I to be in each other's store on a very regular basis. We became good friends as well as business partners as we worked together in our meetings and then travelled together to Headquarters on our Weekly Managers Meetings. We also 'socialized' often with our wives too.

Fridays were the days we met to 'plan and coordinate' the newspaper Ad for 3 weeks ahead of us. This 'lead time' gave us the chance to order the product and plan the displays and allow the local newspaper to 'lay-out' the Ads for us. We usually met weekly at my store or his store on Friday afternoons.

One Friday, I loaded up my things and drove to Emmett's store for the weekly Ad Meeting. I arrived about 10 or 15 minutes early, so I looked around in

Emmett's aisles for a few minutes. I wanted to make sure I had not missed any Price Changes or overlooked a new way of displaying products on the shelves (called Shelf-Sets). I could usually get an idea or two from Emmett. He was a 'Good Operator'.

When the time of our meeting arrived, I went to Emmett's Office for the start of the meeting. As I walked up the stairs to the office, I could see a 2'x4' piece of wood standing in the corner. It looked to be about 5 or 6 feet long and it had a hole drilled on one end with a wire running through it. On the end of the wire, I could see a single 'Silver Key' shining in the light.

I said "Hey Emmett, what's with the key?" Emmett very calmly replied back "Rick, I am so tired of my guys taking the pop machine key home with them at night, I fixed it so they won't do it again. They will have to work like Hell to get it in their car and then maybe they won't take it home."

It was a great 'quick fix' for a problem born out of frustration. It seemed a bit odd, but it must have been working for them. It was a funny moment.

It must have struck Emmett how funny it was also, because we both had a great round of laughter from it and then had our meeting. The key stayed on the board until Emmett and his crew moved to a brand-new store the following year. I never saw it after that.

I suppose they figured with a new 'Multi-million Dollar' Operation, they had come to the point of having a few more keys available--or at least the need to look more organized anyway.

It was not 'The Key To Success',

but rather it was...

'The Success To The Key'...

“Oh, The Sweet Taste Of” ...

For as long as Hy-Vee has been in business, there have been instances where there ‘Was a caper to solve’... It might have been mice...It might have been a leak...It might have been Shoplifting...It might have been someone trying to pass a Bad Check or it might have been Employee Theft...

But, for sure, ‘There’s always been a caper to solve’.

Hy-Vee’s roots in Southern Iowa and Northern Missouri in the 1930’s lent itself to stores who knew all of their Customers and Crew and believed those Folks to be deserving of ‘some discretion’ when things happened in the stores with its Crew or a good Customer. Sometimes it was someone ‘snitching’ an apple, a candy bar or even a bottle of pop, but usually, things ‘came to light’ and whatever it was, it was soon in the past.

The ‘discretion’ part of these issues usually came about because Hy-Vee felt (and still does feel) that the negative image of an incident would cause embarrassment to a local family or individual who was really not part of the problem. Hy-Vee believes in being ‘discreet’ and when a person got involved simply by ‘name association’ with the ‘guilty party’, it causes an undeserving shadow on them. It has proven to be an ‘Honorable Path’ to take for nearly 90 years.

The incidents that happened were sometimes 'funny' and this story is about one of those 'funny incidents' that came about and made for a good 'whodunit story' in the process for the Hy-Vee History Books.

This was 'The Caper'…

In Hy-Vee's Newton, IA #1 Store, the Store Manager, Al, kept getting reports that someone was drinking Chocolate Milk in the Milk Cooler and then leaving the 'empty cartons' lying around… Having a thief in the Crew is a lot like having a mouse in your house. When you know that someone is 'grazing' on the store's products, it sort-of starts 'wearing real thin' on a store's Management Team.

It's true that if you allow it for one person, the other members of the Crew will eventually believe that if it is tolerated for one person, everyone else can do similar things. When that happens, all attempts to keep everyone honest seem to fail quickly. So, with Honesty being a real 'core value' of Hy-Vee's Heritage, Al knew he had to deal with it and he made his mind up that he was going to catch the culprit.

So, he made a plan.

Al drove to the local Police Department and he talked to a friend there he knew could help him and his friend obliged. He obtained 'The Stuff' he was advised by his friend to use and he returned to his store. It would be a bit of a 'wait and see' issue, but Al had the patience to let it take whatever time

necessary to stop the 'Thief in the Milk Cooler' that was bothering him and hurting his store's morale.

Several days went by and nothing happened. Each of the scheduled persons who normally worked in the Milk Cooler stocking the cases with fresh milk were beginning to work their shift and the exposure to 'the culprit' was beginning to play out. 'Who would it be?' and better yet, 'Would Al's Detective Work find the answer?'

Late one afternoon about 5 or 6 days into the 'Detective Work', Al walked back to the Backroom to go to the Men's Restroom. As he passed through the Backroom and the door to the Milk Cooler, a young man came out dragging some empty wire milk crates along on the floor with the wire hook used for that...

Bingo!

Al knew immediately that this young man was his 'culprit'... 'The Chocolate Milk Bandit' of the Milk Cooler...Al immediately walked up to him and boldly announced "You—are the Chocolate Milk Thief" and pointed his finger directly in the young man's face. Being totally surprised at Al's accusation, the young man sort of 'shot back'... "No, Al...it's not me!".

And with that, Al took a hold on the young man's elbow and said "Come with me" ... And they walked to the Men's Restroom where Al 'squared' the young man right up in front of the mirror and he said "Look—you are the thief".

As the young man looked at himself in the mirror, he knew he had been 'caught' and there was no denying it...All around his mouth, was the 'Brightest Purple Stain' you can imagine...Al had been 'A Super Detective' and he had solved the caper ...simply and precisely. Nobody was falsely accused and the 'culprit' was found.

Good Work, Al ...

You see, Al had obtained 'Detective Powder' from his friend at the Police Department and he had applied a small amount to the tops of several cartons of Chocolate Milk in the Cooler...The Detective Powder would stay invisible 'until' it came into contact with the lips or skin of the person who was drinking the Chocolate Milk...When the Detective Powder was touched by the young man's lips to take a drink, they changed color immediately.

They became 'Bright Purple'...

The Young Man's Parents were called to come and get him and he 'no longer worked for Hy-Vee'. The Police were not called but, it was quite embarrassing for the young man to be picked up by his Parents with his lips 'Bright Purple' from the Detective Powder. There was no arguing about it. He had been caught and his Parents could easily tell after Al explained how it happened, that their son was the 'Chocolate Milk Thief'.

The story of Al's 'sleuth work' has been told for many decades and it is a good one. Nobody ever drank Chocolate Milk in the Cooler at the Newton Hy-Vee after that...

It was the story of

Not Being Caught 'Red-Handed',

but instead,

Being Caught 'Purple-Lipped'...

"Customer Loyalty means everything to our Store Managers and their Staffs."

Ronald D. Pearson

President, CEO and

Chairman of the Board

(Retired)

"FORE !"...

'The Supply Store' era of Hy-Vee left many indelible marks on the Company that have lasted for almost 90 years. In those early years, several Store Managers would gather on a Wednesday in the Backroom of one of the centrally located Stores and they'd drink 'Gallons of Coffee' and draw-up ads on Butcher Paper that had been laid out on a Post Toasties Carton or other large cases of Cereal.

From those primitive, unorganized 'Managers Meetings' of the late 1930's and 1940's, Hy-Vee's Managers Meetings 'Morphed' over the decades to the huge Meeting Center that was built in 1994 at the New Corporate Headquarters when the Company moved to West Des Moines, IA. The new facility was built to hold the regular Corporate Meetings with up to 500 or so people in attendance. There is a lunch served from a complete kitchen to prepare food from. There are 'State of The Art' Sound and Video Projection Systems as well as plenty of table space and large Restroom facilities.

But that's not how it always was...I was there for 'lots' of Meetings in "lots' of places before that.

It took many 'rented locations' and many 'tries' at finding facilities that were both large enough and well-located enough for getting everyone in to the meetings from great distances. Parking, Table

Sizes, Meals and Restrooms became a 'Central Focus' of these 'Rented Locations'.

When Hy-Vee (then still Hyde and Vredenburg, Inc.) purchased the Chariton Wholesale Grocery in 1945, the meetings moved there for a few years until the new Corporate Headquarters and Hy-Vee Warehouse were built in 1960 at the location of 1801 Osceola Avenue in Chariton, IA. The 'Meetings' were moved there at that time.

As the Managers Meetings grew larger yet and as Hy-Vee's need outgrew the meeting space there in the Chariton Offices, the Main Lodge at Red Haw State Park on Chariton's East Side was used. Then later, at the new Clubhouse at Lakeview Golf and Country Club on Chariton's West Side was used. Lakeview Country Club met the needs nicely for many years. During those times, some of our 'Larger Meetings' were also held at The Inferno Lounge on Des Moines' South Side, The Savory Hotel in Des Moines, The American Legion on 2nd Ave in Des Moines, Adventureland Inn in Altoona, IA and a host of other locations over the years. Many were used.

A 'Growing Company' required more room all the time to get everyone in. As mentioned, in 1994, the Managers Meetings were moved to the new Hy-Vee Headquarters in West Des Moines. The 'Meeting Center' there is where they are still held today.

This story centers around the Chariton Meetings at the Lakeview Country Club. I attended meetings there for nearly 18 years.

Those Meetings held at 'Lakeview' in Chariton were the ones I will always remember the most. I am sure that feeling is 'pretty universal' of the Store Managers of the era. It bordered on 'organized chaos' with a bunch of 'high powered big kids' getting together for a meeting and some time away from the store. It was always an enlightening day and lots of fun and 'lots of Horseplay' too.

Lakeview was a modern Country Club with a nice 'main room' and plenty of parking and adequate Restrooms. There was a kitchen and the staff there always had a nice 'Soup and Sandwich Meal' prepared for us. The meal price was $4.

The Country Club's Meeting Room was all glass on the North side of the room and it was elevated about 15'-18' above the 18th Hole of the Golf Course. On nice days, there were golfers hitting onto the 18th for their 'final hole' and it was always tempting to turn and watch them instead of the Speakers at the podium, which was positioned to make sure the audience was facing to see the Speaker and not to see the golfers. It was a pretty good setup, but every now and then, we'd get a view of the 18th hole that we never forgot.

Sometimes, right out of 'clear blue' a golf ball would come crashing through the window and land on one

of the tables in the audience or on the floor. Of course, there was a lot of glass that came with it and it just scared the 'B'Jeezers' out of everyone. It would totally disrupt the meeting and there was a need to stop everything, sweep up the glass, brush the glass off a few people, put some cardboard over the hole and 'Oh, yes' ...take a 'Pee Break' to calm everyone's nerves.

We never knew when one of these 'Crashings' would happen, but we'd always keep one eye on the Speaker in front of us and one on the 18th Green behind us.

And of course, we always listened attentively for the 'Ever-Threatening Roar' of someone yelling...

"FORE ! ---Oh, No---Look Out !"

"She Probably Talked It Off" ...

'The Family of Hy-Vee' is a well-known slogan used within Hy-Vee to denote the 'Love and Respect' between the Crew at any store. That feeling started all those years ago in 'The Supply Stores' of the 1930's and 1940's. It's not a secret that 'Happy People' will work harder and that 'Happy People' grow to know each other. Over time, 'The Breakroom' in every store has become 'the hub' of information for the store. It was a place everyone 'became a family' at Hy-Vee.

It is in the Breakroom that a few moments of 'Leisure Time' is captured in 'small clippings' of time by every Employee. The Employees from all the different Departments go to the Breakroom for a quick 15 or 20-minute 'paid break' or a full 60-minute period 'off-the-clock' to eat lunch and get ready for the second half of their shift.

Many times, there are 'jokes and pranks' along with serious Family issues that are shared with everyone. It is an interesting 'microcosm' of the personalities involved at the store. It is 'the glue' that holds the Crew together as 'The Family of Hy-Vee'.

It's a very strong bond...In every store, the group that seems to interact as a 'Family' in the Breakroom will be centered around the 'happenings' of those Employees and many times, it is like small 'soap operas' for the rest of us listening. I say 'soap opera'

in that things will seem to continue on for 'days or weeks' at a time by the same person or persons. Most days, the same people are there at the same times, so the stories get very 'over and over' in nature and that's where the 'soap opera' atmosphere comes in. Gossip and open criticism got into the mix on a few occasions and that would cause problems along the way too.

One such 'Soap Opera' happened in 1978. I was not able to keep my mouth shut any longer and 'my comment' got repeated very quickly... and to 'everyone' in the store!

Here's how it went.

I was the Store Manager of the Ottumwa, IA #1 Hy-Vee Store from 1977-1981. Although I tried not to get directly involved in the Breakroom conversation, every now and then, I would accidentally get right in the middle of it and it would 'resonate' through the store. Sometimes, I might as well have announced it over the loudspeaker. You can be sure, 'whatever' the Boss says, will be repeated.

Our longtime Cashier, Etta, was married to a great guy named Frank. A few years before I started in Ottumwa, Frank had become the victim of 'Diabetes Issues' that had necessitated the amputation of his leg.

Now, Etta was perhaps one of the 'sweetest and most loyal' members of our Crew and everyone loved

her, but she couldn't open her mouth without talking about Frank and him 'losing his leg'. It went on nonstop. Frank and his one leg...

Etta would come to the Breakroom for her Coffee Break and she'd sit and smoke and get everyone in the Breakroom to listen to her stories about Frank's leg. As she talked, everyone would "Mmmm" and say "Uh-huh" and shake their heads the whole time until her Coffee Break had ended and then she would go back to work and everyone would look at each other wondering "???". Everyone was thinking something, but nobody would ever say anything.

This is 'how that all changed'.

One day in the Breakroom, I happened to be up there through the lunch hour and Etta had come up for her 15-minute break to have a smoke and a cup of coffee. We always had 'Free Coffee' in the Breakrooms. While there, Etta talked 'non-stop' to the 10 or 12 people in there and it was all about Frank's leg. So, after listening to it for nearly 15 minutes, she finished her Break and returned to work at the Front-End.

Whew!... We all looked at each other with 'total amazement'...How could one 'Sweet Little Lady' talk so much? We were all thinking 'something'.

And then I 'stepped right in it' ...

About 10 seconds after she left the room, I quietly said "It's no wonder the Poor Guy's only got one leg, she probably talked the other one off." ....

OH BOY! ... The roar of laughter was so loud. I am sure it could be heard all over the store.

It took about 15 minutes for my comment to reach Etta and I learned 'the hard way' that 'whatever the Boss says', will get around pretty quickly. All the remaining years of my career, I watched very carefully what I said in the Breakroom...I had 'Learned My Lesson'.

Etta asked me later that afternoon about it and I said "Etta, you know I love you dearly, but you do like to talk." Then, I hugged her and she laughed along with me and we went about our work. Somehow, that moment seemed to bring us closer together.

We were "Great Friends" after that day.

In the years after, I was always careful what I said in the Breakroom... Those types of 'Lessons' were always the ones with a 'story to go with 'em'.

Once in a while, it would come up in conversation by the Crew at the Ottumwa Hy-Vee...We'd all laugh and I'd remember back to the day

I Was Kicked In The Pants

By A 'One-Legged Man'...

"Where Did They All Go ??" ....

In the nearly 90-year History of Hy-Vee, there have been "Many-Many" fun times with events going on in the Communities that Hy-Vee has stores in. Those times of 'Excitement and Fun' are usually the product of a 'Famous Event' or a 'Famous Person' visiting the store and there are so many 'Special Preparations' made to go along with it.

In some cases, Hy-Vee gets to 'host' some of the people involved as the 'Guests' of the area and that can be very good for the 'Public Relations' parts of the 'Community Involvement' that Hy-Vee strives for. Hy-Vee wants to be 'deeply involved' so that the Community looks at Hy-Vee as a 'Center for Good' to their Customers.

It's a great position for a Company.

Hy-Vee feels so strongly about all of this 'Community Involvement' that it has even created an 'Annual Award' to be given to the Hy-Vee Store Manager or Headquarters Staff Member that has excelled in their Community to be involved in as much as they can. This 'Annual Award' also recognizes those who have been 'Leaders' in creating something so big in their Community that almost everyone in town knows about it. It is a very big award and a very prestigious award to receive.

I was the Store Manager at the Ottumwa, IA Hy-Vee #1 Hy-Vee Store when an event happened in 1979

that came as a 'direct result' of the 'Community Involvement' Hy-Vee had displayed over many years in a largest city Hy-Vee city.

Here's what it all came down to...

Pope John Paul II announced to the World that he would be making a 'historic' visit to America. It was not the first time a Pontiff had ever been to America, but it was the first time The Pope had ever been to Iowa.

The 'Official Plan' was that he would stay in America for several days and during his stay, it was decided that he would hold some 'Outdoor Mass Ceremonies' in which the General Public would be invited to attend. One of those stops was to be on October 4 1979. It was a very 'big deal' and it was his stop at Iowa's Living History Farms in Urbandale, IA. It truly was 'Historic'.

Now, The Living History Farms is a very large and popular attraction 'right smack' in the center of Iowa's Polk County. From all indications, it would be 'huge' and it was 'then' and is 'to this day', the largest 'Outdoor Event' ever held in the State of Iowa.

The 'Community Involvement' of Hy-Vee in The Des Moines/Polk County Area had been so 'Strong and Supportive' over the years, that Hy-Vee was invited to be 'The Vendor' for the huge crowds that would be there for Pope John II's visit. What an 'Honor' it was to not only be recognized as a Business Leader for

the State, but the request to have Hy-Vee be 'The Vendor' for all the food items and stands ...It spoke loudly as to the respect Iowa and Des Moines have for Hy-Vee.

It was also a great 'Business Opportunity' for Hy-Vee.

So, with plenty of advanced notice of the Pope's visit, many plans had to be worked out and the Des Moines Area Hy-Vee Stores got 'real busy' figuring it all out and dividing up the jobs that would need to be done.

In a group of then 12 stores in the area, one of the big questions had to be 'How will we divide it?'...You know, 'The costs and the revenues'. 'Will we divide It according to an even split?'.... Or 'Will we divide it on A 'pro-rata share' basis?'. Pro Rata Share meaning that it would be all be divided according each store's percentage of the total sales that the stores produced over a month or quarter. Larger stores would 'pay more and get more' and smaller stores would 'pay less and get less'... All based on the group's ongoing sales totals as a percentage.

After working it all out to everyone's agreement on how the 'Costs and Revenues' would be split, they were on to the task or 'Figuring Menus' and 'Procuring' all the items to sell to everyone. With over 300,000 people estimated to be in attendance, the potential was 'Huge'.

Locations of the 'food stands' were drawn out on maps of the Living History Farms' grounds and

‘menus’ were decided upon for the aspect of a ‘quick pay and go’ sale. Getting the food in ahead of time and keeping it all in the best condition became a concern too.

Then, came the decision of ‘How would the money be protected?’...That was a huge decision because of the potential amount of cash that would be on hand and the cash being vulnerable to theft or robbery.

Special ‘Drop Cans’ were designed for ‘skimming the cash’ from the food stands at regular intervals and therefore protecting the ‘Loss Potential’. It was all well-thought out and all of it seemed so perfect...

But not so fast...

On the day of the Pope’s visit to Iowa’s Living History Farms, over 350,000 people showed up and the crowds were ‘absolutely overwhelming’. There was hardly enough space to move around the Farm for a spot to hear the Pope’s Mass and His Holy Comments. The problem with the event as far as Hy-Vee’s plans were concerned was that the ‘people didn’t come to eat, they came to see the Pope’... And with that, they bought very little of what Hy-Vee had prepared...

It was a ‘Bust’ for sure. The stores ‘lost their shirts’.

I moved to Des Moines almost a year and a half later and the Store Managers were still talking about it. By April of 1981, Pope John Paul II’s visit was moving to the ‘Funny Stories’ Column and away from ‘The

Losses' Column. I'd heard much of it already as my older brother was a Store Manager at the Urbandale, IA Hy-Vee Store and he had been involved in all of it. He had filled me in all the details...

The jokes in all of the Des Moines Area Ad Meetings about 'Pope-Corn', 'Cans of 'Pope' and 'Pope-sicles' along with lots of other words created out of the word 'Pope' were tossed around a lot. I found the whole event to be amusing and a great way of getting the Ad Group to 'be quiet' and 'not so critical at times' of my ideas.

I used it as 'ammunition' at times.

Yes, I stood my ground in those meetings and when I needed to quiet anyone or the group down a bit, I'd come up with a "Yeah, remember the Pope" or "That's about as good an idea as when the Pope Came" ... We'd all laugh and then go on with the meeting.

It was the time in Des Moines when the Store Managers

'Prayed For A Hail Mary'...

“The goal should be to buy it and sell it before we have to pay for it.”

Marion M. Coons

Senior Vice-President

and CFO

(Deceased)

“According To The List” ...

Since the early 1930’s and the days of the Hy-Vee Founders, Charles Hyde and David Vredenburg, most Daily Routines in Hy-Vee have been completed by the use of ‘Lists’. You know, a ‘List’ to order, a ‘List’ to remind ourselves of an impending job and a ‘List’ of ‘To Do Items’ to serve as a ‘Work List’ for the Crew of a store. All kinds of ‘Lists’ have been religiously used in the nearly 90 years of Hy-Vee’s existence and some of those ‘Lists’ were pretty primitive compared to the ‘Electronic Age’ of gadgetry being used today.

Scraps of Butcher Paper, box-lids, spiral notebooks, the palms of people’s hands and even old used ‘computer cards’ and ‘shelf tags’ have been used for making ‘Lists’. It didn’t ever matter what was used for the ‘List’ to be written on, it was ‘What was on the List’ that really mattered. Nobody cared about whether it was ‘fancy or simple’... Just ‘write it down’ and ‘get it done’. That was it.

In all the decades, each day in Hy-Vee has been full of ‘Lists’ of one kind or another and ‘occasionally’, they were almost a ‘story of their own’ by the time the tasks on that ‘List’ were accomplished.

This Story is about one of those ‘Lists’ and here’s how it happened...

According to ‘The List’.

I was the Store Manager at the Ottumwa, IA Hy-Vee for several years in the mid-late 1970's...We had a beautiful new 'State of The Art' Hy-Vee of 25,000 square feet with all the new Departments Hy-Vee was offering in those days. We had complete Meat, Produce, Frozen Foods and Dairy Departments as well as a 'Scratch Bakery' and a 'New Deli/Kitchen Department' that served 'ready-to-eat' foods such as Fried Chicken, Salads, Sandwiches and Cold Fountain Drinks. We catered a lot of large parties and functions from our Deli/Kitchen and there were times it got hectic.

In the Summer of 1978, our Deli/Kitchen Department had been contacted to do an outdoor meal function at the Davis County Fairgrounds in Bloomfield, IA, which is about 18 miles South of Ottumwa. It was planned that we would feed about 3500 Customers of The Rural Electric Cooperative (aka The R.E.C.) as a gesture of that company's 'appreciation to their Customers'. It was going to be a 'Huge' catering and we had a lot of planning to do.

With the 'Big Event' only a couple of weeks in front of us, we got busy planning the menu of Ham Sandwiches, Chips, Potato Salad, Baked Beans, Cole Slaw, Chocolate Chip Cookies and Beverages. It would require a lot of 'extra help' from our Crew and we began lining up the numbers of people we would need to make the 8 Serving Lines we thought we needed for the ease in getting everyone through the lines at a good pace.

We needed Supplies like Plates, Cups, Plastic Tableware and Napkins. It was all well-thought out and all the Supplies and Food Items started rolling in as ordered. Plans were underway to have a 'Crew' come in during the overnight hours and make all the Ham Sandwiches and prepare the Beans, Cole Slaw and Potato Salad. Then, another large 'Crew' would take it out to The Davis County Fairgrounds and serve it late in the afternoon.

It was a 'Real Production' to make 3,500 Hoagie-type Ham Sandwiches with Lettuce, wrap them and then stack them carefully into clean sturdy cardboard Apple Boxes to be kept in the Cooler until needed. Along with the Ham Sandwiches, the Cole Slaw and Potato Salad were prepared by hand and also stored in the Cooler. The Baked Beans were readied during the night for the ovens. They would go in the Bakery Oven at mid-day and would then be transported, while hot, to the Fairgrounds and the 3500 hungry people waiting 18 miles away. It was a 'fun event' for all due to the size and 'ring-up' it would produce for the Deli and the store.

The job of the Day-Crew coming in was to organize the Supplies such as Plates, Napkins, Plastic Dinnerware and other necessary items that were needed for the eight serving lines at the event. There were massive numbers of each and it was important to make sure nothing was left off the 'List' or left behind at the store.

All of this was a 'Huge List' of stuff to do.

So, on the day before the big 'R.E.C. Catering' was to be held, all the Supplies were in, organized and ready to be loaded on the trucks for the Catering. The food items were in the coolers at the store and would be finished that night for the big event the next afternoon. Everything was really looking good. The final plans were starting to 'Come to Life'.

On the morning of the big 'R.E.C. Catering', one of the Department Managers asked me if I'd seen Ted's (the Deli Manager) 'List of Events'. That 'List' was hanging on the wall for his Kitchen Crew to see... Apparently, everyone but me had seen it and it was the 'talk of the store' in a very humorous way.

Since I had not seen it, I sauntered over to the Kitchen Prep area and looked around. There it was, 'In All of its Glory', taped to the wall by the phone and it was exactly what I'd been told it was and it was 'quite humorous'. All the details of 'what things were to be done' and 'when they were to be done' were on 'The List'. It was the last item on 'The List' that had gotten everyone's attention.

It was Ted's personality that made the whole thing even more of an 'event' because we could all envision his mindset as he wrote 'The List'. He was in 'High Gear' and 'READY'. He had 'tunnel-vision' of the event for sure.

Now, I knew our Crew well enough to know that the last item on the list was going to be the one that everyone was focused on and 'one by one', I could see and hear the Department Managers and other Full-timers making arrangements to be at the Kitchen at the designated time of 3 PM for the last item on 'The List' to occur. My guess was it would be a huge crowd in the Kitchen at 3 PM sharp.

And it was going to be 'Wild and Funny'...

So, here we were. It was the 'Big Day'. All the plans and all the items on "The List' were there were in 'Time Order' of scheduled occurrence starting at 1PM with the loading of the dry Supplies in one of the Store vans. Ted had it all organized right down to all the boxes and bags being numbered to designate which of the 8 serving lines they went to. The Ham Sandwich Boxes each had a precise number written on them designating how many sandwiches were in each of them. The names and scheduled times for the added Crew to report for work were on 'The List' and it was coming right down to the wire.

By 2:45 PM that afternoon, everything was to be loaded on the trucks and the only thing left to do was to load the Baked Beans that were still warming in the ovens. We were now down to that last item on 'The List', so our Department Managers, Full-timers and others, who could be freed up from their work duty and I started to 'congregate' in the Kitchen Prep Area. It was easy to see Ted was getting nervous

and concerned about how many people were there. He was already nearly worked into a 'frenzy' and he was really taken back with all of us there.

So, with an extra 'audience' of about 30 people just standing there looking at Ted, the Baked Beans came out of the ovens and they were sent out to the waiting Vans that were ready to go to 'The R.E.C. Catering' 18 miles away.

With how things go with 'Human Nature' and as it does in lots of cases, 'Curiosity' had gotten the better of Ted and he sort of blurted out "What are all of you doing here?" and then he waited for some kind of response.

With that, I walked over to 'The List' he'd taped on the wall a few days earlier and I looked at him and I said "We came to see the last item on this list happen. We've heard about this all of our lives and we don't want to miss it" With that, I peeled the list from the wall and I waved it around in the air for everyone to see and then, I very loudly said "Your list says '3 PM---All Hell Breaks Loose'."

Ted was caught a little off-guard and he laughed as loud as the other 30 or so people who were gathered to see it. We all roared out loud. It seemed to be very soothing to Ted's nerves and it was the 'final thing' that really got everyone 'Revved Up' for the big 'R.E.C. Catering'.

We laughed for a few minutes and then we all piled in the Vans and our cars and we 'took off' in a caravan for the Davis County Fairgrounds. We started serving from 8 serving lines at 4 PM and it was a 'Huge Success'.

Ted took a pretty good 'razzing' about all of it, but like usual, he 'gave as good as he got' and it was a fun time for all. We heard 'lots' over the next months about the great job our Ted and his Kitchen Crew had done at the big 'R.E.C. Catering'. We were proud.

We were also proud that we'd been witness to History. We'd been witness to something few people ever get to see.

We'd seen 'All Hell Break Loose'...

(And It Did It In Ottumwa, IA)

“Put your shoulder to the Wheel, your nose to the Grindstone and keep your ear to the Ground.”

Dwight C. Vredenburg

President, CEO and

Chairman of the Board

(Deceased)

“Hey, There’s A Guy Out There With A...” ... (Bang-Bang)...

Every Hy-Vee Store has ‘neighbors’ and these ‘neighbors’ are either in the form of ‘private residents’ or they are in the form of ‘businesses’ that have opened near Hy-Vee for the overflow traffic of Hy-Vee’s Customers. At either side of the ‘neighbors’ type, there are some ‘Really Fun’ and ‘Funny’ people who are an ‘Everyday Part’ of the Hy-Vee store and its ‘personality’.

When the Ottumwa, IA #1 Hy-Vee Store was purchased in 1957 from Ray Benjamin, it was already located on Albia Road in South Ottumwa. It was ‘On the Road’ to Albia, IA (or ‘Al-bee’ as it was called by the ‘Old Timers’) and when the State of Iowa built a new and faster route through Ottumwa, it was a faster trip East and West for travelers on the new U.S. Highway 34 and it ‘bypassed’ the old route. The old route then became known as ‘Old Albia Road’. That’s where Hy-Vee was...1527 Albia Road.

The ‘Old Albia Road’ location was nestled right into a fairly heavily populated residential area and it was a very successful store for Hy-Vee, both in Sales and Profits...Until it burned ‘completely to the ground’ on July 3, 1974. In that fire, ‘everything’ was lost, with the only exception being an Olivetti Divissuma electric calculator that was at the repair shop for service.

It was 'The Lone Survivor' of the fire.

Within days of the fire, the decision was made to not only replace the store right on the same location, but to purchase the homes that were behind the 'old store' and then remove them for the new building to be 'set back' on the full square block, thus allowing for a bigger store and a huge parking lot. All of the eight houses were 'negotiated for' and finally purchased at premium prices and their removal started immediately. Plans for a 'State of The Art' 25,000+ square foot Hy-Vee were decided upon. It was a store built completely off of the blueprints for the recently new Marion, IA Hy-Vee store. They were both beautiful stores with all the 'new things' and 'new departments' that Hy-Vee was starting to add to their stores in 1974.

The only home that had been an 'obstacle' in the group of eight that were purchased was owned by an elderly Italian man named Tony. Now, Tony was not interested in moving and at near age 90, his family stood firm with him on the 'no move' part. He'd lived in that house for nearly 65 years and it was his 'home'. So, after Hy-Vee 'met and met and met' with Tony about the purchase, he agreed to sell it with the stipulation that he got to live there 'Rent Free' until he died. So, with Tony already being near 90, Hy-Vee felt it would work 'just fine' and for the 'most part', it did.

Our 'Neighbor Tony', was very active for a man at nearly 90 years-old. He mowed his own grass, shoveled his own snow, tended to his repairs on the house and in his 'spare time', he liked to sit out in his yard and have a few 'Cold Ones' and enjoy the scenery of all the Customers coming in and going out of the store. He loved the activity.

I was sent to Ottumwa to be the Store Manager of the Hy-Vee there in early 1977. The Store was doing less Sales than it needed to cover the expenses and I knew that getting to know every Customer I could would help in one way or another and that we could get the store to higher levels. It proved to be the way to go and we prospered.

So, I walked over one afternoon to meet Tony and he said to me "Come over and have a Beer with me. That other Store Manager wouldn't do it." ... So, I decided I try to "have a beer" with him whenever the late afternoon opportunity arose and I did. I would sit with him and have a beer and then go right home. Sometimes, I would take a 'six-pack' over and other times, I'd just go over and drink one of his, but we got to be pretty good friends and I was glad I'd made the effort. Tony was a lot of fun.

Like he had always done, Tony still did the things in his yard that he'd been doing for nearly 65 years. 'occasionally', one of the things he did would cause a 'real stir'. The 'beer drinking' along with the 'routine things' were fine, but there was 'one thing' he did that

really got the 'hair up' on the backs of everyone's neck...and he did it often.

Here's one that is 'Classic Tony'.

One Fall day, I was busy at my desk which overlooked the entire Front-End of the store and I saw Hy-Vee's Senior Vice-President and Treasurer, Marion Coons come walking through the front door with his wife, Peg. They were walking briskly and unlike other times of them being in, they headed straight for the Office. I knew something was up.

I walked down the Office steps to greet them and when I got close enough to shake hands, Marion sort of blurted out... "There's a guy out there shooting a gun." It had really gotten Marion and Peg's attention. I thought I could diffuse the feelings a bit, so I said "Oh, that's just Tony shooting Squirrels. He does it all the time."

I could tell by the instant look on their faces that it was in the 'unbelievable category' that someone was shooting Squirrels 30 feet out the front door of the store. After a few seconds and a couple of other 'soothing comments' by me, they got used to the idea that it was not a threat and things went back to the 'Courtesy Visit' we were getting by one of the Hy-Vee Executives on their way through Ottumwa.

We visited and I walked around the store with them and made sure they got to see and talk to as many of

the Crew as possible. It was a great visit.

In the years after that visit, Marion would occasionally ask me...

"Been Squirrel Hunting Lately?"

“Just because I didn’t hit the Bullseye every time, doesn’t mean I wasn’t aiming for it.”

Jack H. Compton

Store Manager

(Deceased)

"Hocus Pocus"...

As the decades of the 1930's and 1940's moved along, 'The Supply Stores' of Charles Hyde (Hy) and David Vredenburg (Vee) moved along nicely in Northern Missouri and Southern Iowa. The Founders of the fledgling Company they'd started had 'visions' into the decades of the 1950'-1960's and 1970's with their Company and they dreamed of 'Big Things'. The name, 'Hy-Vee' was still into the future and did not emerge until the year 1952, but so many things were beginning to look like 'hard work' and 'diligence' would pay-off and they would grow and prosper right along.

They were right.

The money that was starting to 'flow-in' was looking more like the possible 'target' of Robbers of the day. The routines were changed and the security of the money started to take center stage by the growing Company. They had devised a good system of protecting the money, but by the 1970's, the need for a 'more advanced plan' to protect the money was needed.

So, in 1973, the Company now called "Hy-Vee" decided that things were happening in the 'Losses' areas and that Hy-Vee needed the help of a Full-time Security Department that could help the stores and Hy-Vee Corporately with Robberies and Cash Shortages. 'mysterious disappearances' of

merchandise seemed to be getting more numerous as Hy-Vee grew too. The growing company needed a professional way of dealing with these issues so as to solve them, but keep 'Employee Morale' at a high level.

In other words, Hy-Vee needed an "Honesty and Integrity" Department...

So, a Nationwide Search for a person to 'head-up' the newly conceived Department was undertaken. After an extensive search, Law Enforcement Veteran, Joe Smith, was hired to 'start-up' and 'head-up' Hy-Vee's new 'Safety and Security Department'. It is a department in Hy-Vee that has grown and developed into a top-notch part of Hy-Vee and it has helped solve the 'capers' of Hy-Vee over the last 40 years. Whether they were 'outside losses' due to Robbery or Shoplifting or whether they were 'inside losses' like Employee Theft of cash or merchandise, it was all within the new Department Hy-Vee had set in motion. It has 'paid its way' every day of every year since 1973.

Now, Joe Smith had come to Hy-Vee after being in Law Enforcement and then branching out into Private Investigations. Joe had also served as a Private Investigator in Detroit, MI and Kansas City, MO and both were tough areas. Joe had really been 'around the block' on his way to Hy-Vee. Ironically, in addition to his Private Investigator work, Joe was an Ordained Minister and preached on Sundays at a

small rural church in Southern Iowa. He was perfect for the job.

This story deals with a 'caper'... Here's how 'The Case Went Down'...

In 1978, I was the Store Manager at the Ottumwa, IA #1 Hy-Vee Store. The store sat on Old Albia Road on Ottumwa's South Side. The Store Manager at the Ottumwa #2 Hy-Vee Store on North Court Avenue on Ottumwa's North side was a great guy named Emmett. Emmett and I had lots of communication so we could keep our stores together on policy and pricing as much as we could. It was necessary so the people of Ottumwa (both Customers and Store Crews) knew we had uniformity in the stores.

One day while talking to Emmett on the phone, he confided in me that Joe Smith was coming to his Store to investigate a lost Bank Deposit bag that one of his Management people had put into their Bank's Night Depository 'drop-drawer' the evening before. The bag contained the day's receipts and it was a large sum of checks and cash that was missing.

Obviously, the person who was responsible for the Deposit to the Night Deposit drawer reported that he had driven it to the Bank and put it in the drawer by using his key to the drawer. This person had been questioned at length about it and he had never had reason to be doubted for his honesty, so Emmett decided to get Joe involved. Maybe a Bank employee had taken the bag and kept the cash ? ... or maybe it

really never did get in the drawer the night before ? Joe would need to get involved and find out where the missing bag and money were at. These were 'touchy' situations.

So, Joe Smith from Hy-Vee's Safety and Security Department arrived in Ottumwa and after visiting with Emmett for a while to get the details, he interviewed the person who had taken the bag to the Bank and deposited it. He then got into his car and drove over to the Bank and interviewed all the people who would normally handle the bags coming out of the Night Depository drawer. Nobody 'fessed-up' on anything of an illegal nature, so Joe went back to the Ottumwa #2 Store for more interviewing and more conversation with Emmett and the young man who 'swore' he'd put the bag of missing money in the Bank's Night Deposit drawer.

There was no progress being made, so Joe went to the Bank again and interviewed the people at the Bank. One more time... No progress there either.

It was at this point that Joe decided he'd 'dummy-up' a bag for the Night Deposit drawer and then take the young man to the Bank to have him 'demonstrate' how he'd deposited the bag in the drawer. As they arrived at the Bank, Joe observed the layout of the bank wall and the drawer and where it was located. After an examination of the drawer, the young man took his key out and opened the drawer and then put the 'dummy bag' in the drawer and shoved it closed.

The Night Deposits were usually pretty big and like usual, the bag in the drawer was a tight fit for the drawer and it required a pretty good 'shove' to get it to close and go down.

The two men walked to the inside of the Bank to retrieve the 'dummy bag' only to find that it had vanished! There was no sign of it on the inside of the Bank Deposit drawer vault, so they 'dummied up' another bag and returned outside to 'shove' it into the drawer only to see it vanish too!

What was happening?

At this point, Joe asked for the Bank President to come to the area and they covered the saga to that point. A Bank Vault repairman was called in and 'Lo and Behold', there were the missing Bank Bags...The two Dummy Bags, The missing Deposit Bag from the night before and Even a 'Bonus Bag'!

You see, inside the Deposit Drawer, it was discovered that a weld had broken on the bottom of the drawer and when a bag of 'oversize' or 'extra weight' was shoved through, the bottom of the drawer would separate and that bag would drop into the inside of the brick and concrete pillar wall it was part of... 'Magically Disappearing.

The 'Bonus Bag' found that day turned out to be a missing Bank Bag from the same Hy-Vee from 9 years earlier that had 'disappeared' and had never turned up. Hy-Vee had assumed that the Bank had a

dishonest worker because the Bank had covered the loss to the store and everyone thought then that it was the 'End of The Story'. It wasn't.

Now, with the missing bags in hand and the recovery of the missing bag from 9 years earlier, the 'Saga was Over'...

It became the Ottumwa #2

'Hocus Pocus--Now You See It'...

(and Now You Don't) Incident...

"My Legs Were Shaking So Bad" ...

'Frugal' is a simple word, but it can be a 'Lifestyle' for some people. Much of what a person is in their Character has to do with where they were during their formative years and also what 'values' were dominant in their homes and surroundings. Many factors will form these traits and those factors include, Heritage, Religion, Financial Resources while growing up, Sibling Rivalry and an entire group of other lesser things.

Hy-Vee emerged as a small partnership company in 1930. It was a partnership between Charles Hyde (Hy) and David Vredenburg (Vee) and in the early years of the 1930's, it was called 'The Supply Stores'. These two men, along with their wives, endured the hardships of staying in business during The Great Depression of the 1930's. The children of these people endured those 'hardships' right along with their parents and the 'frugality' of their ways stayed with them all of their lives.

Dwight Vredenburg (David and Kate's Son) so loved the Grocery Business that he decided to 'cast his lot' in the Business along with the Hydes and the elder Vredenburgs. Dwight obtained a College Degree at Graceland College in Lamoni, IA and it prepared him for the 'journey' his life would take him on... All over the World.

As the years rolled along and The Supply Stores grew, the money aspects of the company grew right along as well, but the ways of the 'Frugal 1930's' never left Dwight and so many others from that era. Those frugal ways stayed 'center stage' in their habits and those habits shaped the company we know now as Hy-Vee, Inc. In its nearly 90 years of operations, Hy-Vee has endured through some tough times financially. Sometimes in 'humorous ways'...

And that's what this story is based on.

Now, I mentioned the 'frugality' of the times and people' of Hy-Vee and it was always fun to watch as things unfolded. One Hy-Vee Executive of the times, Marion M Coons Vice-President and Treasurer, wanted a new car, but he didn't want to look extravagant. So, when he ordered it, he ordered it with 'Black-Wall' tires' which were almost unheard of at the time. 'Every' new car had 'Whitewall Tires' and then Marion would drive up in his new big Oldsmobile 98' with 'Black-wall' tires' on it. We all laughed, but only because we knew full well that 'frugality' was still 'Alive and Well' in Hy-Vee.

One 'lecture topic' we all seemed to get a couple of times a year had to do with not being 'flashy' if you were doing well in your store. We would be told that "You don't want to be seen doing too well in your store or people will think you're 'gouging' them on prices". And the joke among us was always... "It's okay to own a Cadillac...Just don't drive it."

Here's the story of one such 'Frugal Instance' and it's a good one.

Now, Hy-Vee has rewarded its Associates with Service Awards for many decades. These Service Awards are given at 5-year intervals of Full-time Employment and they are awarded at a special Dinner to honor the recipients. These Awards Dinners are held in various locations around the 'eight states' that Hy-Vee does business in and the Officers of the Company are at each Awards Dinner to 'congratulate' and help 'honor' the years of Service for a Company Associate. They are proud times for the recipient and for Hy-Vee.

When I was the Store Manager at the Ottumwa, IA Hy-Vee #1 during the late 1970's, the Service Awards Dinner for our area was held in Burlington, IA and it was a distance of about 100 miles for us. Hy-Vee's Headquarters was still in Chariton, IA at the time and Chariton was another 47 miles added onto the 100 for us. That meant that the Executives were another 47 miles West of Ottumwa. Most of the Executives still drove many of the places within Hy-Vee then and they would drive home after the Awards Dinners. It was usually late and they were tired after a rigorous day.

When Company Cars were ordered every other year or so, they were usually the most 'stripped down' versions of the Chevys for the time. No extras. There were no exceptions to this guideline and it didn't

matter 'who' it was...Dwight's Rules said so. 'Plain Jane Cars'...

Now, the night of the Awards Dinner in Burlington, my wife and I were there with our store's recipients and we had a nice visit with several of the Executives and it gave us a chance to say "hello" to the wives of the men we saw each week and knew pretty well. We always enjoyed that very much. It was nice for 'all the wives' to know each other too.

After the Dinner that night, we all drove back to our respective towns and the Awards Dinner was over for another year. It wasn't until a day or two later, that we heard that Dwight and Ruth had a car accident on their way back to Chariton. They were not injured, but it sent a 'scare' and a 'shock' throughout Hy-Vee.

The following week, there was another function that we were at and our wives were with us again. The wives of the Executives were also there and as we encountered Ruth Vredenburg, my wife said "Boy, we're glad your accident last week didn't injure you two." And Ruth's reply was one that will live in my heart forever. She said "We are too...You know, when I hit that deer, Dwight was asleep in the back seat of the car and by the time I got the car stopped, my legs were shaking so bad I could hardly push the clutch in."

HOLY COW! ... A Clutch?...

No Automatic Transmission for the CEO?

In Dwight's 'Never-Ending Quest to Be Frugal', he'd opted to take one of the Hy-Vee stripped-down 'Pool Cars' to Burlington and not to drive his own late model Chevrolet. You know, the one with the extras like 'Automatic Transmission' and so forth? And on top of that, he'd chosen to drive home and not spend the money for a motel in Burlington.

All 'Classic Dwight'... The 'Tightwad' we all loved.

To this day, when I catch myself 'scrimping on something', I think of Dwight and Ruth all those years ago...

When Ruth's legs were "Shaking So Bad", she

'Could Hardly Push The Clutch In'...

“Attitude is not the number one thing…

It’s the ‘Only’ thing.”

P. Lynn Blanchard

Store Manager

(Retired)

“You Bought How Much ??” ...

All the way back to 1930 and the early years of ‘The Supply Stores’, the Holidays have been coming every year... ‘always hectic’ and ‘always exciting’. In those small Southern Iowa and Northern Missouri towns, the Founders of now Hy-Vee tried hard to ‘always’ have the right things to sell their Customers so the Customer would not have to shop elsewhere. It served several purposes. Sales were perhaps the ‘biggest’ of them.

It’s a huge understatement to say that the Holidays are really stressful for a Grocery Store. So many things can take a fun time of the year and make it a real ‘chase-your tail’ event. It all starts in early-mid November and the Customers start buying the ingredients for the baking and recipes they want to get ahead on for the Holiday Meals and Parties. Cookies, Candy, Cakes, Special Soups, Turkeys, Party Mix Snacks and a huge list of other things were the focus for the Holidays then and now...Almost 90 years later.

It’s fairly simple to know what items to buy to sell to your Customers, but one major problem in a Grocery Store is knowing ‘how much’ of those items to order so you don’t run out. I have always said that running a Grocery Store is the best example of ‘organized chaos’ that you’ll ever see. Scheduling ‘issues’ like sickness taking large numbers of good employees out for days at a time, out of town family parties that

employees like to go to, weather related issues, school parties to attend by the young parents and grandparents are just a few of the obstacles faced by a Grocery Store at Holiday time. And these items don't even take into account 'The Business Side of the Business'.

The Newspaper Ads around the Holidays will most times, be the factor that determines how much of their total order that the Customers will spend in your store instead of 'the competition' in your town. These ads 'must' contain the 'right items' at the 'right price' for the choices the Customers will make. There really is only so much money in a household budget and the store that 'competes' for that money will get the business.

'How much merchandise' to buy is as important as anything else you do. If you advertise an item and then don't have it, you really add to your problems. Now, you have not only sent them to your competitor's store, but you have made them mad while they made the trip. The Customers would also find items in the competitor's store that they would have bought in your store and you'll miss those sales too.

If only you would have ordered enough.

There has been an 'old adage' in the Grocery Business that says "If you buy the Customer's business at Thanksgiving, you'll get their business for Christmas." This simply means 'Do everything

you can to be right at Thanksgiving and the Christmas Business will flow to you naturally'. The 'right items' at the 'right prices' and 'don't run out'.

This next 'event' happened at Thanksgiving in 1978 and it is funny now, but it was not so funny back then. Well, it was 'Sorta' funny.

This is the story...

About 4 weeks ahead of an Ad, 'pre-order sheets' come out from Hy-Vee's Headquarters so the stores can 'pre-order' the items they will need for the Ads coming up and it helps the stores plan and it also helps the Warehouse plan how much to order so the stores will have enough. It's not always a 'perfect science' because the warehouse will have 'extra' beyond pre-order amounts on hand, but they don't always order enough either, so pre-orders help everyone to ensure there will be enough for the Customers to buy.

A year prior in the Holiday pre-orders for 1977, we had failed badly on the pre-orders for one of the big items... 'Frozen Whipped Topping' for the Pies, Cakes and other Desserts for the Thanksgiving Table. Everyone buys it. We had run way short and it 'did' send our customers to our competitors to get it.

I was extremely unhappy about it.

So, with having 'stubbed our toe' so badly the prior year, when the pre-orders for Thanksgiving came out in late October of 1978, I said very boldly "Well, I'm

ordering the whipped topping because I'll be Damned if we're going to run out this year." So, I did order the whipped topping and I sent it in.

Oh Boy! ...

Within a few days, I was 'paged' for a phone call and the voice on the other end of the phone said "Rick, this is Jim from the Frozen Warehouse in Chariton. Can you talk for a minute?". Jim was the Head Buyer for the Hy-Vee Frozen Warehouse in Chariton. A 'big operation'.

I said "Sure, Jim, what's up?" So, Jim went on to say "I was looking at the pre-orders from the stores for the Holidays and there's a number on your Frozen pre-orders that doesn't look right. Your store ordered 800 cases of Hy-Vee Whipped Topping. Did you mean 80 cases?"

I thought for a minute and then I replied to Jim "The 800 number is right, Jim. We ran out last year and I said I'd be Damned if we were going to run out this year."

Jim hesitated for a moment and then he said. "Well, that's your decision, but I will tell you that that's more whipped topping than all 12 of the Des Moines Area stores ordered in total."

Then he waited for my answer...

So, what I said next sort of sealed my fate. I said "That number will be fine, Jim. Just leave it at 800

cases." Jim acknowledged my decision and he reminded me that once we got it, it couldn't be returned because it was perishable item. For that moment in time, it seemed like the thing to do.

So, the week of Thanksgiving, the Frozen Food Deliveries came and 800 cases of Hy-Vee Whipped Topping consumed every bit of freezer space we had 'and then some'. We had Whipped Topping 'everywhere'. We had it in the Freezer, in The Milk Cooler, in the Produce Cooler and even some in the Meat Cooler.

By now, I was pretty sure I'd 'messed up'!

Thanksgiving 'came and went', Christmas 'came and went' and then Easter 'came and went' before we 'finally' cleaned up the inventory we had on Hy-Vee Whipped Topping. We all laughed so much over that six-month period about the 800 Case order of Whipped Topping. I took a real 'razzing' over it.

In 1979, I let someone else decide how much to order...

I'd proven it shouldn't be me.

My Whipped Topping Order Had 'Gone Over The Top' ...

“Sell it as low as you can and still make a profit.”

Dwight C. Vredenburg

President, CEO and

Chairman of the Board

(Deceased)

“Let’s ‘Pop-A-Top’ ” ...

It’s an important thing to be part of the ‘Business Community’ in any town that you are part of in Hy-Vee...The people you meet and the ‘good-vibes’ you create will pay dividends in lots of ways. It’s a great way to meet a lot of influential people too.

Even way back to 1930, Charles Hyde (Hy) and David Vredenburg (Vee) believed that ‘The Supply Stores’ needed to be part of the communities they served. You know, be involved with their time or donations of products to help out. It seemed to bode well for the ‘image’ of the stores and it has continued as a Company Philosophy for all these years since. Nearly 90 years later.

Now, most communities that Hy-Vee does business in have some organizations that are very popular and it’s good to be seen ‘out in the community’ partaking in the endeavors of those organizations...Those endeavors might be for fund-raisers, community betterment projects and the strengthening of the local businesses. Organizations such as Toastmasters, Rotary Club, The Chamber of Commerce and many other ‘Civic Projects’ that come up for a specific purpose such as a park project or a memorial are popular too.

I was the Store Manager at the Ottumwa, IA #1 Hy-Vee from 1977-1981. It was my first Store Manager assignment and I wanted to be involved to strengthen Hy-Vee in Ottumwa so, I got involved in an organization there in town.

Ottumwa is a Southern Iowa town of about 25,000 people. It has two Hy-Vee Stores and the store I was at happened to be on the 'South Side' of Ottumwa which was designated that way because it sits on the 'South Side' of the Des Moines River which runs right through the middle of town. The other store, Ottumwa #2 Hy-Vee, is on the 'North Side' of Ottumwa for the same geographic reason...Thus, 'North Ottumwa' and 'South Ottumwa' as the two sides of the city are known locally.

Traditionally, the North Side had always been viewed as more the 'White-Collar' side of town. The South Side had always been viewed as the 'Blue-Collar' side of town. The factories and meat processing plants that had been a big part of Ottumwa's economic history were mostly located on the South Side and their employees lived there too.

So, when we moved to Ottumwa and I took over the reins at the 'South Ottumwa' store, I was quickly asked to become part of the Chamber of Commerce 'Ambassador Committee' and I gladly accepted the offer. Both Hy-Vee Stores were large employers and a big part of the community and major members of The Chamber of Commerce.

The Chamber's Ambassador Group is the 'Red Jacket' group that makes 'visits' to the new businesses in town and issues a formal "Welcome to

Ottumwa" greeting and then presents them with a framed 'First Dollar of Profit' and a Chamber Certificate to be hung in their business for a display of their 'acceptance' into the Business Community. Usually, there was a picture taken of the Ambassador Group with the new owner or manager and it was in the Ottumwa Courier newspaper too.

I enjoyed the group of about 30 or 40 well-known Business Leaders and it was a very fun group. At 26 years-old, I was, perhaps, one of the 'Youngsters' in the group and I enjoyed that too because I felt sort of 'special'. I was treated very well by everyone.

Sometimes, the 'Calls' we made were lots of fun and we remembered them vividly...One such 'Call' made a 'memory' I'll never forget.

It 'came off like this'...Literally.

I had been in Ottumwa and on the 'Ambassador Committee' for about two years when we all got a call one day from the Chamber Office asking those who could make the 'Call', to 'meet and greet' a new Lounge called 'The Pop-A-Top Lounge' on Ottumwa's far West End. I agreed to go and the time was set for 2 PM the same afternoon. So, I planned my day accordingly.

Now, Ottumwa has had such a long history of having a 'honky-tonk' segment of population, that a new Lounge seemed to fit right in with the 'hundred or so' other bars and lounges in town. All of them seemed

to do well and we had no reason to think this one would do any different or 'be' any different...

Oh, how wrong we were...

At about 1:30 PM, I stopped what I was doing at the store and put on my 'Red Sport Coat' and took off for 'The Pop-A-Top Lounge' which was not all that far away, but I wanted to allow some extra time because we always met in the parking lots and walked in as a group. It made a good impression and we liked that.

So, we all met in the parking lot and gathered our 'framed certificate' in hand and went in...Holy Cow, it was a 'Strip Club Lounge' and of course the name 'Pop-A- Top Lounge' had a dual meaning... 'Popping Beer Pull-Tops' and also 'The Dancers' Tops' were going to come off too...

When we entered, there was a 'really cute young girl' on the stage wearing nothing but a pair of 'skimpy shorts' and a 'pair of roller skates'. Of course, we were interested 'from the git-go'. Boy, did she have a body and a great roller-skate routine to music.

We made our 'Official Presentation' of the plaque and then we all 'settled-in' to a group of tables. We all ordered a Beer and we sort of 'got engrossed' in what was happening on stage. We even saw that our female 'Ambassadors' were having a great time too. It was an enjoyable change from the mundane 'Calls' we usually made and eventually, each of us had

consumed a few Beers. We stayed until around 4:00 PM and then we all went home.

It was 'great'...

But the story gets even better...And much more exciting.

The next day was a Friday and that evening was a pre-planned 'Picnic Party' for the Ambassador Group and their spouses at the home of a prominent member who owned a local Miller Beer Distributorship. There were perhaps 50 or 60 people in attendance, counting the spouses. We had a nice meal and everyone enjoyed a few drinks and eventually, the subject of the prior day's 'Call' to The Pop-A-Top Lounge came up and somebody said "Hey, let's all go Over and check it out! ... We can take the wives and hubby's and show them."

And that's where it all started 'To Go South'. And 'South' it went' ...IN A HURRY!

We quickly cleaned things up at the party and about 40 of us got in our respective cars and we all took off for 'The Pop-A-Top Lounge'...When we got there, we all got parked and gathered as a group to go in. When walked in, the same pretty little gal was on the stage doing her 'roller skate routine' to music. Again, she was adorned only in the 'skates' and some 'skimpy shorts'. We found enough tables for all of us and we settled in to watch the show. We watched intently and again the 'little gal on skates' put on a pretty

good show for all of us and the other '75 or so' patrons that were in attendance...Mostly guys.

Within about 30 minutes, 'The Little Skater' announced that she was done until 10 PM and she exited the stage...What happened next was like something from 'The Old West'.

It was WILD!

A 'scantily dressed' young man of about 30 years-old came out onto the stage and he started to dance to music and then he began to 'take it all off'...I could see our group starting to look at each other very 'warily' when all of a sudden, a chair 'whizzed past my head' and hit the male dancer on-stage. Then 'another' chair and then 'another' chair went whizzing by...

Control had been lost for sure...

It looked like the saloon fights in the 'TV Westerns' because 'All Hell Broke Loose' and there was the wildest 'brawl' going on you have ever seen in your life. Chairs, bottles, cans, drink glasses and 'anything else' not nailed down were being thrown at the stage...The poor young male dancer had made his exit very early in all of it, but it was all still in protest of him.

The term 'Rednecks' pretty well described the group now squarely in control of 'the brawl' going on at The

Pop-A-Top Lounge...So, along with most of our group, I grabbed my wife to protect her and as we turned to 'head for the door', I ran physically 'smack into' the Chief of the Ottumwa Police Department, Willie, whom I knew 'very well' as he had two daughters that worked at the store.

The Police had been called at the 'throwing of the first chair' and about 6 or 8 Officers along with Willie had responded. As I bumped into Willie, his eyes got as 'big as saucers' and he sort of shouted "What the Hell are you doing here?"

It was a question I had asked myself only a few seconds before...

With that, we all ran outside and the whole 'fracas' was soon quelled and 'peace' was restored to The Pop-A-Top Lounge... After it was all calm, I had some 'esplainin' to do to Willie as to 'why' his daughters' Boss was there, so I quickly told him the 'two-day saga' and once he heard it and saw who else was there, he understood... And then it got funnier as it went along over the next few days.

There we all were...The Chamber's Pride and Joy... 'The Ambassadors. Everyone in the group was supposed to be 'The Best of The Best' in Ottumwa's Business Circles and we found ourselves to be part

of the next night's newspaper article on "The Brawl At The Pop-A-Top Lounge" ...

We laughed a lot about it over the years and it has always been funny whenever it was referred to.

It was the night We 'Skated On Out'

Of The 'Pop-A-Top' Lounge !

"It Did What ??" ...

After the 'fragile years' of 'The Supply Stores' of Charles Hyde and David Vredenburg had passed into 'The History Books' of Hy-Vee, the need to have stores designed specifically for food sales was much greater. No longer could 'just any old building' be taken over and made into a 'Supply Store'.

So, into the 1940's buildings were drawn up on 'blueprints' and then 'built to the prints'. It was costly, but successful operations of the prior decade had made it financially possible to do it.

The future Hy-Vee, Inc. was 'on its way'.

Hy-Vee's stores of the 1970's and earlier, were sometimes in neighborhoods that were heavily populated and because of the population, it sustained the store's sales for many years. There were stores in Shopping Centers and on large lots close to Shopping Centers, but they would not become more of 'the norm' for a few years yet to come... More into the late 1970's and 1980's

In the Spring of 1978, something happened at the Ottumwa, IA #1 Store that I was the Store Manager at and it still 'boggles the mind' when I think about it today. It was almost 'stranger than fiction' and it makes you realize the force of Mother Nature.

This is 'how it all piled up' on that Spring Day...

When the 'old store' of Ottumwa #1 Hy-Vee burned completely to the ground on July 3, 1974, the decision was made to buy all eight of the houses behind the old store and then 're-build' the store with a 'State of the Art' 25,000 square foot store where the houses had been at the back of the block. The area of the old store was then paved for a large 270 car parking lot. It was beautiful.

The new store was a 'red-brick' building with white lettering for "Hy-Vee Food Store" across the front. From Old Albia Road, it looked very 'majestic' sitting at the back of the entire 'square block' it now covered.

Well, parking lots can be 'tricky critters'. The water-flow from them is extremely important for the safety of the cars and the Customers using the lots. Concrete was usually poured in sections and the slope was very important for the drains that were installed 'strategically' over the entire lot. There had to be a slope, but the snow-plows also had to be able to get a good flat 'blading' across the lot too.

When the Ottumwa #1 parking lot was poured in 1974, it was poured in the usual sections and if you had gotten down to ground-level and looked horizontally, it had a bit of a flat 'w' shape to it...Maybe a little too much 'w' shape in our case. The 'w' shape allowed for the water to run to the low spots and then into a sewer drain and the water disappeared.

Now, as it happens, on this Spring Day in 1978, Ottumwa got a rain like nobody had seen for many years. It was compared by many in town to the flooding of the 'Flood of '47' in Ottumwa that saw water as deep as six feet in parts of the Business Section of South Ottumwa. It wasn't nearly as bad as that flood, but this rain did get the talk about the 'Flood of '47' going around town. You know, 'nostalgia' took over.

So, with a downpour of 4 inches of rain in about a one hour or so period, it 'washed' everything and sent it everywhere in the yards and parking lots. It was almost phenomenal. We all stood inside and watched because nobody was about to step out into the 'deluge' going on outside. As we stood there and watched the rain fall, we saw it flowing in river-like form across the parking lot and we could see it directing itself to the drains, but not all of it. There was no way the drains could handle it all.

When the rain stopped, and the water appeared to be flowing through as it was designed to, the phone rang and I was 'paged' to take the call. The lady on the phone identified herself as our 'neighbor' there at Hy-Vee. Her house sat right across the street to the side of the store and one of the entrances to Hy-Vee from the side street was immediately across from her driveway. A straight shot across the street.

Our Customer/Neighbor was really talking fast and I could tell she was 'rather angry' as she relayed what

the rain had done to her driveway. Finally, I said "Why don't I just walk over and we'll look at it together?" She said that was a good idea and we hung up the phone.

I took off on foot for her house with my Assistant Store Manager, Gary.

As we started down the sloped entrance to Hy-Vee from the small side street we shared, we could easily see the problem. The rainfall had 'roared' down the entrance like a 'chute' and the 'deluge' of rain had taken all of the 'marble-size' gravel in her driveway and shoved it all the way into her garage. There looked to be about eight or ten tons of gravel just shoved into the garage and it was all around her car. The floor of her garage had gravel piled about 8"-10" deep and there was no way the car or anything else was going anywhere. It was a sight to behold. The driveway was nearly stripped of all gravel and it was pretty much mud at that point.

As our Customer/Neighbor met me near the driveway, I said "Wow! ... This is a mess!" and with that, she acknowledged the comment. I went on to say "Well, I hope you know that we'll get it straightened out and it won't be any expense to you." She gave me a rather 'accepting smile' and I went on to assure her that we'd 'get right on it". I wanted her to know things were on the way to being 'fixed to keep a good relationship.

Gary and I walked back to the Store and sat down to put together a plan. We called about six 'husky' young guys that already worked for us and we lined them up to report for work in old clothes the next morning. We asked them to bring shovels and garden rakes with them. We lined up a couple of good sturdy wheel-barrows and then we waited for the next morning.

Most of the next day, the guys worked to rake, scoop and haul all of the gravel from the garage back out into the driveway. They worked hard and it looked great. I then arranged for a large load of gravel to go on top of the old for thickness and then 'it was done'.

Our Customer/Neighbor was very happy again.

We never had another 'deluge' like that one while I was at the Ottumwa #1 Store, but I did always watch that entrance pretty closely in heavy rains after that fateful day in 1978.

I am always reminded of that day whenever I hear that song from the late 1960's ...

"Who'll Stop The Rain ?"

“Always pay your bills on time and take advantage of all discounts when you can earn them.”

Marion M. Coons

Senior Vice President

and CFO

(Deceased)

“Where’s The Restroom ?” ...

Things happen in Grocery Stores that you would ‘swear’ are ‘made-up’ and they are ‘Stranger Than Fiction’ in lots of ways. When you deal with 400 employees and literally, ‘tens of thousands’ of Customers ‘week after week’ and ‘year after year’, the odds increase that some of those ‘Stranger Than Fiction’ stories will happen.

You can bet on it and win.

In 1978, I was managing Hy-Vee #1 on Ottumwa’s South Side on Old Albia Road when one of those stories crept up on us and it got right in on the ‘History’ in that store. It involved the Restroom or ‘lack of’ the Restroom in this story.

In those days, Hy-Vee’s Restrooms were in the Backrooms of the stores. They were generally in a corner of the Backroom and ‘tucked away’ out of plain sight. In many stores, the Restrooms were located in the Backroom near the Produce Trim Room. There were no Restrooms on the Sales Floors of the stores then and it made it sort of complicated when trying to explain the location of the Restroom to a customer who hadn’t used our Restroom before.

The Produce Manager of the Ottumwa #1 Store was a longtime Hy-Vee Employee named Doug. Doug was a really smart guy and he was the kind of a Produce Manager that I could always count on for great results... ‘month-in’ and ‘month-out’, he always knew how to generate Sales and Profits for the Store. Doug was a good 'team player' and he was liked by everyone.

Now, Doug loved to play practical jokes on people and people liked to play them right back at Doug. He laughed a lot and he knew just how to 'get under' some people's skin while playing a prank on them. In turn, the others loved to play those pranks on him and it seemed like a 'win-win' for anyone watching. There was never a dull moment in the 'prank department' at the Ottumwa #1 Hy-Vee.

So, one day, I was working on some paperwork in the Office when Doug came roaring up the Office stairs and I could tell by the look on his face and the mood he brought with him, that something 'big' was up. He was 'stammering' and 'sputtering' and rambling' about "I Never", "Who?", "Why?", and "Can You Believe It?"

It wasn't making any sense.

Whatever it was...It had gotten to him in a 'REALLY BIG WAY'. All I could do was wait for his composure to come back and then, I would find out what was going on. As I watched him wave his arms around, I listened to him and then, suddenly, he blurted out "I just found a human turd on the floor in the Produce Trim Room!"

OMG! It wasn't anything I would have expected to hear and so I said… "Well, who in the Hell would have done that?".

He didn't speak…He just 'shrugged sis shoulders' and looked at me.

Now, in all the years I have known Doug, it was the 'only' time I ever saw him when he was speechless. He just plain didn't know what to say.

At this point, Doug was starting to make some sense in what he said and he'd come to the conclusion that 'someone' had done it on purpose to get under his skin and he was just dumfounded on who it could have been. So, I told him to sit down and we talked about it for a few minutes and then he went back to work still muttering about "Who" and "What" and "Why" it all happened. The whole story had a lot of travelling to do in the store before it was over. Everyone eventually knew it happened.

The next day, we had a little meeting of the Department Managers and we had a discussion of the 'Turd in the Trim Room' situation. We really laughed, but then we had a serious talk about other possibilities for it happening …besides a prank on Doug.

There were only a few possibilities. Obviously, a prank was a possibility, but there may have been 'another' logical explanation of it. 'What if?' …Just 'What if?' a Customer had asked where the Restroom

was and was pointed in the direction of the Backroom and told that it was "In the Corner" in the Back Room? And 'What if?' in the Customer's frantic attempt to find the Restroom, the urge to 'go' had gotten the best of them and so, they found a quiet and secluded place in the Produce Trim Room 'Corner' to relieve themselves?

Could it be? ... Hmmmmm...???

Yes, a 'What if?' had come into the realm of a possible answer to the 'Turd in the Trim Room' ordeal, but could we be sure? Well, the answer would eventually lie with whoever the 'Teller of the Turd-Tale' was when it was repeated. 'some' loved to tell it as a prank on Doug...And 'some' loved to tell it that is was a 'miserable' Customer looking for the Restroom.

You make the call...

No matter how it came down while being repeated, the real story was the day it 'Came Down and Landed' on the Produce Trim Room floor...

One thing was for sure... It was 'always' a story for laughs.

'Holy Crap !'... It Really Was

'Stranger Than Fiction'...

“Be Careful What You Say” ...

Lessons in Humility can come at a ‘very high price’ sometimes and the things people say can (and most times do) come back to haunt them for many years to come.

Hy-Vee had ‘grown its roots’ in small towns in Southern Iowa and Northern Missouri. The lessons learned in those towns had set the tone for the humble attitudes of the Hy-Vee People. The ‘journeys in time’ through those years of building the business by way of the loyalty and trust of the Customers and Crews at Hy-Vee had taught that sarcasm and snide remarks had no place in Hy-Vee. “Just Work Hard, Be Humble and Be Appreciative” were The Founders’ beliefs.

It is a ‘winning’ philosophy.

Oh, it happened occasionally that someone would say something ‘bold’ or ‘brash’, but it was always discouraged in ‘day to day’ routines over the years.

Now, it has been said many times about “Someone getting too big for his britches.” and that’s what this story is about...Not physically getting ‘too big for the britches’, but that egos got ‘too big for the britches’.

One glaring example of an ‘ego comment’ came by way of the entry of Hy-Vee into the Des Moines Area around 1960.

This was “The Story Heard ‘Round’ The Midwest’.

In Hy-Vee, we were 'reminded' many times over the years about that 'ego' element and we were always 'schooled' to "Keep a Low Profile". Another of Dwight Vredenburg's (President and CEO from 1938 until 1989) favorite expressions was always "Keep your nose to the Grindstone, Your shoulder to the Wheel and your ear to the Ground" ... Then he was quick to 'chuckle' and say "It's actually pretty hard to work in that position."

But we got the message... 'loud and clear'.

Around 1960, Hy-Vee purchased a store in Johnston, IA. And another came soon at Altoona, IA. It was purchased from their owners. One of whom stayed on to become the Store Manager. It was a great move for Hy-Vee and for Des Moines and Polk County Area residents. This move 'sparked' a comment in the Des Moines Register newspaper by the owner and President of Dahl Foods there in Des Moines. His name was W.T. Dahl. Dahl Foods was a 'major factor' in the Grocery Business in Des Moines then and was quite successful to that point in their history.

Referring to Hy-Vee's 'entry' into the Des Moines Area, W.T Dahl was quoted in the Des Moines Register as saying that "Hy-Vee won't make it in the city. They're nothing but a bunch of 'Cornmeal Merchants' from Southern Iowa. People in the cities don't want all that 'friendliness and down-home stuff'."

It was an 'ego statement' for sure that he'd wish later he could take back...Many times, in fact.

Hy-Vee acted quickly in those years of the early 1960's and by 1970, there were about eight stores 'open and doing well' in Des Moines and its close-by suburbs. Many more stores followed in the years ahead.

It was starting to shape up that Hy-Vee and Dahl's were the 'two biggies' in Des Moines and with Dahl's philosophy of 'No Advertising', every piece of advertising Hy-Vee put out actually seemed to push Hy-Vee a bit farther ahead in their market-share in Des Moines. W.T. Dahl and his people could see the future shaping up to be 'tough' for Dahl Foods.

With their 'Shoulder to the Wheel', the Hy-Vee People of Des Moines and Polk County kept 'chipping away' at Dahl's sales base and by the early 1990's Hy-Vee was the 'largest' Grocery factor in the market. All others in town had fallen to much smaller segments...Especially Dahl's.

With forward momentum at a rapid rate, Hy-Vee continued to open stores all over Des Moines and by the time the year 2000 came, Dahl's was in 'Big Trouble'. Their slogan of "Ultimately Dahl's" was being overtaken by Hy-Vee's "A Helpful Smile in Every Aisle" slogan. The two slogans, in comparison, were seeming to have 'opposite' connotations. Dahl's seemed to say "Ultimately, you'll be good enough to shop at Dahl's" whereas, the successful

slogan of Hy-Vee's 'A Helpful Smile In Every Aisle' told the Customers just the opposite... "Come to us and we'll treat you right".

After the year 2010, Dahl's would seem to be fading fast and in 2015, they 'closed their doors' forever. They are now just a 'memory' of those years in the decades prior when they dominated the Grocery scene in Des Moines.

There is an 'irony' to all of it as it happened and that 'irony' is that 'ego drove them down'...Yes, just plain 'ego' and by the time they realized they were in trouble, they already had 'two feet in the grave'...

The Moral of This Story? ...

'Keep Your Shoulder To The Wheel'...

(With Your Mouth Shut) ...

"Be Careful Who You Make Mad" ...

Armed Robbery... When a masked man points a gun at a Cashier and says "Okay, put it all in the bag and nobody gets hurt!"

These are words that every Store Manager fears and they are words that will change a Crew and the Customers of a store...Forever.

Even back in the 1930's, Robbers were 'sticking-up' businesses and Charles Hyde and David Vredenburg taught the Crews in 'The Supply Stores' to just 'give them the money' because no amount of cash was worth 'somebody's life'. That thought has been 'embedded' in the Philosophy of Hy-Vee for almost 90 years now and it has saved many lives over those years. A 'simple, but safe' practice.

Stores that sit in affluent areas or stores that are located in Shopping Centers seem to have fewer robberies than stores out on a city's edges or even stores that are in neighborhoods. The plain truth is... 'Robbers don't like audiences'.

I was the Store Manager at the Hy-Vee in Pleasant Hill, IA from 1981 until 1987 when I moved to Moline, IL to manage a new Hy-Vee Store being built in Moline. We knew from the first day we were open at Pleasant Hill, that the day would probably come that we'd be 'robbed'.

The Store was on Des Moines' far East Side and it sat all by itself on a major road leading out of Des Moines. That road leading out of town would make a great 'escape route' into hundreds of rural side roads and places to hide for a few hours until the "Heat Was Off". It was 'ripe' for it all to happen to us.

In preparation for the 'robbery' that we always knew might come eventually, we had Store Meetings and we had set into motion some policies that were to help keep our Store Crew and our Customers safe. Those policies included lots of things that we tried to instill in our Store Crew and procedures we practiced religiously every day.

There was no doubt that we had a lot of cash on hand and the potential 'big losses' could be minimized by 'skimming' the cash down each day at certain times to get some of each Cash Register's 'excess' cash into the Safe for protection. Rarely would a robber take the risk of forcing a 'Safe Opening' because that meant they would have to get too far into the store and that left too much distance to the door for a quick 'getaway'.

In case we were 'robbed', each Cash Register also had some 'cash in a bundle' that was to stay in that drawer all the time...The Serial Numbers on those bills were recorded by us and Law Enforcement could later identify it as Hy-Vee's money for proof of a robbery.

We had talked at length to our Store Crew about "Always giving the money" to a robber that was threatening in any way. It was much easier to cover the losses of some cash than to have a Crew member or a Customer hurt or killed because they felt the need to protect the money. It just wasn't worth it. So, "Always giving them the money" was the first rule of the Robbery Scenarios we told our Crew about at our store.

There were other things that we really pushed into our Crew's heads about a robbery. Things like, paying close attention to see just what the robber looked like and characteristics of the things they saw in the robber. Eye color, height, approximate weight, ethnicity, hair color, noticeable scars or tattoos, any voice patterns or accents, jewelry worn, weapons displayed and right down to which hand seemed to be their dominant one. Were they right-handed or left-handed when they moved around to gather the money?

Yes, it would look like a Cashier was helpless, but if they were 'protecting themselves and the Customers' by giving up the money, they were also being the 'best help' to Law Enforcement Officers that would need to solve the case. At least that's how it's 'supposed to be solved'...

But not always...

One Saturday evening around 6:30 PM and after a particularly busy day in the early Spring of 1987, 'The

Robbery' we feared 'reared its ugly head' at the Pleasant Hill Store and it became the 'Big News' of the week'...Both in town and on television newscasts.

The 'Big Caper' went down like this....

The robber who came into the Pleasant Hill Store on that Saturday evening had parked in what was apparently a good spot to view into the store. He was waiting for the best time to enter for the actual robbery. Timing is always the top element for the robber... In and out...'Quickly'...

Now, if you were 'casing out' the store for a robbery, the parking lot would be the first thing to look at by the robber... or robbers. Where could a person 'get in', 'park' and then 'get out' of the parking lot with the least likelihood that they would be seen and leave witnesses behind. Also, the activity level on the Front End of the store would dictate the quickness for the robbery too. More people also meant 'more witnesses' too.

So, at 6:30 PM on that Saturday evening, our robber must have waited and watched in the parking lot for a while. We were also pretty sure that the robber had waited until it looked as though the Front-End of the store had slowed down a bit to come in for the robbery. The partially hidden view of the last half of the Cash Registers must have kept our robber from seeing that the entire Front-End was still pretty active and that all 10 Cash Registers were busy with

Customers. It was not just the 3 or 4 he could see from the parking lot. The timing for him could have been much better, but once he was in and had the robbery was underway, he had to 'live with the situation' and the 3 or 4 Cash Registers he could see from the outside were the only ones out of the 10 that weren't busy at the moment. There were lots more people than he must have anticipated when he entered. Fully 'masked' at this point, he entered the store carrying his shotgun.

As I already said, he was 'committed' by this point and upon entering the Front Door area near the Cash Registers, he yelled loudly to all people to "Stop everything." and for everyone to "Put their hands in the air." as he pointed his shotgun at people. Then, moving about rapidly, he had each Cashier empty their Cash Drawer into his bag as he went from 'register to register'. When he had been through all 10 Registers, he backed himself to the door still pointing his shotgun back and forth at everyone. When he hit the door, he ran away and vanished into the darkness and to a waiting car.

When the person 'In-Charge' of the store at the time of the robbery gathered his thoughts, he quickly asked everyone if they were 'okay' and he told everyone to please stay for a few minutes to be interviewed by Law Enforcement when they arrived. A '9-1-1 Call' was quickly made and within a minute or two, the Police Squad Cars started converging onto the parking lot.

The 'investigation' was underway.

Interviews, accounts of the robbery by witnesses and official reports were all followed by the television Crews who came to cover the story. It was a regular 'Soap Opera' of events and the remainder of the evening was finished with the necessary paperwork and phone calls to 'upper management' at Hy-Vee's Corporate level... We were glad nobody was injured or 'badly traumatized' to cause issues in other ways.

It was a robbery of the best kind 'OVER WITHOUT INJURY'.

As the weeks rolled along, it became pretty obvious that it had been a 'clean getaway' and that no real trace of evidence or viable witnesses had seen the robber's getaway or even the car involved...His body and face had been covered so there was not much information about him either. All that was known was that he was a 'right-handed' 'white male' of 'medium height and weight' with 'blue eyes'. That description seemed to fit 'quite a few' people in Iowa.

But, could it have been that 'clean' of a robbery'? ...Now that's where this story gets real interesting.

The answer didn't come from any form of 'investigative practice'... No, it came in 'The U. S. Mail' about 6 weeks later... A letter prompted by 'someone mad at someone else' came to me in the mail giving the name of the robber. Yes, 'a simple letter' with a man's name, address and 'the facts' of

his parole a few weeks earlier from an Iowa Prison told the 'whole tale' of the robbery...

'Case Solved'...

The 'WHODUNNIT' had been revealed. Not by witnesses, forensics or even by good 'Police Work', but by someone wanting to 'Get Even'...

Yes, it came from someone who was 'MAD'...

So, 'Be Careful Who You Make Mad !'...

"You only get one chance

to make a first impression."

Ronald D. Pearson

President, CEO and

Chairman of the Board

(Retired)

"Cook It ??" ...

As early as 'The Supply Store' History of the 1930's, new products in the stores became a 'Way of Life' for Hy-Vee. The absolute best way to get a product into the Customer's grocery cart was to get the product into the Customer's mouth and in turn, that would make the sale of 'an extra item' get into the Cash Register for the store. Most times, the cost of the product and wages for the person doing the sampling were usually funded by the company that made the product.

Why wouldn't a store want to do it?

Usually, the 'sampling' takes place on weekends, holiday times or other busy times for the store. A person is either supplied by the store or is hired by the company that makes the product and that person is to stand with the product and either 'cut it up' or 'prepare it fresh' as the Customers go by. Some of the usual items are pizza, pop (sodee pop), snack foods, salads, fruits or cooked meats.

The sales generated for the store are always a very nice 'boost' for the week and it really was a 'win-win' situation for all. The company sells lots of 'extra product', the Customer gets a 'free sample', the store gets lots of extra sales and it provides a job for the person 'sampling' the item.

In our store, we always had a nicely dressed and 'especially friendly' person to sample the food. Their job was to cook it (usually in an electric skillet or in a

Microwave Oven) and then cut it into pieces and serve it on a stick pretzel if needed. The 'demo person' would then offer samples on a plate or napkin to the Customers. Usually 'one piece' or 'sample' was all that people took, but there were always those that wanted to have their 'lunch' with the free samples. Of course, we never really minded because it is just part of the 'sampling process' in the stores.

Sampling is 'Successful for Everyone Involved'.

One weekend, while I was the Store Manager at the Pleasant Hill, IA Hy-Vee Store, we 'sampled' a new Bratwurst item for one of the Meat companies. As normal, our 'Sample Person' opening the packages and cooking it in an electric skillet and offering it to our Customers. It seemed to be going over 'very well' and it 'tasted great'. Then, a story 'crept right into' the History of the Pleasant Hill Store.

Here's 'The Meat' of the story.

Late on a Saturday afternoon, our Meat Manager, Fred, came bounding up the steps and he hurried into the Office. After entering the doorway, he blurted out "I have now heard everything!" So, I asked what he was talking about and in between his laughter and cackling, I heard the story.

A phone call that had just come in to the store been given to Fred and it was from a Customer. It was a man on the phone and he was very unhappy. Fred had asked him to

explain why he was unhappy so he could help him. Fred was really good at handling these types of calls.

"I bought some of that Bratwurst you were sampling." The man said "It's terrible. It doesn't taste anything like it did at the store." So, Fred asked him a logical question in response "Well, how did you cook it?"

And with that question, the 'Statement of the Month' was given back to Fred by our unhappy Customer...

The man replied "Cook it? I didn't know you were supposed to cook it! Nobody told me that. You should tell people they have to cook it." Hiding his laughter, Fred explained how to "Cook it"... and then offered a free package when he came in next.

DUH! ...

It was one of 'The Best Stories' all year at the store and whenever things got a little dull,

Someone would always say ... "Cook it?"

“Customers will go where they are invited and they will return to where they feel welcome.”

David M. Vredenburg

Hy-Vee Co-Founder

(Deceased)

“Do You Smell Something Hot ??”

From those early days of The Supply Stores of the 1930’s, the ‘Line of Authority and Responsibility’ got passed down when the Boss went on vacation or had to be out of the store for a few days.

It is one of the ‘most important times’ in the life of an ‘Assistant Manager’... when the ‘Manager’ is on vacation. The Assistant usually ‘comes in earlier’ and ‘stays later’. They usually worry more about the Business and they have to handle many more problems than they do if the Manager is there. It can be a real ‘eye-opener’ for the Assistant and usually produces some memorable times for the store.

Some funny ones too...

I was the Store Manager in the Pleasant Hill, IA Hy-Vee Store from 1981-1987. In 1984, our Bakery Department Manager, Mary, went on vacation. With Mary being gone, that left our Assistant Bakery Manager, Merlin, in charge of the Bakery for the entire week and what a week it turned out to be!

Merlin was coming in early and staying late and the expectations of his performance were multiplied by the desire he had to show Mary he was getting close to being able to be a Bakery Manager himself. Merlin had managed the ‘personnel issues’ and written out the ‘production lists’ and he was really in complete control of what was happening in the Bakery. Sales

were good, Labor Cost was under control and the overall operation was very close to normal.

And then it happened...

Merlin had gotten busy with another project and had forgotten that he had biscuits in the Bakery Oven that needed to come out pretty soon. As the time went on, he was unaware that the biscuits were going from a 'white color' to a 'beautiful golden brown', to a 'dark brown' and then to the dreaded— 'Burned Black' !

The biscuits were ruined.

So, when Merlin remembered the biscuits, he went into a 'near panic' as he tried to decide what to do--- He could only remember two things: #1 The old 'adage' of training Bakers by standing them at the oven and saying "Brown they're done----Black you're done!" and #2 If the girls in the Bakery knew what happened, they would certainly make sure Mary found out and then he was in 'Big Trouble'.

He was in a 'tough spot'.

So, Merlin did some quick thinking and decided he would 'rush' the pans of 'now smoldering biscuits' to the store's trash compacter in the Backroom and 'dispose of the evidence'. It was a great plan, but it had one flaw.

Merlin didn't know that Frank, the Produce Manager, had 'just' been to the compacter and dumped a large bunch of cardboard apple boxes in there. Now, in itself, that's not all that bad, but when you remember that the 'premium' apples were packaged with an 'individual tissue paper' around each apple, 'THAT WAS A PROBLEM'.

Merlin dumped the biscuits into the compacter and 'quickly' went back to the Bakery as though nothing had happened. No, it hadn't happened 'yet', but about 5 minutes later, the Smoke Alarm sounded signaling a fire in the Backroom and with that, everyone raced back there to see what was on fire.

It was obvious the fire was in the Compacter, but by then it was so hot and had 'sprung up' so fast that nobody from the store could do anything to extinguish it. The Smoke Alarm had triggered the local Pleasant Hill Fire Department which in turn had alerted the Police Department and 'suddenly', the whole town was at Hy-Vee's back door to see what was going on.

The Fire Department, the Police Department, kids on bikes, neighbors and 'lots' of people just driving by had all stopped as well. The Firemen came in 'all dressed up' in their fire gear and they tried to put the fire out. They could only spray water from the inside of the store, so there was a 'real mess' developing there and in the end, the only way they could put the fire out completely was to totally unhook the trash compacter box from the 'ramming unit', pull it away from the building and then 'Spray' the inside of the compacter.

The Fire had gotten so deep into the trash compacter, that 'Fire Axes' had to be used to drag the

flaming boxes out of the compacter box and onto the parking lot to be extinguished. So, after about 20 minutes, the fire was out and our compacter and parking lot looked similar to the 'Chicago Fire' with burned smoldering remnants of cardboard boxes and garbage laying everywhere.

At this point, nobody knew the cause, but a 'quick investigation' showed the origin of the fire to be the 'Burned Biscuits'. Merlin was forced to 'fess up' about what happened.

Obviously, the threat of danger was over and the whole thing became 'hilarious' to all of us. Merlin was so embarrassed and being the 'perfect gentleman' that he always was, he got 'red in the face' and laughed along with the rest of us. It was now a story for 'The Ages' in the Pleasant Hill Hy-Vee.

The 'Burned Biscuit Fire' story seem stay alive all year and we used this event to 'Honor' or 'Roast' (you choose the term) Merlin at the annual Store Christmas Party. A fairly 'windy' lead-in by me to the award was made to the group and Merlin was 'officially' presented with a Radio Shack Fireman's Helmet complete with a 'Red Beacon' on top and a very loud 'Siren'. He was forced to wear it and it was a perfect way to remember the events of the year. His being the most memorable for sure.

All evening during the party, you could see the 'Red Beacon' flashing and hear 'The Siren'...

It was Great!

Merlin was a real 'Good Sport' about it and the story lives on in Pleasant Hill Store's History....

We'd often times remind Merlin to

"Get 'Em While They're Hot !" ...

"You say that's not very much money?... Then, write me a check for it."

P. Lynn Blanchard

Store Manager

(Retired)

“Here Kitty-Kitty” ...

In almost ‘nine decades’ of doing Business, ‘millions’ of Customers and Crew members of those 1930’s ‘Supply Stores’ and later Hy-Vee, have left behind some really great stories and ‘Folk History’ along the way. Starting in those very primitive ‘Supply Stores’ of Charles Hyde (Hy) and David Vredenburg (Vee), things have happened that will forever be ‘along the pathway’ of the Company we now know as ‘Hy-Vee, Inc’.

They are fun to remember.

Hy-Vee opened the Pleasant Hill, Iowa Hy-Vee Store in the early Summer of 1981. Earlier that Spring, I was fortunate enough to be selected as the Store Manager. It was fun to be involved with the ‘Opening’ of the store and in the three months ahead of the ‘Grand-Opening’ of the store, I was able to build a very good rapport with the newly hired Crew and we got to know each other pretty well.

Now, the Part-timers in any store are lots of fun. Their energy levels and excitement are contagious. The conversation is usually about cars, sports, school, girls, guys or ‘what’ they were going to do after work. They are rather ‘carefree’ and almost always enjoy pulling a ‘fast-one’ or a prank on each other. So, when this story unfolded, I played right along.

Here’s ‘the way it all came ‘roaring’ down.

In the Breakroom one day, some of the Part-time guys were talking about "The lady with the Lion". Now, I sensed I was being set-up for a prank on me, so I listened and I didn't say too much at first, but when the conversation went on for a few more minutes, I asked some questions. You know, the usual ones... "What lady?" How big is this Lion?" "How does she bring it to the store?" "Is it friendly?" I thought these questions might confuse their story and expose the joke, so I waited as I heard more of their story.

The Part-timers kept on talking and I continued to think they were 'messing with me', so I finally said "Okay, the next time she comes to our store with the Lion, I want you to call me to see it." I figured this would stop it and I would not end up being the object of their joking.

But not so fast...

About three or four weeks went by and I heard nothing more about 'The lady with the Lion'. I was pretty sure by then that there 'was no Lion' and that I had somehow 'loosened myself' from the 'grips' of their joking. So, one day, I was in the Office and I was paged to the private 'store phone'. One of the young guys said "Hey, hurry and get up here---the Lady with the Lion is here!"

I immediately headed for the Front-end of the store to see "if" there was a 'Lady with the Lion' at all.

I arrived at the front of the store in time to see a lady by the Front Door with two of our young guys and a large cart of 'bagged groceries'. They were waiting on me so,

I quickly said "Hello" and introduced myself to the woman standing there. With that, we walked outside to a 'waiting' Chevy Station Wagon.

In the back of the large Chevy Station Wagon, there was a huge, full-grown, female Lion. Yes, a 'live' female Lion. I was flabbergasted. I was amazed by this magnificent creature. I was also a bit in 'awe' of its 'size and beauty'. I was probably equally in "awe' of the fact that this 'magnificent creature' was 'right smack' in the middle of Iowa Farm Country and it was a sight that few people ever see outside of a Zoo. The Lioness looked very comfortable in the car as she watched all of us strangers gawk at her.

The Lioness looked to be about 300 pounds and she had a head as big as a bushel basket. This 'cat' filled nearly all of the backseat and rear area of the Chevy Station Wagon. The Lioness was 'rather reserved' and appeared to be very docile, but for safety, the woman always loaded the grocery bags into the car herself as the Clerk handed them to her.

Like the young guys normally did, I handed the bags of Groceries to the lady and she loaded them into the back of car. As we loaded them, the lady talked about "How much fun it was to go places with a full-grown Lion in the car." Seems the lady lived just East of the store very near the little town named Runnells, IA. She apparently shopped about every-other week and she would bring this 'full-grown female Lion' to the store in her Chevy Station Wagon for an 'outing'.

Our Customer said people didn't seem bothered by her Lioness and she said having 'her' (The Lioness) as a pet was like having "An Overgrown Kitty". It was obvious the Lioness was a family pet and was 'loved very much'. We had a nice conversation and she soon left to go home with her Lioness.

Again, 'The Joke' turned out to be on me.

From this point on, I had to really think hard as to whether the Part-timers were telling me the truth on some story or if I was being 'set-up' for another joke. What I thought was a prank, in this case, turned out to be a 'factual story' and it only set me up to be 'had' again later. There really was a Lion.

It was a 'Great Story' and

They Weren't 'LION' After All ...

“Hurry...Get To The Store !”

Back in the 1930’s when Hy-Vee started out in those small ‘Supply Stores’ of Southern Iowa and Northern Missouri towns, the people who lived in America had no Television to get ‘News and Happenings’ from. It was all radio and newspapers then. Television would come along in the 1950’s and it would ‘Change the World Forever’.

In those days of the 1930’s, the news on the radio was listened to very carefully and newspapers were read thoroughly ‘several times over’ for the news. Entertainment in people’s homes was a combination of things...games were played, books were read, baking and cooking were prevalent and small repair jobs were done with light from small electric light bulbs of the day. ‘Evening Radio Shows’ were listened to by the whole family.

Things were primitive by today’s standards.

One of the ‘Coldest Winters Ever’ recorded in the Midwest was the Winter of 1935-1936. It had come on the heels of the ‘Hottest Summer Ever’ in 1934. In some cases, the ‘Record Lows’ of that Winter of 1936 stood in place for decades and may still be ‘Records’ today in some places. It was brutal and it took a lot of work and personal sacrifice by those early Store Managers to keep everything in their stores safe and warm. With heat in the stores coming solely from a ‘Pot-Bellied Stove’ in the middle of the Sales area of

the store, it was necessary to 'stoke' that fire often. Lots of coal was used that Winter.

Hy-Vee's future President and CEO, Dwight Vredenburg, was the Store Manager in the Unionville, MO 'Hyde and Vredenburg 'Supply Store' at that time. There were about 15 small stores in those years. When the Company 'Incorporated' in 1938, Dwight became President and he stayed at the 'Helm' until 1989 when he retired with 54 years of Service to Hy-Vee.

During that Winter of 1936 though, Dwight was like everyone else in Unionville. They were all nearly 'Frozen to the Bone' and his job as the Store Manager required that he keep the store 'safe and warm'. To keep it warm that Winter was nearly as important as keeping it safe. Keeping it warm required him to get up from bed twice each night to go to the store and 'stoke' add coal and 'stoke' the fire in the Pot-Bellied Stove there so the cans and jars wouldn't freeze on the shelves. Many nights, the items on the shelves would be moved 'closer to the stove' to protect them. It was just that brutally cold.

With Radio being the 'Cutting Edge Medium' in America then, the Citizens really listened to what they were told by the Radio Announcers. That cold Winter, they were told many times to 'Get to The Store' and to 'Stock-up' so they wouldn't be stuck at home with no Food or Supplies. The radio broadcasts

were essential for survival and the Customers knew it.

As the decades rolled along, television came into existence and then the 'live broadcasts' were 'watched' and 'listened to' as well as to radio. It seemed a bit like a 'double broadcast' sometimes, but during inclement weather, it kept people safe. Now, in the year 2017, along with radio and television, personal computers, 'smart phones and even wrist phones keep people 'in the loop'. Times have changed so much.

Something happened in 1982 that 'stormed right in' to the Hy-Vee History Books for many stores and it needs told...

This is how it all came down...

(Or 'didn't' as it turned out.)

In the Winter of early 1982, I was the Store Manager at the Pleasant Hill, IA Hy-Vee. We had already seen the beginnings of a 'Tough Winter' and people were already very 'edgy and concerned'. Even in a 'normal' Iowa Winter, roads were bad, power outages happened and people got 'stuck at home' for days at a time, so with an already 'Bad Winter' started, when the forecasts started coming in for a 'Big Storm', people nearly 'panicked' and it got wild.

It was starting to be 'reported' that it would be a "Snow Storm of Record Proportion". People were being told to "Get to the stores and stock-up". It

didn't matter what radio station or television channel you turned to, there it was, the prediction causing 'Wide-Spread Panic'. It looked bad and most people took it all very seriously ...As they should.

Now, we had opened the Pleasant Hill Hy-Vee the previous June as a 'new store' and 'new town' for Hy-Vee. We had established our Sales numbers at a respectable level and we had pretty good knowledge of what each week would be. We had no idea of what was to come from the 'dire prediction' though and it was more than we ever imagined.

All evening and into the night, the newscasters were telling everyone of the 'Terrible Weather' coming and they stressed it 'over and over and over'. It was to be widespread as far West as Nebraska and as far North as South Dakota and Minnesota. All Hy-Vee Stores in those areas were getting 'blitzed' by their Customers.

'Panic Buying' had ensued in Central Iowa and our Customers came to the stores in record numbers. They were buying everything from batteries to canned goods to frozen foods, milk, bread and just about anything else you can think of. The only things being passed over were things like soaps and cleaning items. It was the 'survival stuff' going out the doors. Even 'Rover' got a 'stockpile' of dog food in many households.

This evening ended for us at 11:00 PM and by 7AM the next morning, there were still regular newscasts predicting the "dire situation" that was to come. As we unlocked the doors for the day, we began to see people coming through the doors in 'larger numbers' yet and they were buying very large orders. We called in all the 'extra help' we could muster and the whole day saw every one of our ten Cash Registers 'going full blast' with big orders.

By about 5:00 PM that day, the store was about as empty as I had seen it since before we stocked it up for the Grand Opening seven months prior. The shelves were very bare and the real 'key items' were gone. The Milk Case was empty, the Meat Case was nearly empty, the Produce Rack was nearly empty and all the Dry Grocery shelves were so empty they all got a 'good wipe down" with a wet rag the next day because there were so many gaping holes of 'Just Bare Shelves'.

The whole thing was like a page out of a 'Bizarre Book'...

At about 5:00PM (or close), I 'made the rounds' in the store and I was trying to survey the damage. I had our Order Man going through the aisles and putting together an order to go in to the Hy-Vee Warehouse as soon as he was done. It was going to be a huge order. We needed everything.

As I went by the Milk Case, there was a man about 60 years-old 'sitting' in the bottom shelf of the case itself with his feet out onto the floor. He was just sitting there with his forearms resting on his knees and he was smoking a cigarette. He was waiting for his wife.

To see someone sitting like that in a cold case made to hold milk, looked really odd and humorous, so I said "Makes a pretty good chair doesn't it?" He replied "Yes, it's actually not too bad. It doesn't look like you're using it for anything else?"

We both 'chuckled'.

So, with really nothing else to do, I walked over and sat down next to him in the Milk Case and we talked about the 'Weather Melee' that we were both witnessing. We had a nice conversation for about 10 minutes or so and then his wife came by and we both got up and went our separate ways. Him to the Cash Registers and me, 'to the Office' to make sure the order for Groceries was getting transmitted to the Hy-Vee Warehouse in Chariton, IA.

We finished that day and it was the biggest Sales Day we had ever had. It was even bigger than Grand Opening had been. The day totaled up to 'over half' of our normal 'weekly' totals. Reports were coming in from the Hy-Vee Stores all over Iowa, Minnesota, Nebraska and South Dakota. There were some 'unbelievable' Sales numbers being quoted and it was true because we saw it and we could feel it in our store. Our Crew was 'tired', our store was 'empty' and we would have about three days of hard work to 're-stock' everything. There was as much hard work

ahead of us as there was that 'day and a half' now behind us.

The irony of it all...?

As 'Fate' would have it, the Weather forecasters were 'wrong'...The snow that came was 'very light' at about 1" or 2" and 'very easily' maneuvered in for everyone...Oh, some of the Northern and Western stores of Hy-Vee got some heavier snow, but overall, 'It was a DUD'!

All we could do was to just shake our heads and say...

"Darn, All This Work And Not Even

Enough For A Decent Snowman."

“We’re not looking for dollar bills, we’re looking for twenty nickels.”

Charles L. Hyde

Hy-Vee Co-Founder

(Deceased)

"I Lost My Billfold" ...

It didn't take very long for Charles Hyde and David Vredenburg to learn that a 'Grocery Store' is pretty much a 'side show goin' on while you're selling groceries'. Whether it was 1930 and those 1200 square foot stores or now in 2017 with those 'monster' 100,000 square foot stores, there's always 'something happening behind the scenes' that makes people laugh and enjoy the fun of working with so many great people.

In addition to all that's going on, one other thing that's 'for sure' about working in a Grocery Store is that everyone knows (or will soon find out) most of the supposed 'secrets' or 'funny happenings' of the Crew in the store... It doesn't matter what the issue, if one other person finds out about something, you may as well 'post it on the bulletin board' in the Breakroom.

It can all get rather comical and sometimes even embarrassing.

Now, the Part-timers in any store are a really fun and they are a very important part of the 'personality' of a store. They are energetic, excitable, hard-working and they can 'dish-out the fun' as well as having it 'pointed at them'.

I was the Store Manager of the Pleasant Hill, IA Hy-Vee Store from 1981-1987. Pleasant Hill is a Des Moines, IA suburb on the far East-Side of Des Moines.

It is a town that gives a 'small-town' atmosphere while 'nestled' into a larger metropolitan area. It is a great town.

One of the funniest things that ever happened at the Pleasant Hill Store involved a Part-timer named Paul. He had come to us through the acquisition of a small Super-Valu Store we purchased just before the opening of the Pleasant Hill Store in the Spring of 1981.

Here's how it went down... 'Literally'.

Paul was 17 years-old and was a really great kid. He was smart, good-looking and really had a personality 'well-suited' for working with other people. I really enjoyed him and he proved to be a great part of our Crew.

One day, while I was doing some paperwork at my desk, Paul stuck his head in the Office door and said... "Rick, has anyone turned in a billfold?" I sort of shrugged and said "No Paul, but I'll keep my ears open for anyone finding one. Why don't you put a note on the bulletin board in the Breakroom? Maybe somebody will find it and return it." Paul was fine with that and he took off for his shift and I went back to my paperwork.

So, a note went up on the bulletin board and 'the word' went out to keep an eye out for Paul's billfold. Unless a customer had found it and had taken it, it was probably somewhere in the store and it would most likely show up sooner or later.

A couple of days later, the Produce Manager, Frank, said that the toilet in the Men's Restroom was acting up and not flushing correctly. We always took good care of the toilets because they really could bring things to a halt if they didn't work right. I said to Frank "Do we need to call a Plumber?" Frank said "No, I'll watch it for a few days and see if the issue resolves itself. If not, we'll need to call though." It was a problem for all the male employees and everyone knew there was a 'growing issue' that didn't seem to be getting better. We were just hoping it wouldn't require the 'expense' of the Plumber.

After a few days, Frank said he thought we needed the Plumber after all, so I called and got them 'on the way'...The next morning, the Plumber showed up and began investigating the toilet. It's not always a clear-cut reason and it can take a while. After about two hours of working on the toilet, the Plumber 'sent word' to have me come to the Men's Restroom. He had found the problem.

So, I made my way to the Men's Restroom and as I went in, I could smell a terrible and stinky 'manure smell'. The Plumber said... "Well, I found it. The toilet was plugged about 3 feet into the sewage pipe, but here it is...It won't give you any more problems." and with that, he handed me (or tried to) a 'wet

human-waste covered' object. I shrugged and said "What is it.?" He replied "It's a billfold."

Then, it 'clicked' and I chuckled inside... I knew whose it was.

So, I got a large Ziploc bag and the Plumber put the billfold into the bag for me. Now, with the billfold safely sealed in the Ziploc bag, I took it the storage area across from the Office and close to the Breakroom. I knew I could have some fun with it. I would make a 'presentation' of it at 'just the right time'.

Two days later, I saw the Part-timers gathering near the Breakroom to get ready to 'clock-in' for work and I saw Paul among the group. I headed out of the Office and I stopped really close to the 8 or 10 kids gathered there.

It was great...I was 'on a roll'...

I spoke to everyone and said something about work that night and then I said "Oh, hey Paul, I have your billfold. It was turned in."

Paul was really excited. I said "Wait here, I'll go get it." So, I went to the storage area and I got the Ziploc bag with the 'squishy' feel of water and the human waste attached to it. I came back and then I said... "Paul, we found out what was plugging the toilet in the Men's Restroom...Next time you have to take a

crap, make sure your billfold is still in your pocket when you pull your pants up." Then, I handed him the 'Squishy' Ziploc bag.

The kids all 'laughed and laughed' and Paul took it all really well. He got used to the idea that everyone was going to know that his billfold was the problem in the Men's Restroom 'plug-up'.

All the employees soon learned the story and it was 'instantly' a piece of the History of the Pleasant Hill Store. Paul heard about it quite often by the Store Crew and it was funny 'every time' it was ever brought up.

I'd hear the Kids say (and Laugh out loud)

"Hey Paul...

Do You Have Your Billfold?"

“If you don’t know how to do something well, be sure to hire someone who does and then get out of their way and let them do what you hired them to do.”

K. Donald Canfield

Store Manager

(Retired)

“In God We Trust” ...

Counterfeit Money...A Retailer’s Nightmare.

Since the ‘human being’ started figuring out ways to ‘Swindle’ other people out of anything of value, it’s been something to reckon with to protect yourself in Business. There’s a thief around every corner. Even back in ‘The Supply Store’ Days of the 1930’s, ‘Swindlers’ were out there trying to get ‘something for nothing’...The whole ‘Swindle Game’ goes on everywhere today. Nearly 90 years later.

Retailers everywhere ‘cringe’ at the thought of receiving ‘bogus bills’ that will ultimately cost them time, effort and money which equates to ‘lower profits’. Over the decades, the problem of Counterfeiting and ‘altering bills’ got so big in the United States, that the Federal Government assigned the whole problem to The United States Secret Service to ‘investigate and control’ from a prosecution standpoint. These Officers of the Secret Service take their role in this very seriously and occasionally, it gets rather interesting.

One such incident happened to me and this is how it ‘cashed out’.

In 1984, I was the Store Manager at the Pleasant Hill, IA Hy-Vee. We did our Store Banking at The First National Bank of Des Moines which had a Branch Office immediately across the street from our store. We had an account there to which we deposited Daily

Sales Receipts and obtained currency and coins from to meet our needs in doing our Business. It was a good relationship, and we knew them pretty well at the Branch Bank.

One day, I received a call from one of the representatives at the Bank and she said she was calling to let me know that she was going to 'charge' our account for an 'altered $20 bill' that had been received by our store. We discussed it for a moment and then I asked for the bill to be returned to us for my inspection and records. She said that was fine.

Within a day or two, the 'altered $20 bill' came back to us and I got to see it firsthand. It was a $1 bill that had been made to look like a $20 bill by the cutting and then the 'gluing' of a real '20' over each corner. Each of '20' emblems on the bill had been removed from an actual $20 bill and then 'glued' over the "1" to make it look like a $20 bill when passed in a group of bills. It required removing one corner from each of four different $20 Bills and then the original bills could still be passed and they would be accepted as payment. Anyone (Hy-Vee in this case) accepting the now altered $1 bill would lose $19 on the transaction.

So, as Hy-Vee people usually do, we tried to make the best of the situation and I decided I could use the 'altered bill' in the 'training' of our people. We instructed them that when they received several bills in a transaction, they should separate the bills enough to make sure they were real $20's. It was a

good plan and I used it for a year or so as a 'training tool'.

In the training, I would sit down for a quick meeting with new Cashiers and I would briefly go over the training they had received from our 'Checker Trainer'. We talked about the losses on 'altered and bogus bills' and I would use the actual 'altered $20 bill' as an example. It worked well to have the $20 bill for an example and it was proving to be a 'good tool' for our training.

Then, one afternoon, the lady from our Bank called and informed me of a counterfeit $100 bill that one of our Cashiers had taken. I agreed to the 'charge' for the loss on the bill and like the 'altered $20 bill', I requested that she return the counterfeit $100 bill to us along with our other receipts and papers for the day. She said she couldn't return it as it had to go to the Secret Service for 'investigation'.

I told her that it didn't seem right and that she'd returned 'other' money to us before. I reminded her about the 'altered $20 bill', but it was obvious I wasn't going to get the counterfeit $100 bill back. So, I finally said that I would be 'OK' with it and just to charge us for it and give us a receipt for it. She said that was fine and that was the end of the conversation with our Bank about it.

Nothing more happened...until about 6 months later.

I had pretty much forgotten about the counterfeit $100 bill as time went along until one day, I was called on the private Store Phone by one of our Crew working at our Customer Service Counter. She told me there was a man there to see me and he was from the United States Secret Service. Not even considering the counterfeit bill, I wondered why someone from the Secret Service would want to see me. I walked to the Customer Service Counter with my Assistant Store Manager, Ray, at my side.

As I rounded the corner from the Backroom and out on to the Sales Floor and to the Customer Service Counter, I could see a very nicely dressed man in a suit and tie and one of our Staff at the Counter sort of 'motioned' that he was the man who wanted to see me. I acknowledged her and approached the man standing there waiting for me. I spoke first.

I stuck out my hand and I said "Hi, I'm Rick Lampkin the Store Manager. How may I help you?" With no hesitation, the man replied "I am John Jamison (not his real name) with the United States Secret Service and I'm here to get the 'altered $20 bill' you have here at your store." It sort-of caught me off-guard a little.

As I stood there for only a split-second thinking of my reply, he said "You do have the altered $20 bill, don't you?" and it was necessary for me to reply, so I said "Yes, I have an 'altered $20 bill', but I don't want to let go of it as I use it for training purposes for new Cashiers. We teach them what to look for in bogus

money." Thinking that would suffice, I stopped talking.

Again, with no hesitation, he simply (and rather rudely) said "I want you to know that we can do this the easy way or the hard way, but I'm going to get that $20 bill. You can make it easy and give it to me or I can arrest you, handcuff you and we'll go Downtown and I'll get it anyway... You choose."

He had made 'no pretense' of being polite, courteous or even respectful. He had thrown the 'weight of the Feds' out like a 'shield' and he had pretty much 'strong-armed' his way through on the conversation.

I was furious inside.

Perhaps I was furious more for the 'lack of respect' that he had for an 'honest retailer' or another person than for anything else. He was just 'arm-twisting' and it was anything but the way it should have been handled. It was so opposite of everything Hy-Vee tries to be in Customer Service to others.

Now faced with the impending situation, I said "Ok, I'll give you the $20 bill...I do want a written receipt for it though." The Secret Service Agent grimaced a little and then he said "I'll have to go to the car to get you one." I acknowledged that him going to get one was fine and I set off to go to the Office to get the 'altered $20 bill'. The Secret Service Agent took off walking out of the store to his car. At that point, I wouldn't have cared if he had to walk 50 miles to get

it. He wanted the 'altered $20 bill' and I wanted a receipt for it. I was going to make him do part of the work.

I was back to the Customer Service Counter before he was, so Ray and I just waited there for him. As he walked up the first aisle of the store from the front door, I could see he had a piece of paper in his hand. He walked up and presented me with the paper and I quickly read it. It was the signed receipt I wanted. I folded it and put it in my shirt pocket.

I let a few seconds go by and I could see he had no other comments for me, so I asked him "Are we done here?" He nodded and said "Yes, we are." It was obvious that there would be no "Thank-you" from him to me, so I said "Well, if we're done and you have what you need, I want you to turn yourself around and hike your 'A$$' right out that front door." Then I looked him 'straight in the eye" for a response.

A look of 'sheer surprise' came over his face and he replied "You don't need to be nasty about it." And with that, I said back to him in a calm voice. "I'm not the one who started the 'nasty' part of this. You have been rude since I shook your hand. Just leave. You represent the Secret Service and I run this store. We are done here with your Business and you're not welcome here anymore."

With that, he left and we watched him walk back up the first aisle and out the door. I looked at Ray and he was as 'white as a ghost'. He quickly blurted out

"Have you lost your mind, Rick? All I could think of was how I was going to explain to Headquarters that you tossed out the Secret Service and got arrested for it?"

The Staff at the Customer Service Counter stared at me in disbelief. Nothing moved and nobody said a word.

I looked at Ray and I grinned. I said very softly "Sometimes you gotta' do certain things to make sure you still have some control." We both laughed and we went about our 'afternoon business'...

I never heard any more about it.

It was the day I met the Secret Service and

The 'Altered' $20 Bill Almost 'Altered' My Freedom...

“We have a definite Operating Philosophy. If you’re going to have a Hy-Vee or a Hy-Vee Drugstore, the store is going to be clean, neat and bright…and the employees are going to be friendly.”

Ronald D. Pearson

President, CEO and

Chairman of the Board

(Retired)

"Well, It Sure Wasn't Him" ...

'Kids Will Be Kids'... (So, they say.)

For as long as young people have been working in the stores, there have been things happen that led to funny stories for 'The Ages'...Oh, those stores of the 1930's, were smaller and had a 'closer-knit group' in the Crew, but there were kids always trying to find ways to have fun and be mischievous just the same. It's in their nature.

In the 1930's the young people were employed to do things like 'bagging sugar, bagging potatoes, sweeping-up the sidewalks, delivering small orders by bicycle and even getting pails of water from the town water pump that was usually not a great distance from the store. In fact, none of the stores had running water then and I can even remember that when I became a Store Manager in 1977, Hy-Vee in Cainsville, MO was still getting their water from a 'town pump' in the middle of the Business District.

In those very early days, most of the 'fun stuff' that the kids found to do was usually confined to practical jokes, loafing a bit, sneaking a cracker to eat from the cracker barrel, grabbing a piece of bulk chocolate or even 'snitching' a pickle from the pickle barrel. It was, just the same, still considered taboo and usually, the 'offense' of not paying for something had to be dealt with through some type of punishment. In those days, most times, the punishment was a 'verbal reprimand'.

Things started changing in the stores for the young people as America started building 'Self-Serve Stores. 'The Supply Stores' followed along in Southern Iowa and Northern Missouri as the trend of 'Self-Serve Stores' came to fruition for the Customers in those small stores and towns. Centerville, IA was the location of the first 'Self-Serve Store' in the Company now known as Hy-Vee, Inc.

Yes, nearly every aspect of those 'Small Little Stores' of the 1930's was changing.

As the decades started rolling along for Charles Hyde and David Vredenburg in 'The Supply Stores', the sophistication of nearly everything 'sold' or 'purchased' for use in those stores grew very rapidly. Things like 'pre-packaged' bags of flour, sugar, salt, cake mixes and canned goods of every kind came along and there was no longer a need for the very 'labor intense' ways of having someone bagging all those things as the Customers asked for them. The jobs for the young people turned to stocking shelves, carrying out Groceries for the Customers, cleaning-up spills and many other 'menial jobs' that didn't require a lot of sophisticated training to do.

In the larger stores, there were more people because there was more Business and the aspects of having lots of young people was starting to change too. It was easier and more 'cost effective' to have a few

'Full-time People' and more 'Part-time People'. After all, one good 'Supervisory Person' could easily keep up with 15 or 20 Part-timers and delegate Jobs and responsibilities and everything got done at lower hourly wage averages. Efficient stores at 'Lower Costs' meant 'Lower Prices' for the Customers. It was all starting to fall in place.

It was in this 'mix' that the young people would occasionally fall victim to 'too much idle time' and 'too little supervision' and then there would be something happen that would 'cause a problem'.

One such event in 1985 happened with a Part-timer and it was talked about for many years. The story is still going today almost 30 years later.

This is what happened.

I was the Store Manager at the Pleasant Hill, IA Store from 1981-1987. We had a mix of about 25% Full-timers and 75% Part-timers in our Crew. The Full-timers were in positions that required a skill such as Meat-Cutting or Baking from Scratch. Some were also in positions of "Supervisory" responsibilities and that was more handling large numbers of Part-timers and getting multiple tasks completed with those people. Of this group, almost all were young people working about 15 to 20 hours per week and in school at either high school or the college level.

In this story, my Supervisory Crew kept reporting to me that they were finding cans of refrigerated

Whipping Cream with broken seals in the Backroom Milk Cooler where they were stored until they were stocked to the self-serve Milk Case. It did not appear that they were empty, but they were opened just the same. These opened containers coupled with returns we were getting from Customers who said the cans were open and they wouldn't spray the Whipped Cream out as normal, made us realize that there was something else going on.

We had a hunch as to what it was.

We set out on a 'plan' to find out just what was going on and why these cans were open. What we found out sort of 'charted a new course' for watching the 'abuses of substances' and products we sold in the stores.

We had all known for many years that certain kinds of glue could be sniffed for a 'High" and pure real Vanilla had alcohol in it that would make someone intoxicated. We knew too that certain kinds of mouthwash would get someone drunk, but none of us knew that aerosol cans of Whipped Cream would be the 'target' of the kids like those other items.

So, as we set up our plan to catch our 'culprit', none of us knew that when we caught him, he'd be 'higher than a kite' and it would take a while for him to 'come down out of the clouds'...

But, that's what happened.

Our Dairy Case Part-timer, Jerry, was opening the seals on the Whipped Cream aerosol cans and then sniffing the propellant gas 'Nitrous Oxide' that was used in the cans to push the Whipped Cream out. This 'Nitrous Oxide' could be sniffed and it was 'completely intoxicating'.

So, we caught Jerry 'sniffing the gas' from the spout into his nose and we brought him to the Office and waited on his Parents to come and get him to take him home. He was certainly not in any shape to drive and it would take a few hours to get him 'sobered up'.

Who knew?

Within about 30 minutes or so, his Parents came and they took him home. I told them that I'd like to see them all the next afternoon after school and they left. I am sure he slept very well that night. I wasn't sure as to his Parents' overall reaction, but I figured we could talk about it the next day and we went about the duties of 'running the store' and taking care of the Customers...

The next afternoon, Jerry and his Parents showed up at the store as we had agreed and we discussed the incident. I explained the 'trail of cans' we had found and that we had caught him 'red-handed' with the open can and 'sniffing it'. I even told them that he was done working at the store as I couldn't justify his continued employment to the others on our Crew. "After all," I said, "rules are rules" and even aside

from the sniffing issue he was guilty of opening and consuming the product." ...

His Parents were 'shocked' by it all and his termination was not what they expected. His Dad stayed silent as his Mother argued for the 'salvaging' of his job. She tried every direction to justify him being kept as an employee. She had almost exhausted herself on it when the 'funny' part of this story 'shot right out' of Jerry's Mother's mouth.

What his Mother said next was so funny and so far 'off course' from the reason for his termination that it 'instantly' became the part of the story that got remembered the most. I could hardly contain myself from laughing, but I held out and kept calm.

His Mother sat up real tall and she said "Jerry couldn't have done it. After all, he don't even like Whipped Cream" ...

WHAAAAAT? ... Liking it had nothing to do with it...

I stood firm on my decision that his job was done and they all left the store together. Jerry was quiet, his Dad was quiet, but Jerry's Mom was still 'muttering to herself' about the whole incident as they left.

It was the Day that what Jerry's Mom said

'Put The Topping On It All'...

“No, Not Again ?” ... (Yawn !)

The 1930’s for ‘The Supply Stores’ were a period of ‘Infancy’ for the ‘Great Company’ that would evolve over nearly 90 years into the future. Those primitive small 1200 square foot stores were operated ‘very simply’ and ‘very modestly’. A very large portion of their Sales was done on ‘credit’ and the Customers didn’t use as much cash. Checks were rare and of course, credit cards and debit cards were still 60 years into the future. Things were pretty ‘austere’ from any angle you view them from.

The decades of the 1940’s-1950’s and even the 1960’s saw the increase in Sales by cash and checks and it became necessary to protect that cash by way of ‘locking it up’ in a Safe or taking it to the Bank overnight to get it out of the building. Gone were the days of simply ‘hiding it’ in the store overnight. Besides, the cash and charge tickets had been ‘burned-up’ more than once by a fire in the building or by being ‘burned-up’ when the cardboard box or paper bag the cash was in was disposed of in the store’s Incinerator by mistake.

In the early years of Hy-Vee, the money for the Store’s Daily Receipts was delivered to and from the Bank via one of the Management Employees driving to the Bank in the morning to pick it up after it was delivered to the Bank the night before by the person in charge of the Store and “closing up” for the night. Only a slight amount of cash was left overnight at the

store and it was just enough to get the store open and operating the next morning. It was usually less than $400-$500. As late as 1968, 'burglarizing' the stores happened too. I will recall going into the Washington Store early on a Saturday in 1968 only to find the Safe 'blown-open' by nitro-glycerin jelly and lying in a 'thousand pieces'. The Burglars realized the 'grand sum' of about $400 and some cartons of cigarettes.

Electronics were about to change things in the stores.

As the years rolled along into the 1970's, the stores were starting to be electronically wired with an alarm signal to the Police Department or a local 'Monitoring Company' that made a call to a designated person that the Store's Management had given them and that person made a decision whether or not to make a trip to the store to check things out. A 'Code Question' was given to the 'Monitoring Company' that they were to ask of the designated person and if that code's 'correct answer' wasn't given to the caller from the 'Monitoring Company', then the local Police were called and they would respond to investigate.

One such story of 'The Alarms Going Off' went off like this.

I was the Store Manager at the Pleasant Hill, IA Store for six years beginning in 1981 and I had a good relationship with the Pleasant Hill Police

Department. When the alarm 'went off' on our Safe, they were notified along with me by the 'Monitoring Company' and we went to the store together to investigate. I felt safe doing this and it was usually a short call for the Police. It worked well.

During one stretch in 1984, the 'safe alarm' went off on 22 consecutive nights and it was just about to 'drive us all crazy'. It was always between 1:00 AM and 2:00 AM and it was really aggravating. Not only had I met with our Crew about it, but I had asked the 'Monitoring Company' to have their Service Crew come out and check the alarm system to make sure it was operating properly.

It was operating just as it was designed to do.

So, we went through the whole 'gambit' of things to look for on it and we 're-visited' our routines internally and then we just had to rely on the 'electronic wiring' as the problem, so I made arrangements to have some new wires run from some 'point A to point B' type spots in the store and I was hopeful that would help. The 'Alarm Company' had given us a date they would come to work on it and it was still a couple of days off, so I just figured I'd tough it out and live with it for a couple more nights.

As I went to bed one night still a day or two before the date to have it worked on, I dozed off and then I seemed to 'sit straight up' with the solution to the whole thing. It had come to me almost 'out of the

blue' and it was the only logical answer after everything we'd been through.

With my 'revelation' fresh in my head, I got up and I got dressed and drove to the store. When I arrived at the store, I surveyed the situation to my hunch and it seemed 'highly logical' that I was right. I made the adjustment and then I went back home to bed. Within an hour or so, I got the usual call I'd been getting and I jumped out of bed, got dressed and headed over to Hy-Vee.

When I arrived at the store, the Police Squad Car was there too and we entered the store together and we walked straight to the Courtesy Counter where the Safe was...And sure enough, there was the answer. A 'Dead Mouse' in the mousetrap I had set an hour earlier. The 'little devil' had apparently been living under the Safe and when people were around, he stayed tight in his 'small nest' under the Safe.

Then, when everyone went home, the 'little devil' would wait for a while and when he was 100% convinced the 'coast was clear', he'd take off to find food and 'Voila' the alarm would sound. Of course, he'd run and hide when that happened.

I was so proud of myself for figuring it out...Twenty-two consecutive nights I had been 'interrupted' to go to the store because of the Security Alarm. I was

getting to a point where I was willing to spend a lot of money to have the wiring changed and I think everyone else involved was 'worn out' too.

Oh, those next few nights were 'GREAT'....

No interruptions...Just Sleep!

It became known as

'The Mouse That Roared'...

“We remind our Store Managers to make today’s decisions for tomorrow’s Customers.”

Ronald D. Pearson

President, CEO and

Chairman of the Board

(Retired)

"Oh, Those Red-Hot Chili Peppers" ...

'The Breakroom'... Ah yes. In every store, it is 'The Information Center of The Store'. It's like a 'Newspaper with Tables and Chairs'. Something said or done in the Breakroom will be 'all over the store 'Instantly!'

During all the decades of Hy-Vee's existence, the Crews in all the stores had a place in the store where they could 'take a break' and relax for a few minutes. A cup of coffee, a cigarette, some lunch or a bottle of pop could all be found in the 'Break Area' of those early stores. In those days, it was simply an area of the Backroom with a picnic style table and benches, but it was 'used by all'.

As time went along, the new stores were built with a separate room in the Backroom as 'The Breakroom'. The newer designs gave a more pleasant atmosphere and it always has a sink and a coffee pot. Generally, there is a microwave oven and a pop machine. Food may be brought from home, the store's Kitchen Department or any other part of the store for a quick meal.

Conversations in the Breakrooms range pretty much to all possible types. Jokes, family stories, dates, cars, girls, guys, grandchildren and many other endless topics. It's truly 'all over the board'. The Meat Department Crew at Pleasant Hill always bought a paper and worked the 'Jumble' every day.

As a Store Manager, I always tried to get 'in and out' of the Breakroom during almost all times of the day. Mostly, I was 'in and out' quickly and I took enough time in there to have a half a cup of coffee and to catch 'most' of what was going on. Sometimes, someone would bring something from home as a treat for everyone and a couple of times each year, we'd have a 'Pot Luck Meal' for the day and everyone would bring a dish for the Breakroom. Relish trays, crock pots, cakes, pies, cookies and all sorts of other 'Pot Luck Items'. Those meals were always lots of fun and we got to see 'Who' the Gourmet Cooks were in the store.

It was always a fun day.

Something that one of the Crew brought in as a 'treat' for all of us turned into a 'great memory' for me and for several others in the store at Pleasant Hill, IA in 1984. I'll remember it for a 'long-long' time to come.

It was 'served-up' like this...

I was the Store Manager at The Pleasant Hill Hy-Vee from 1981 until early 1987. The store was new when we opened in mid-1981 and we had a 'huge' Grand Opening and a great Store Crew. The usual jokes and 'minor pranks' were played on each other and at times, 'The Boss' (Me) became the target and I laughed right along with the rest of them. They were fun times for sure and those times together always seemed to 'pull' everyone together as a team'.

One morning, Chris, one of the young men that worked in our Bakery Department was telling everyone in the Breakroom about the 'Red Hot Chili Peppers' that his Grandpa grew and then 'packed in jars' each Summer. He kept stressing just how "Blasted Hot" these Cherry Peppers were and how he didn't see how any human being could ever eat one.

So, like I did on many occasions, I 'put my foot right in my own mouth' and I said... "Bring us some and we'll see if they're as hot as you say." Well, Chris agreed to get a jar of them from his Grandpa and I figured it was a bit of a 'longshot' that we'd have to try the Hot Cherry Peppers.

Several days went by and one morning, Chris stuck his head in the Office doorway and said "Hey Rick, I've got a jar of Grandpa's Cherry Peppers in the Breakroom...Come on in and have one."

So, I agreed that I'd be 'right in' and I got up and went into the Breakroom. When I arrived, there must have been 10 or 12 people in there and the conversation was centered on "Just how hot those Cherry Peppers were.' Everyone was raving about them. They all said "Nobody had ever had Peppers that hot before."

I poured myself a cup of coffee and sat down.

Not to be considered a 'pansy', I said "Do you really think they're that hot? I've had lots of hot things over the years and they can't be any worse than some of that stuff." And I no sooner got the words out than

the lid came off the jar and I was 'offered' a Cherry Pepper. Of course, everyone was watching. It was like 'The calm before the execution'.

Everyone knew it...Except me...

I took a hold of the fork that was on the table by the jar and I picked out a medium sized Cherry Pepper. I stabbed it and pulled it out of the liquid to let it drain off. I could smell the liquid in the jar and I knew it was going to be hot, so I rationalized in my own mind that if I chewed it and swallowed it quickly, it would be less painful and I'd look 'Tougher'.

Wrong, Wrong and Wrong Again...

With the 10 or 12 people in there all looking on eagerly to see 'The Boss eat a hot pepper', I stuck it in my mouth and I quickly chewed it several times and then I swallowed it. 'My God', whatever had possessed me to do it, I have no idea, but I was now 'stuck' and there was 'absolutely no way' that I could let them know how miserable I was. So, I played 'Tough' and I commented on how 'good' it was and how 'hot' it was and then I made my exit to the Office with an excuse of an 'impending call' from the other Store Managers in town.

When I got to the Office, which was about 25 feet away, I was sure the top of my head might blow off and if that didn't happen, a hole would burn right

through my stomach and it would open up. Either one would have been a relief for the 'agony' I was in and I could do nothing but 'suffer though it' for whatever time it was going to take me to recover.

I truly wanted to 'scream', but I had an idea that somehow, they'd all hear me and I'd be 'forever teased' about it. So, I just sat at my desk in misery taking occasional gulps of coffee and wiping my tongue with a paper towel.

Whenever I heard the door to the Breakroom open and close, I'd straighten up and act like I was busy and doing fine. As soon as the person or persons walked by the Office, I was back to trying to get the 'burn' out of my mouth. I knew I'd have to deal with the 'stomach burn', but that didn't hurt as bad at the moment as my mouth did.

Within about 45 minutes, I was 'settled down' enough to at least feel 'close' to normal and I had overcome the bad burning feeling in my mouth. I had conquered it 'so far'. My stomach burned and churned for about an hour longer and then I was fine.

But, 'Thank Heaven' it all stayed down.

It was the last time I ever 'Hung Myself Out to Dry' like that on a food item in the Breakroom. I made sure in the years after, that whatever the item was

that I was eating was an item I didn't think could cause my 'Ultimate Demise' like the 'Red Hot Chili Peppers Of 1984'...

It was another time I opened my mouth and

'I Thought I Was A Gonna' Die!'

“Shhh ! ... Don’t Let Ruth Hear You ...

The ‘frugality’ of Dwight C. Vredenburg, the man who became Hy-Vee’s President and CEO for 51 years, has a ‘legacy’ that transcends mortality. Dwight’s Guidance and Leadership from the mid 1930’s until his retirement in 1989, is so ‘Legendary’ that his name is spoken in Hy-Vee with a ‘Reverence’ that is nearly unequalled in all of Hy-Vee’s History. Hy-Vee was incorporated in 1938 and the man we all knew and still know as ‘DCV’ was at the Helm.

Dwight’s insight and ability to bolster large numbers of people into the most loyal and devoted group a Company could ever want, was a ‘Gift’ that he was given ‘Divinely’ and he built upon those ‘Divine Gifts’ with many traits he picked up along the way.

Dwight just plain ‘had it together’ in all the right areas needed to turn a ‘small little’ 1930’s Partnership/Corporation into a complete ‘Powerhouse’ now a dominant force in the 21st Century Grocery Industry of America. He was known ‘Internationally’ in his lifetime and it all was born out of the depths of The Great Depression of the 1930’s. Dwight and his wife, Ruth, were there at the ‘Top of The Ladder’ and yet, they still knew ‘Every Rung’ on that ‘Ladder’.

Yes, the legacy of Dwight’s frugality lives like a ‘kindred spirit’ in the History of Hy-Vee. Some of the other stories of his frugality will be covered in this

book, but one particularly 'enlightening' example came to the surface by a mere coincidence of a bit of misfortune and the 'Right Persons' coming along at the 'Right Time' to help.

This piece of Hy-Vee History happened in the late 1970's...

It went like this....

Chariton, IA is a small rural community of about 5,000 people. It is located about 55 miles South and a little East of Iowa's Capitol City, Des Moines. The two largest employers in Chariton and Lucas County (besides Agriculture) are the Johnson Machine Works, Inc. and of course, Hy-Vee, Inc. Hy-Vee would be the larger of the two. The town of about 5,000 people is pretty tied to these two Companies. Hy-Vee's Headquarters was still in Chariton at this time and the Executives all still lived in Chariton.

Now, Chariton is close enough to Des Moines that lots of people from Chariton and Lucas County would go back and forth to 'shop' and have a nice meal out or take in a movie. As a city, Chariton is in a pretty good location for that. It did require about an hour's drive though and that's not bad as it has good roads back and forth.

There are many people around the Hy-Vee 'Territory' whose 'roots' are in Chariton and their 'travels' have taken them to new towns and places away from home. Those people came from all over Hy-Vee's

'Territory' to get back home and see Family there as well. The whole 'In and Out' thing with Chariton has been real common over the decades...

One of Hy-Vee's most successful people came from down in Lucas County. His name is 'Mike' and he married a girl named 'Nancy' and she was from nearby Wayne County. Mike and Nancy's trips home to Lucas County to see Family were pretty common over the years. Mike was the Store Manager in Hy-Vee's largest Sales Volume store the time of this story. That store was located on Des Moines' far East Side. Des Moines was also Hy-Vee's largest Market at the time.

So, at around noon on one pretty Sunday in the late 1970's, Dwight and Ruth decided to go to Des Moines after Church and enjoy 'a day in the City'. Perhaps a 'meal out' or 'a movie' or just some 'shopping' was their destination there. Their trip would not be a long one and they could easily go and come home in an afternoon.

Coincidentally, on this same day, Mike and Nancy decided to go from 'The City' to see Family in Lucas County and have a nice meal and some 'Family Time' with them. It was a day of the 'In and Out' thing about Chariton and Lucas County that I mentioned previously.

Little did either carload of people know that they would 'meet in the middle' and that this day would

'go down' as legendary in the stories of Dwight's 'frugality', but that's what happened.

A 'Legendary Story' was born out of 'Sheer Coincidence'.

Headed Northbound and about halfway to Des Moines, Ruth and Dwight's car 'blew a tire' and so Dwight had pulled to the side of the road to put on the spare tire. Ruth sat patiently in the car as Dwight got out and started the process of the tire change. At this same approximate time, Mike and Nancy, with their car full of their children, came from the opposite direction heading Southbound to Lucas County. As they passed by, Mike and Nancy saw Dwight out of the car with the back lid up on their very old and very small Chevy Wagon. He needed help.

Mike and Nancy immediately turned their car around and pulled in behind Dwight and Ruth's car. Mike could see that Dwight had the Jack handle in his hand and he was having difficulty with prying the lid from the spare compartment located below the back floor of the small Chevy Wagon. Mike got out and told Dwight that he would change the tire and get him back on the road.

Now, with Dwight's 'advancing age' and being 'dressed in a suit' and with Mike at a 'much younger age' and dressed more casually, Dwight welcomed Mike's help. Dwight stood and talked with Mike as

Mike got the spare tire out and began the jack set up for the change.

It was about this point in the changeover, that Mike noticed something really concerning… Dwight's car tires were almost bald. There seemed to be little, if any, tread on them… Any of them! So, weighing his words well, Mike said "Dwight, do you know how bad these tires are on this car? They're almost bald and they're not even safe."

Dwight's response is so 'Dwight' that Mike still tells the story 'several decades' after it happened… Dwight responded "Shhhh… Don't talk too loudly, I don't want Ruth to hear this. Yes, I know they're pretty bad, but I think I can get a couple of hundred more miles out of them."

Mike said he stared back at Dwight in 'total disbelief'. With Dwight's comment, he was realizing the depth of Dwight's 'frugality'. Mike got the tire changed and each car then went their respective ways. Dwight and Ruth again headed Northbound to Des Moines and Mike and Nancy with their kids again headed Southbound to Lucas County.

It was a day that Mike will never forget.

He was able to help his 'Dear Friends' out of a small 'squeeze' and also learn a little more about a man he

already loved and respected. He now understood even more about the stories he'd heard of what a 'Tightwad' Dwight could be. This day had confirmed it.

It was the day when...The Rubber 'Almost Didn't' Meet The Road...

“Up-Up And Away” ...

In the beginning, the small little Corporation known then as ‘Hyde and Vredenburg Supply Stores’ was not much of a factor in the world of ‘Retail Grocers’. Most Customers in the towns and cities of Southern Iowa and Northern Missouri were shopping with the ‘Big Guns’...The Great Atlantic and Pacific Tea Company (aka A & P), Super Valu Stores, United Foods, the Independent Grocers Association Stores (aka IGA) and a few others were very much in control of the areas that ‘The Supply Stores’ were in. There were also ‘lots’ of privately owned ‘Independent’ stores too.

There just wasn’t a reason for the Suppliers and Big Companies to pay much attention to ‘little’ Hyde and Vredenburg in the rural towns. That would all change dramatically over the years and all of the attention started shifting towards Hy-Vee and its stores and Store Managers. In fact, as the 1950’s, 1960’s and the 1970’s rolled along, the ‘Wining and Dining’ of the Hy-Vee People became so prevalent, that Hy-Vee felt the need to ‘limit the extravagance’ for the protection of the Company itself. It was correctly believed that too much ‘showering of gratuities’ to the stores would lead to ‘favoritism’ and that would eventually lead to products being carried or promoted because of what the Supplier could do for someone instead of what the customer wants to buy. Rules were put in place to limit the contact and the ‘gratuities’ accordingly.

There were things that were not looked at favorably or approved. Overnight trips, expensive items and things deemed 'lavish' were not allowed. They were the sort of things that made someone on Hy-Vee's end of it feel 'obligated' and that was the entire reason for the Rules to begin with.

On the other side of it all, afternoon golf outings with a meal afterward or a tour of a plant or factory with a meal afterward went along fine with what was believed to be appropriate. Lots of things were deemed appropriate because the function was not really something to make Hy-Vee or its Store Managers feel especially compelled to do something in return later.

Once in a while, there were things that came along too, that were very good for the relationships between companies. Those would be some 'social events' that helped build good relations at no real obligatory cost. Usually, they were lots of fun for both parties and we got to know each other as 'people' and 'friends'.

All of this 'scrutinizing' of the 'extras' that came along was very good for Hy-Vee in many ways. It kep the system 'pure'.

In 1984, when I was the Store Manager at Pleasant Hill, IA Hy-Vee, one of those 'special social items' was offered to a few of us that turned out to be one of those 'Memories of a Lifetime' and it is one of my favorites today nearly 35 years later.

This is the story of 'How it all went up'---and it was... 'Up-Up and Away'.

The National Hot-Air Balloon Championship events were still being held in Indianola, IA on the Campus of Simpson College. It was a week-long series of daily (mornings and evenings) Hot-Air Balloon Races, Balloon Tethering events and just plain 'viewing' of the festivities.

Each morning and evening, hundreds of huge and colorful Hot-Air Balloons would start the process of unpacking and then filling their 'Colorful Billowy Balloons' with hot air. Then, when ready, each one would take- off out of Indianola and across Warren County, Iowa. They were headed to areas of open fields with plenty of good roads around to serve as 'viewing spots' for the 'thousands' who would come to watch. From those 'country roads', one could see the ascension of a 'hundred or more' Hot-Air Balloons in the air and going along with the wind. Each looking for their own 'Chase-Vehicle' that followed a Balloon's every move and drove along those 'country roads' to be there when the 'touchdown' was made.

It was 'MAGNIFICENT'.... One of the most 'Beautiful Sights' a person will ever see.

So, one day early in the week of the Balloon Races, I was called to the phone and it was Gif, the President of Mid-Continent Bottlers there in Des Moines. Gif called wanting to know if I would to bring my wife and 10year-old son to Indianola "For A Balloon Ride".

He said that we'd be joined by Hy-Vee's CEO, Dwight Vredenburg, and his wife, Ruth, whom we knew well. Gif said we'd also be joined by two other Store Managers along with one of their wives. I 'jumped' at the chance and said "Yes" and we lined up the time and location for the events of the evening for the ride. I was excited to go home and tell my wife and our son.

On the evening of 'The Balloon Ride' and our visit to Indianola, we drove the 15 miles to Simpson College. We were approved for entry to the grounds and we quickly located our hosts and the other Hy-Vee People. We were to ride in two Balloons that Mid-Continent owned. One was a very large red, white and green '7-Up' Balloon and the other one was a bright red 'Like Cola' Balloon that they owned.

The '7-Up' Balloon would hold quite a few in its 'Basket', so Dwight and Ruth, along with Dick, Joyce and Bob were quickly put in the 'lineup' for that Balloon and the three of us in my family were 'lined-up' for the red 'Like Cola' Balloon. After some simple instructions on 'Balloon Safety', we were each given a "7-UP tee-shirt" to wear and keep. So, everyone 'slipped on' their tee-shirt' as we prepared for a wonderful evening as guests of Mid-Continent Bottlers of Des Moines. The weather was 'perfect' for a Balloon Ride. It was 'sunny and clear' and about 75 degrees.

When the organizers of the event 'signaled' to our area for the 'Balloon Ascension', we all climbed into our respective Baskets of the Balloons. The two balloons were ready and full of hot air. They were 'standing tall' from the gas burner 'blasts' used to create the Hot Air. 'One by one', the 50 or so Balloons in our area hit their Air Furnaces and 'took off'...rising quickly into the air.

We were so excited...

The two Balloons we were all in stayed in close proximity to each other and we waved at each other as we climbed to an altitude of several hundred feet. The beautiful Iowa Country-Side was a wonderful backdrop for the now 'hundred or more' colorful Balloons in the air. Big Beautiful Balloons of every design were everywhere around us as we floated along very quietly. It sure was peaceful up there. We were close enough to other Balloons that we could 'holler' back and forth with a few of them as we floated along. It was very surprising just how quiet it was up in the air like that.

We were 'airborne' for about 50-55 minutes and then, as the Pilots saw their 'Chase Vehicles' on the road below, we looked for a place to 'set down'. So, with pre-arranged approval from some local Farmers to land on their property, the Pilots put the Balloons in a descent pattern and we floated down to the ground to the waiting help of the 'Chase Crew'. Our ride was over.

What a ride...It had been 'Wonderful' !

Our bright red 'Like Cola' Balloon had set down pretty straight-up and we landed with no difficulty. The '7-Up' Balloon, however, was carrying a few more people and a heavier load and as it hit the ground, it tipped over sideways sort of 'spilling' its riders a bit. As it went over on its side, the Ankeny, IA Store Manager, Dick, landed squarely on top of Dwight in the 'spill'.

Everyone recovered quickly and of course their focus was on Dwight and Ruth due to their advancing ages. When they indicated that they were "a little shaken, but okay", things went on from there and we were all relieved there had been no injuries.

After the flights, we were all then 'gathered together' and we were 'ceremoniously' told the story of how Hot Air Ballooning had started in France in the 1880's and we were asked to get on our knees for a 'Traditional Blessing' of Balloonists Worldwide. As we all knelt together on the ground, we were 'Christened' with cold Champagne dribbled on the backs of our heads and we were 'Congratulated' for what our Pilot said was "Our entry into the 'Ranks' of the small number of people who will ever ride in a Hot Air Balloon". Then, as a 'finale' of the ceremony, we 'toasted' each other with a few sips of Champagne.

We felt honored.

We stayed around and talked for a bit and then we all 'headed home' with all the visions of the 'Magnificent Experience' we'd just enjoyed still very vivid in our minds. We followed all the 'Balloon Events' for the remainder of the week as they were covered on television locally. We now had a new perspective on it all.

The next Wednesday at the weekly 'Managers Meeting', Dwight told the entire group of our 'experience' and he shared all the details right down to the Champagne on our heads. I sort of 're-lived' it all as he told it. It was a 'Great Memory' for sure.

When Dwight began to wrap up his comments, someone in our Managers Group spoke up and said "They'd all heard that his Balloon had 'hard-landed' and tipped over and that he and Ruth may have gotten hurt?"

The room listened carefully to his answer. Dwight and Ruth were 'Iconic' figures in the eyes of all Hy-Vee People and there was genuine concern for their well-being.

Dwight told the Manager group that "Yes, we landed a bit hard' and we got 'jostled around' pretty well, but that he and Ruth were just fine and no injuries" ... Then, he quickly added "I will say though, after Dick landed on me, I realized Dick needs to lose a little weight."

I will never forget the conversation and to this day, I can still see Dwight standing at the Podium 'chuckling' over his comment about Dick.

Everyone "Roared with Laughter" and poor Dick got 'red-faced' and then had to endure everyone telling him to "Lose a little weight" ... It went on for weeks. Dick sure was a 'Good Sport' about it.

It's a 'memory' I will always cherish and the 'fun of the ride' was 'equaled' only by the 'presence of the people' we got to share the ride with...It's a part of my 'Hy-Vee History' that will always stand-out among most others.

It was the time Dwight said Dick was

"Full Of More Than Hot Air" ...

“Watch (for) The Pennies And Nickels” ...

Hy-Vee was born in the ‘depths’ of The Great Depression of the 1930’s. In those years during the beginning of the partnership of Charles Hyde (Hy) and David Vredenburg (Vee), the Business was run on a real ‘shoestring budget’.

In those early years, almost daily trips to Kansas City to get Fresh Produce and other trips to various local suppliers to get fresh milk, eggs and meat items all took up gasoline and labor expense. Those expenses, along with rent and electricity costs, local advertising costs, left the two Founders very ‘strapped’ for cash sometimes. Not only were they starting a new fledgling company, but they were doing it at America’s worst Economic Depression... ‘Ever’.

Charles and David believed that ‘Integrity’ was extremely important and they firmly believed to always pay their bills ‘on-time’. That is a philosophy that still lives strong today in Hy-Vee nearly 90 years later.

Frugality became a ‘way of life’ for them and soon, certain expressions began to emerge...Sometimes out of frustration and sometimes to bolster their own spirits to keep them moving in the ‘forward direction’ to their eventual ‘success’. These little sayings and expressions 'molded' the Company philosophies forever.

Some of the things they used to tell themselves and their Crew were things like... "We're not looking for dollar bills, we're looking for twenty nickels." and another also got bantered around a lot and it was "A quick nickel is better than a slow dime." There were others too, such as the one this story is based on... "Watch the pennies and nickels and the dollars will fall in place" ...

Yes, 'pennies'.

During those early 1930's, David's son, Dwight Vredenburg, was still in his late teens. He worked around his Father, David and his Mother, Kate, in the stores and he watched and learned from not only his parents, but from Charles and Mrs. Hyde as they worked their 'corner' of the new company as well...A young, Dwight Vredenburg learned those 'philosophies' and some have said "They became so embedded in him that he carried them all of his life. Long after the financial need to do so."

In 1938, when the Incorporation came about, there were 15 Original Stockholders. The 'Originals' had all been 'part Owners' of the stores and in some of those stores, the ownership had gotten complicated due to each owning 'part of this store' and 'part of that store' so the Incorporation made it easier to detect the 'Ownership'. New shares were sold for $100 each and the number of shares of the stock issued was given based on what everyone involved agreed was the 'Ownership' that a man already had in the 'total'. It seemed to work for all concerned.

Dwight was elected to be the President of the 'New Corporation" and he stayed as CEO until his Retirement in 1989. For 51 years, Dwight's philosophies of 'The Future Hy-Vee' influenced the Company in many directions.

Frugality reined with Dwight in charge.

Much has been said over the years about Dwight and his 'Penny-Pinching'. And what I was able to witness for several years told me that those stories... 'Were pretty well true'—He loved a bargain and he loved to 'Save Money'!'

Hy-Vee benefitted by those habits of his and Hy-Vee as we know it today has had the 'Successful near 90-year run' that it has, in part, because of those 'frugal habits'. Yes, "Don't spend it if we don't need to." is widely known in Hy-Vee.

We heard many times over the years about "The Leakey Barrel Theory" as Dwight called it... He'd say often to all of us... "You don't have to dump as much water in the top of the Barrel to fill it, if you can plug the leaks in the Barrel." His References were saying "We don't need as many Sales if you can control the expenses and wasted spending". Said 'Perfectly' by Dwight and we always got his 'message' very loud and clear... 'Be A Spendthrift'.

Charles Hyde's philosophy of "The Pennies and Nickels" came out of Dwight again in a very unusual setting one day and I am happy to say that I was there and I was a 'direct part of it'...I remember it well.

Here's how 'the pennies" added up...

I was the Store Manager at the Pleasant Hill, IA Hy-Vee from 1981-1987. One day in 1986, about 12 or 15 of us Store Managers were in Chariton, IA at Hy-Vee's Headquarters on Wednesday for our Monthly 'Profit Review' (called Inventory) with the Executives of Hy-Vee. We were there to have the Accountants figure our Monthly Profit Sheets and then to review them with Ron, Hy-Vee's President. Dwight was still in as Chief Executive Officer (CEO) and he was still very active day to day. He would 'occasionally' even get in on those meetings too.

Now, Dwight regularly parked his car behind the Corporate Office Building in a spot close to the door and it allowed him to be 'close' in bad weather and so forth. There were about four stair-steps in the hallway leading down from the outside parking to the hallway to Dwight's Office. The hallway led right past the Meeting Room where we were all at.

Our group was going over Sales and Profits with Ron as was very normal. When we heard the outside door open and close, we looked up. Dwight entered the doorway to the Meeting Room with his overcoat on and it was apparent by the noise of the door closing

behind him that he'd just come back from lunch or an errand.

As he stood there, Dwight spoke first "Hello fellas! Look what I just found!" and with that comment, he was holding and waving a shiny penny. He was smiling and we knew he was happy to be 'one penny better off'.

I couldn't help myself, so I said "You better put it in your shoe." As soon as it was out of my mouth, I could tell he was going to ask what he did. "Why should I put it in my shoe?" he said and then he waited for my reply. I quickly gave it to him. "Well, haven't you ever heard the old saying 'Find a penny, put it in your shoe...It'll bring you good luck the whole day through?" And then without missing a beat, I added "I found one this morning and it's in my shoe."

I think for a quick moment in time, he was wondering if I was having fun with him, so he shot back... "Well, are you having Good Luck today?" and he walked over to me and looked over my shoulder at my Profit Sheet for the month and quickly said "Yes, you are having a Lucky Day...You had a good month!"

With that comment said, he reached down and put the penny in his shoe and when he stood back up to leave for his Office, I said "Dwight?" and he turned to look at me, I pulled my shoe off and dumped about six or so pennies on the table. Everyone laughed and Dwight chuckled out loud as he said "Well, I hope I

have a Lucky Day, too." And with that, he took off down the hall with his 'penny in his shoe'.

I put my pennies back in my shoe and then slipped it back on all to the amazement of the other Store Managers and Ron...It had been fun to see the way Dwight handled it all.

I still do put my 'found pennies' in my shoe and I usually have more than one in there. I have to admit, every time I find a penny and I lean over to put it in my shoe, I think of Dwight. I learned so many things from him and I think I will always feel that I am a 'product' of his philosophies in many ways.

I am a 'tightwad' and I do 'pinch pennies' and I fix things myself to save money whenever I can. I have found myself 'doing without things' many times because I couldn't bring myself to spend the money needed. I will always feel fortunate that my life 'Mixed Together' with Dwight and Hy-Vee...I am far better because of.

I have no idea where I'd be or what I'd be doing had I not gotten into Hy-Vee. Oh, I suppose I'd have 'made it somehow', but I don't know.

To this day, I 'Smile' to myself and think of Dwight when someone says

"A Penny For Your Thoughts" ...

“Doing What At The Party ??” ...

If ‘ever’ there were a successful Sales Promotion in the entire History of Grocery Retailing, it has to be Hy-Vee’s Annual ‘Salute to Spring’ called “Springtime Party”. It has been a ‘50 Year Party’ that has brought ‘millions’ of Customers to Hy-Vee over the years and it’s a ‘WINNER’!

Winter in the Midwest can be ‘brutal’...It snows a lot, it rains some, it sometimes gets real cold down to a frigid -20 degrees, the winds blow and ‘everything’ gets covered with a dirt and grime. That dirt and grime can be seen everywhere. Oh, don’t misunderstand, Winter has been affecting the Midwest for millions of years and it’s no different now, but anyone will tell you “Once the residents of the Midwest get a smell of Spring, it all ‘shifts gear’ and they’re ready”.

Yes, ‘Ready for Spring Cleaning’...

In the early 1960’s, Hy-Vee hit upon the idea of having a ‘Spring Party’ to clean-up from Winter and help the Customers ‘change their mindsets’ to a more upbeat attitude. The first time ‘Springtime Party’ occurred, little did anyone know of the ‘Powerful Tool’ it would grow to be.

It is AWESOME !...

For well over 50 years now, plans start in ‘early-Winter’ in every store for what they will do for

'Springtime Party'. Plans are made for a Store Theme, Decorating Ideas, Employee Costumes and a 'huge' Newspaper Ad to 'wake-up' the Midwest. The 'First Week of May' is the target date and by then, the weather usually cooperates and it is a fun time...

Fun for everyone... 'Customers and Crews alike'.

On the outside of the stores, the parking lots are 100% cleaned and some are even 'washed' by arrangements with some local Fire Departments. Donations are made to those Fire Departments and the parking lots are cleaned from one end to the other. Fresh new paint on the parking lot lines goes on in every store's lot and any repair or 'fix it' type thing on the outside gets a makeover.

On the insides of the stores, the 'endless list' of things needing done is in the 'crosshairs' and each Department is charged with the responsibility of getting 'their corner' of the store cleaned, decorated and 'READY'.

Special Tee-Shirts are ordered in some cases, costumes are reserved for rental and all the decorating that will be done for 'Springtime Party' is organized to be done by the last week of April. Special music and lots of 'Special Events' are planned for the week.

While Springtime Party is going 'In the Stores', only the imagination can limit the ideas of activities to be seen. Face-painting, balloons, hot dogs, popcorn,

soft drinks, eating contests, prizes to register for, famous TV cartoon characters Walking Around the Stores and 'The List Goes On' for about a mile.

It's so much fun, it starts building 'The Excitement Level' early each year.

To coincide with the Retail Stores efforts, Corporately, the stores are divided into geographic territories and teams of Judges are sent out from Headquarters to 'Judge' the stores'. After the 'Judging' is done, the 'Top 3 Stores' in each 'geographic territory' are awarded Prizes for their Winning Results.

Winning Springtime Party is looked at as a very 'Big Deal' in Hy-Vee.

The Winners are awarded a nice Plaque to hang in their store, a cash award for a Summer Picnic and 'lots and lots' of Recognition. Pictures are taken and a 'special issue' of Hy-Vee's Quarterly Company Magazine 'Hy-Vee People' is printed with pictures from all 240 stores.

To win, is also a huge 'status symbol' for the stores and their Crews and they take it very seriously. Store Managers gain 'Bragging Rights' and it is GREAT!

Hy-Vee is shouting to the World... "Hey, we're having a Party...Come See Us!"

Now, as I have said in other places in these stories, each Store Manager 'runs' his or her store with

'independent ideas' and that goes perfectly hand in hand with 'Springtime Party'. Sometimes a Crew member will toss out an 'idea' that will just absolutely resonate with the events planned and it goes viral...One such 'idea' came about in one of Hy-Vee's oldest small Southern Iowa towns and it was "PRICELESS".

This is what happened 'At Their Party'.

Centerville, IA is a small town of about 5,000 people in Appanoose County of Southern Iowa. Hy-Vee has had a store in Centerville for over 75 years. The town has a nice College and has an 'Agricultural Area' around it. It has the 'Colorful History' of being a Coal Mining Town of the late 1800's and on into the 1940's and 1950's. Coal Miners are very fondly remembered and well-respected in Centerville.

So, one year, when the Crew at the Centerville store planned 'their' Springtime Party in the mid-Winter of the early 1970's, they had a great theme and they built a 'special' Newspaper Ad around it all. When they were nearing completion on it, someone jokingly said "You know, we ought to advertise 'X-Y-Z'" and 'by golly', it got into the plans... 'Top Secret', but in the plans.

So, the Centerville Hy-Vee Crew got in 'high gear' and they got their store in perfect shape for the coming Springtime Party Week and when the Wednesday Ad broke in the Centerville Iowegian newspaper

announcing all the 'Festivities', there it was... 'actually in print'...

The Ad read "Topless Checkers From 11AM--12 Noon on Saturday at Hy-Vee."

HOLY COW! ... In Centerville, IA?...

So, the Springtime Party Ad had come out in the Centerville newspaper and the 'whole town' (and surrounding towns) were really getting 'wound up' over the "Topless Checkers" advertised for Saturday.

Talk was everywhere.

So, when Saturday arrived 'hundreds' of people showed up around 10:30 AM to watch and 'Sure Enough', at 11:00 AM sharp, the Cash Registers all stopped at the same time and the female Cashiers went to the Backroom as a group...The 'suspense' was great...And then 'Out came the Topless Checkers'.

Yes, 100% Topless.

There were '8 Topless Men' walking out to the Registers and each one took over and 'Cashiered' until Noon... 'Roars of Laughter, Loud Hoots and Cat-Calls' were all part of the hour-long event. The 'Topless Men' were the 'Center of Everything' in Centerville, Iowa.

It was Hilarious.

It was a 'Springtime Party' talked about for many

years around Centerville. I managed the Hy-Vee in Ottumwa, IA from 1977-1981 and it was about 50 miles from Centerville. 'Topless Checkers' would occasionally come up with a Customer from somewhere in between us and we'd all laugh about the 'Great Memory' of it all.

It became the day the Centerville Hy-Vee

'Took It All Off' For Springtime Party...

“Who Was At The Store ??” ...

Some of the most fun that a Customer or Hy-Vee Associate will ever have at the store is when ‘Special People’ or ‘Celebrities’ come to visit for advertised periods of time. The weekly Newspaper Ads will tell the Customers that “Between the Hours of 2PM and 5PM on Friday and Saturday, the famous ‘X-Y-Z’ Character or Celeb will be here”.

It brings people to the store ‘In Droves’.

Small towns such as the ones Hy-Vee started in Southern Iowa and Northern Missouri all those years ago in 1930, responded very well to that kind of notoriety and excitement. During those times, the store will also try to add some ‘special pricing’ on some items or have ‘hot dogs and pop’, ‘on the spot giveaways’ or a cheap price on something. Popcorn, balloons, prizes and many other things all going on create lots of ‘Customer Enthusiasm’ and Sales to go along with it. It creates that feeling in the Customers of “We better go to Hy-Vee and see what’s going on.”

And it REALLY WORKS!

Some of the ‘Great Characters’ that have been to Hy-Vee over the decades are The Oscar Mayer Wienermobile, Twinkie The Kid, Coach Egg from the Iowa Egg Council, NASCAR Drivers and Team Members, The Iowa Cub, Tony Tiger, Disney Characters, Professional Athletes, Politicians, TV Celebrities and many-many others that draw ‘Big

Crowds'...They are almost too numerous to mention because the list is 'Endless'...

Two of the ones I will always remember the most were at 'opposite ends' of the yardstick and they were so much fun to have at the stores in the 1950's, 1960's and into the 1970's. By the mid-late 1970's, they were both aging to the point that it was hard to get them to do the 'rigorous travelling' that it all required going from 'store to store' and 'town to town', but whenever they were around, 'so were the Customers'...Always!

Measuring up to a full "4' 8" tall, was 'The Little Squirt'...He came to our stores to represent the Squirt Pop Company and he would generally stay at a store for a couple of days at a time. He had a 'Bright Yellow Plaid Suit' and he drove a very special early 1950's Metropolitan car painted 'Squirt Yellow'...For those of you who don't know what a 'Metropolitan' car is, think of it like this. It's a 'couple steps smaller' than an early Volkswagen Bug...That's right... 'even smaller' and it was just a bit larger than 'a shoebox with wheels'.

The Little Squirt's 'Metropolitan' was bright yellow and had the Squirt Logo on the sides. 'The Little Squirt' would give free rides in his 'Metro' to the kids in the crowds and they 'grinned from ear to ear' and waved to everyone as they'd circle around in a designated area of the parking lot in the bright yellow 'Metro'. Everyone wanted to get their picture taken

with 'The Little Squirt' because he just seemed so 'cute and cuddly'.

Now, over the years, 'The Little Squirt' gained lots of attention in the Hy-Vee Stores of the Midwest. He 'lives on' today as a sort of 'Folk Hero' to many people who are now 'middle-aged' and even older. At 4' 8" tall, 'The Little Squirt' still stands 'Like a Giant' in the Hearts of many Hy-Vee People and Customers.

And 'Speaking of Giants'...

Henry Hite or better known as 'The Wilson Giant' stood tall at 7' 7" tall and with his 'Purple Velvet Cape' and 'Jeweled Crown', he was well over 8' 2" tall. Henry was employed by the Wilson Meat Company of Cedar Rapids and he was also a 'favorite' of Hy-Vee Customers and Associates in all the stores. Henry was 'quite the showman' and a he was a wonderful representative of The Wilson Meat Company.

Henry would come to our stores for a few days at a time. During those days, Wilson Meat Company would 'team-up' with Lowenberg Sunbeam Bakery from Ottumwa, IA and together they would provide the people to make 'Ham Sandwiches' and sell them for 10 cents each. They would be 'bagged' in large numbers and these sandwiches 'sold like crazy'. Sometimes, 15,000 or 20,000 Ham Sandwiches in a 3-day period. During these big Sales, Henry would be at the store for about 4-6 hours during each of the three days and he'd walk around the store wearing

his Velvet Cape and Jeweled Crown. He'd meander out into the parking lot and he'd 'pose for pictures' with people who had come to see him. Most times, he'd even show everyone how he could 'touch tall things' in the store...Even the ceiling in some stores. He was a 'Sight to Behold' for sure.

Yes, the fun we all had being part of the 'Shows' put on by people like 'The Little Squirt' and 'The Wilson Giant' will live in my Heart forever. They represented a time in American History when 'Good still won-out over Evil' and 'Doing the Right Thing' was taught to every child. During those great 'Days Gone By', even the teachings of things like Honesty, Hard-Work and Loyalty were alive in America. 'Each and Every Day' of the Year. Thank God, they're still alive at Hy-Vee.

It was a wonderful time in America and in Hy-Vee.

'The Little Squirt' and 'The Wilson Giant' may have had 'different views' of the World from where they stood, but they clearly understood 'The Basics of Customer Service' at Hy-Vee and just like Hy-Vee, they believed in the philosophy of "Making the Customers Feel Like #1 at Hy-Vee"

Just ask anyone who ever saw them. 'The Wilson Giant' was pretty 'Down to Earth' and 'The Little Squirt' stood as 'Tall as the Stars'.

I have great memories of these two

'Larger Than Life' Guys !

"You Shut Your Mouth" ...

For a few decades, I have repeated something I heard from a great mentor, Don Canfield of Iowa City, IA. I heard him say many times "Hy-Vee is in the People Business. We just sell Groceries on the side".

Don's right and the longer you're around, the more you realize he's '100% Right'. You see, Customers come in all 'sizes, shapes, personalities and with 'stranger than fiction' actions. They have come that way for the nearly 90year History of Hy-Vee. Even since those early 1930's and 'The Supply Store' era, Hy-Vee People have been going home and telling their Families "You won't believe what happened today". I know I have said it "MANY" times.

Most times, a person couldn't 'make it up that good'.

In my 34-year career with Hy-Vee, I sometimes felt as though I was in charge of a 'Circus' instead of a Grocery Store. Almost daily, you could look at things happening and you'd feel like you should announce to everyone in the store "Ladies and Gentlemen, in Ring #3, The Idiots are performing". Now, as I said, it's been going on for almost 90 years and it will go on for as long as Hy-Vee is in 'The Customer Business'. But, it is 'SO MUCH FUN' to watch and be part of.

In 1983, I was the Store Manager at the Pleasant Hill, IA Hy-Vee and we had established ourselves in our Trade Area as "The Local Supermarket" in Pleasant Hill and the East Side of Des Moines. Perhaps even

Eastern Polk County too. We had Customers who were 'regulars' and we got to know them pretty well.

As with every Store in Hy-Vee, things would happen at the Pleasant Hill Hy-Vee 'Right out of the Blue' and you'd look back and say "What Just Happened?" and "Did It Really Happen?" We sometimes couldn't figure it all out and we just shook our heads.

One such incident involved a Regular Customer named Walter and it still gets talked about in Pleasant Hill all these years later.

This is what happened.

It begins with a simple explanation of how Hy-Vee sold Fresh Chickens in those days. The Chickens came in to the stores as 'Fresh Whole Chickens' and some were sold as a "Whole Chicken". They were bagged whole and then weighed, priced and put right out in the self-serve Meat Case for sale. Other 'Fresh Chickens' were sold 'cut-up' and they were cut up by the Meatcutters in our store, then arranged and packaged on styrofoam trays. After that, they were overwrapped in plastic wrap, weighed, priced and put out in the self-serve Meat Case for sale. Right next to the Whole Chickens. Cut-up Chickens carried a slightly higher retail price due to them being 'cut-up' and the expense to do that. Usually, the price difference was about 2cents per pound.

It seems like a 'simple deal'...But, don't count on it.

So, I was working at my desk early one afternoon in 1983 when I was 'paged' over the store microphone to come to the Courtesy Counter "Immediately".

Now, we had always instructed our Staff at the Courtesy Counter (or anywhere else in the store) that when they added the word "Immediately" to any 'page', we'd know right away that there was a serious problem. So, when I heard the word "Immediately", I headed for the Courtesy Counter at 'almost' a dead run.

As I got to the door to the Sales Floor, I could hear someone screaming loudly and using lots of profanity and just plain 'out of control'. I pushed the door open and turned the corner to see two of our Ladies that worked at the Courtesy Counter standing helplessly behind the counter waiting for 'Help' to arrive. I also saw a man I knew to be Walter 'jumping about' and 'screaming and hollering' about our 'Price' on Chickens.

He was acting like a 'Wild Man'.

I quickly and loudly said for him to "Calm Down" and for about 30 or 40 seconds, he did. I asked him what his issue was and he 'hollered' that we were "Charging too much for Cut-Up Chickens". And with that, he went right back into his tirade and got even louder and more violent in his actions. At this point, I tried to tell him "Yes, we do charge 2 cents per pound more for a cut-up Chicken than a whole Chicken" I tried to tell him that it cost us more to

process the Cut-up Chicken because we had to pay a Meatcutter to 'cut it up' and put it on a tray. My explanation landed on 'Deaf Ears'.

He didn't care. He was 'MAD' ...

It was at this point, I realized his wife was there and I asked her to help calm him down and she quickly said she couldn't control him when he got like this. So, I said to Walter that "I wanted him to leave the store." He quickly said "He was going nowhere". At this turn of events, I told the two gals at the Courtesy Counter to "Call the Police and get them headed our way".

Then, I took a hold of Walter's arm and told him he needed to go home and I started him to the front door which was about 100' or so away...Suddenly, he got physical and 'The Fight Was On'...By this time, at least 100 people had gathered to watch 'The Circus Act in Ring #3'. They were all very quiet as everyone watched the action.

As he tried to scuffle with me, I finally grabbed him by the back of his sleeveless vest and by his belt and I sort of started 'pushing' him to the door forcefully... All the while, he was 'screaming and hollering' at the top of his Lungs about the "Fresh Cut-up Chickens" and he was making a 'real spectacle' of himself. His wife was in 'hot pursuit' by this time and she was really mad at him. She was hollering at him to "Calm Down".

That was about to change too.

As we neared the Front Door, two Police Officers entered the door and they immediately 'took over'. They knew Walter from other 'incidents' and they called him by name. It seemed to get 'even worse' as they grabbed him to get him outside to the Squad Car. Walter was 'screaming bloody murder' the whole way out the door. Now, by this time, the crowd watching it all had moved outside to see the 'Finale' and 'see it' they did... 'Act Two'...Now in 'Circus Ring #2' was about to start.

When the Officers got Walter outside, his wife had started to get 'wound-up' too'...And Boy, did she ever. As he was held over the hood of the Squad Car for cuffing by the Officers, she started viciously 'wailing on him' with her purse and she kept yelling "You shut your mouth you S.O.B.—shut your mouth". She repeated it about three or four times before they got her pulled away from Walter and then they loaded a 'now handcuffed' and screaming Walter in the Squad Car and 'whisked him away'...Leaving us to deal with his now 'really upset' wife.

The crowd sort of dispersed at this point and I asked one of our Staff to drive Walter's wife to their home about 8 blocks away. They left and things then settled back to sort of a 'Dull Roar' about the whole ordeal.

Geesh! All that fuss over "Two cents a pound on Chicken."

Several days went by and I was told during that time, by the Police, that no charges would be filed due to a 'medical condition' Walter had and that sometimes, he just 'went wild' but, not intentionally.

I was 'Okay' with that.

The real 'kicker' to the whole event came about a week or so later when I got a phone call and the voice on the other end said "Rick, this is Walter. Can I come in to see you?" I replied that he could and he said he'd "Be right over".

In about 10 minutes, the Staff at the Courtesy Counter paged me to the private Store Phone and told me Walter was there to see me. As I walked down to the same Courtesy Counter where he and I had 'dueled' only a week or so before, I wondered what was going to happen. "How would Walter handle himself today?" was crossing my mind.

As I approached him, Walter stuck out his hand and offered an 'apology' for his actions the week before. He said he was "Sorry" and then he asked if he "Could still shop in our store?" My reply back was "Are you going to behave yourself?" Walter very quickly said "I promise I will...You won't have any more trouble with me."

Somehow, I believed him, so I said "Yes, Walter, that will be fine. I do hope you realize what a 'Big Mess" you made the other day though?"

He acknowledged my question and then he made the 'Statement of The Year'. He said... "I'd have been better off to pay the two cents a pound and keep my mouth shut."

We both laughed.

We never had any more trouble with Walter. He went on to be a very loyal Customer and Friend.

It was the day Walter

Acted Like A Real 'Cut-Up' Himself...

“Honesty and Integrity are the Cornerstones of our Company.”

Dwight C. Vredenburg

President, CEO and

Chairman of the Board

(Deceased)

“And Nobody Even Said” ...

In the 1930’s, when ‘The Supply Stores’ were doing business in Southern Iowa and Northern Missouri, Partners Charles Hyde and David Vredenburg had a ‘Vision’ of the ‘Quality Products’ and ‘Good Service’ they wanted to be known for with their Customers. It was their ‘Goal’ to get those Customers to be loyal ‘Year After Year’. And it isn’t an easy thing to do.

The ‘answers’ they found in their quest came from some very ‘common sense’ things in Business. They believed in ‘clean well-stocked stores’ with as much variety in merchandise as they could provide. All of these were to be with the ‘Best Possible Service’ they could achieve.

Now, in Farm Towns, City Towns, Big Towns and Little Towns, people are pretty much the same no matter where you go. The ‘wants and needs’ of the Customers in any store are a ‘responsibility’ and sort of an ‘honor’ that those people trust their Families and their overall well-being’ to the store they feel in their mind is ‘Their Store’...

And we hope Hy-Vee is that store.

Over the years, it has been established that ‘People go where they are invited’ and they ‘Return to where they feel welcome’...Nope, it’s not Rocket Science. You just need to show Respect and Appreciation for the ‘Good People’ they are and the money they spend in a Hy-Vee Store every week. And for that Respect and Appreciation, they will reward you and Hy-Vee with their Business and their Loyalty 'year after year'. They will be loyal for their lifetime in many cases.

Now today, printed newspapers in a given town are not the 'messenger' that they once were, but there is still a lot of information about your Customers in those newspapers...If you just take time to look for it. I'm talking about Obituaries, Special Birthdays, Wedding Anniversaries, Community Recognitions, Terrible Accidents and a 'Whole Host' of other events. That's right...They are all there, they just need to be used.

In every Hy-Vee Store I was the Store Manager at (Ottumwa, IA, Pleasant Hill, IA and Moline, IL), I used the local newspaper as a very good way to 'reach out' to our Customers. It was extremely successful.

One glaring example of the 'big benefits' of communicating with your Customers from the newspaper happened to me in 1993 while I was Store Manager at the Moline, IL store.

Here's the scoop.

I had a really 'efficient and meticulous' Human Resources Manager in the store and her name was Margaret. Now, Margaret was a good as they get and all I ever had to do to get a project handled correctly was to sit down with Margaret and explain what results I wanted. And 'off she'd go'...It would be done and done right.

Margaret was GREAT!

The 'program' that this story tells about involved people whose names and sometimes pictures appeared in the Moline Dispatch newspaper recognizing a couple for their Silver Wedding Anniversary, Golden Wedding Anniversary or another Special Wedding Anniversary or someone for a Senior Birthday at a 'Big Number' or a 'Special Even' like a Promotion or Retirement. There were several each week in the Dispatch Newspaper on Sunday and our 'plan' for those clippings went as like this.

Margaret would get the section of the paper listing these 'special occasions' and she would clip the article out, put it in an appropriate greeting card and also include a quick hand-written Gift Certificate for 'Two Complete Meals and Drinks' in our Kitchen/Deli Café. The card would get a hand-written 'congratulatory note' from me and then it was 'in the mail' to the person or couple celebrating. We sent cards appropriate for other things that happened and that included the passing of good Customers or if someone had suffered an accident or a serious health issue.

We had been doing this program at the Moline Hy-Vee Store for several years and it was a good one. Because of the program, I got to meet lots of our Customers who would ask for me personally to say "Thank-you" or to share a story about our store. It

was fun for me and 'very rewarding' for our store.

So, one day, I was working at my desk when one of the Staff at our Customer Service Counter phoned me on the private Store Phone and asked if I could come to the Courtesy Counter to meet a Customer who was asking for me. I said I could and I went right away to the Courtesy Counter. There, I found a couple about 60 years-old waiting for me. I did what I normally did and I stuck out my hand and offered it to the man and I said "Hi, I am Rick."

The man shook my hand and his wife stood there smiling as the man said "Hi, Rick...My name is John. I wanted to meet you today because you sent us a card for our 35th Wedding Anniversary and we really think that's nice." So, I acknowledged the Anniversary with a verbal "Congratulations" and that's when I got ... "The Rest of The Story".

John went on to explain that he had been an employee of Eagle Food Stores (our main competitor) for 35 years and when the day of their Anniversary came, not one word was said about the 'Special Day' by anyone at Eagle Foods. He then said that when he got home from work that day, his wife handed him our greeting card and said to him "You aren't going to believe who sent us a card for our Anniversary."

John told me that it really humbled them to think that not one person from his company had acknowledged

the day, but yet the 'big competitor' came through with a card, the newspaper clipping, a hand-written note from me 'AND' two 'free meals with drinks'. I could tell they were thrilled.

John's next comment was the one I will remember forever...He looked me in the eye and he said "Thanks Rick, it's this kind of stuff that is the reason Hy-Vee's kicking our tails all over the place." Wow! I was astonished at the sincerity of John and his wife and I knew 'right then' that our outreach of Friendship had 'Hit the Bullseye'.

John and his wife went on to the Kitchen/Deli Café and enjoyed their meals and then got a grocery cart and bought $75 worth of groceries...And we saw them in the store 'often' after that. Our store saw them 'every week' after Eagles went into Bankruptcy and closed their doors forever.

There was one 'humorous' example about our program of sending the greeting cards that I still laugh about and it was the same expression of Hy-Vee's 'good tidings to people'...Only this one 'just about' turned out to be a big 'Negative'.

This is what happened...

I was called to the phone to take a call one evening and the lady on the other end told me her name. I could quickly tell she was mad...Seems we'd sent her

85year-old Mother a card for her 85th Birthday with the usual newspaper clipping, note from me and gift certificate and 'all of that' was fine, but the lady said to me "Thanks for spoiling my Mom's surprise party."

Say what? 'A Surprise Party?' I was a bit confused.

It was at this point, I said to her "Well, I am sorry if the party was spoiled by anything we did, but just how were we to supposed to know it was a Surprise Party? After all, it was an 'Open Invitation' in the newspaper and about 120,000 people got that paper. It said nothing in the article about a Surprise."

I waited to see what was coming next and this is the comment that told me that we had a 'GREAT PROGRAM' going on. She said "Well, Mom lives in a nursing home and she doesn't get the paper, so we put it in the paper because we didn't think she'd ever see it. And besides, people just don't do things like 'sending cards' from a Business. We just didn't count on that and you messed it up".

Yes, I felt vindicated, but I still had the 'chore' of 'smoothing it over' with her, so I said "Well, we are very sorry. Would you like it if we sent a pretty flower arrangement for the table?" That was all it took. We were 'out of trouble' and moving quickly to being 'heroes'.

All was well. Our Customer was happy.

I still laugh about it when I think of it in terms of

'120,000 People

Invited To A 'Surprise Party'

At The Nursing Home'...

“If you don’t have time to do it right the first time, when will you have time to do it right?”

Charles M. Bell

Senior Vice-President

Western Region

(Retired)

“Hey, You Guys” ...

As I have said many times previously, Hy-Vee’s very early Managers Meetings were ‘born’ out of a ‘sharing of ideas’ in the Backrooms of a ‘scant few stores’ in Southern Iowa and Northern Missouri in the late 1930’s and into the 1940’s. These ‘meetings’ developed quietly from the ongoing belief that ‘every’ Store Manager should run his own store’ and these early meetings came about because some of the Store Managers could easily see that there was a ‘wealth of information’ that was there for the sharing.

In those early meetings, ideas got ‘kicked around’ and some Post Toasties Boxes got stacked up to make a table and ideas for ‘Newspaper Ads were drawn with pencils on butcher paper. When the meetings were done, each Store Manager would drive back to his store ‘full’ of the knowledge he’d learned that day. The fledgling Company called ‘The Supply Stores’ got stronger after each meeting.

In the nearly 90 years since, nothing is really different now than those very ‘primitive meetings’ ... Oh, the technology is different and the meeting rooms are different, there are ‘LOTS’ more Store Managers, but the same ‘sharing of ideas’ is a ‘weekly thing’ for Hy-Vee’s Store Managers. As ever, the men and women Store Directors of today go back home to their respective stores ‘fully charged’ and ready to compete against the World.

It is a 'Winning Way of Life' for Hy-Vee.

Now, the Managers Meetings are a serious thing, but it's 'IMPOSSIBLE' to get any number of people together in the same room 'week after week' and 'year after year' without the personalities of the people involved showing themselves in some really fun ways. There are 'talkative' Store Managers and there are 'reserved' Store Managers. There are still more in the categories of 'prankster' Store Managers and even the 'jokester' Store Managers and in the nearly nine decades of Hy-Vee, each has been 'on display' every Wednesday.

Right out in plain sight.

The 'talkative' Store Managers were always quick to 'chime-in' to the current conversation with a comment or two and they'd be the ones to 'occasionally' draw themselves into a discussion of a given topic. They loved being the 'center of attention' and we felt like we got 'entertained' sometimes by their comments.

The 'reserved' Store Managers sat quietly with a thousand thoughts running through their brains, but they weren't going to say anything 'unless' it looked like either of two things was about to happen... #1 They would get drug into the conversation or #2 Whatever was being discussed or voted on was going to cost them money.

Mainly, it was the latter of the two that got them to speak-up the quickest because the very deep-seeded 'frugality' we all know that Hy-Vee has engrained in its 'Soul' came out at the sound of 'money being spent'...

Their money...

The 'prankster' Store Managers were almost always looking for the best prank they could find to pull on the others... It might be to 'scribble all over' somebody's notebook while that Store Manager was in the Restroom or it could have been pouring salt from the shakers on the tables into the coffee of a Store Manager when he wasn't looking. I've even seen someone's notebook 'lit on fire' with a cigarette lighter just to watch the owner 'get excited'...You name it, it probably got done... I remember another instance of a group of Store Managers 'racing' from Des Moines to Headquarters in Chariton, IA. They kept in touch by using their CB Radios along the way. It was a distance of about 55 miles. The lead car kept 'challenging' the others to 'catch up' and they eventually, got so far in front of the others, that they pulled off the road and in behind a Church to hide. Thinking they'd gotten so far behind, the other carload of Store Managers 'sped up' to a very high speed...After they had passed the church, the first car pulled out and went on down the road to find their 'cohorts'.

Now, racing at a 'high speed', the group now in the lead came 'very close' to being pulled over by the Iowa Highway Patrol. Of course, the guys that had pulled in behind the Church thought it was a great prank. It was talked about for years.

But the 'jokester' Store Managers always had a great joke or they were doing things to each other to 'poke fun at' or 'make fun of' someone else...This story is about one Store Manager who loved to make fun of a group of 'someones'.

This 'jokester' Store Manager's name was Jack and Jack managed one of the Cedar Rapids, IA Stores for Hy-Vee. He was probably the 'premier jokester' of the entire group and not a week went by that he wasn't having fun at someone else's expense and 'lots' of it.

Jack's place in Hy-Vee's 'History Books' is 'very solid'...He's in there and this is one of the stories about Jack. Here is a 'great story' about Jack...

And this is how it 'Yukked-Up'.

For about three or four months, Jack's list of 'things to focus on' centered around a group of his 'fellow Store Managers' that he viewed as being 'short—not very tall' and honestly, he never let up. He called us "The '5-7' Club.' (You know 5' 7" tall) and Jack's relentless pursuit of a joke against 'The '5-7' Club' became 'almost legendary' among the Store Managers. It was hilarious.

Jack would roam around the room before a Meeting started and he'd locate each of his '5-7 Club' members and quietly tell them something that would 'eventually' lead to six or seven of guys about the same height coming together...Where he could then have fun by 'reminding' everyone that they were all "Vertically Challenged" as Jack put it.

Sometimes, he'd say "Ron (Hy-Vee's President) wants to have a little 'Short Meeting' with you guys at lunch" or he'd say "You guys need to sit up front today so you don't have to try to see over everyone else." Jack had several 'funnies' to say to everyone...And he loved saying all that stuff loud enough for anybody within 20' to hear it. He kept everyone laughing with his jokes.

We all had fun with Jack. He really had a great 'sense of humor', but the most important thing I ever learned from Jack was not funny at all. It was as 'serious as serious can get'. It was at his Retirement Party in 1993 and being the 'jokester' that he was, we all expected his final comments to his 'Company Buddies' to be funny...But we were surprised and we got to see the other side of Jack.

We saw the 'Serious Side' of a great guy.

On that day of his Retirement and after everyone had spoken about Jack and 'his great success as a Store Manager' over the years, the 'podium spot' was offered to Jack for his comments. As he 'sauntered up' to the podium, we all wondered what he'd talk

about in his final few minutes of the gathering. We thought about his fun with 'The '5-7' Club' and we thought about his jokes about other Store Managers' 'golf games' and his other fun topics.

But that's not what Jack said at all.

Jack took the podium and from the first comment, he was serious. He 'thanked' everyone in Hy-Vee's Corporate Management for the opportunity he'd been given with Hy-Vee...He "thanked" his Family for his happy home-life and then he made a few other comments. It was the last one that will stick with me 'forever'.

It was 'POWERFUL' ...

Jack said that he hoped that over the years ahead, he'd be remembered for his "Contributions to Hy-Vee" and he wanted everyone to know one final thing about him... Jack said "Just because I didn't hit the Bullseye every time, doesn't mean I wasn't aiming at it."

WHOA! 'So Powerful'... Jack had just left his Legacy 'Loud and Clear'...

It was the day Jack Held A Little 'Short Meeting' and 'Hit the Bullseye' ...

“If You Get A Chance” ...

For as many years as Hy-Vee has been in existence, there have been people stealing from the stores. Yes, even those early ‘Supply Stores’ of the 1930’s found themselves losing merchandise through ‘pilferage’. The 1930’s showed merchandise theft to be a ‘big issue’ because of the Great Depression years that plagued America. Nobody had any money, but they needed to eat and feed their Families.

Shoplifting, as it has become known, is a real problem in the Retail sector of American Business. It costs ‘Billions’ of dollars every year and eventually makes its way to the prices on items purchased by everyone in America. It adds ‘many pennies’ to the price of every item sold and it is the goal of every Retailer to reduce their losses.

Hy-Vee has these losses too. This story deals with an incident that happened in our Moline, IL Store.

Here’s how it all came down.

I was the Store Manager in the Moline, Illinois Store from 1987-1999 and our losses from Shoplifting were large. There was a ‘low-income’ Housing Project very near us and we also sat ‘squarely’ in front of the Moline High School with over 2500 kids going to school there. We constantly saw ‘the remnants’ of product

packaging left in the store's aisles. In addition, we saw people doing everything they could to deceive our Crew with products concealed for theft. Labels were changed to a lower selling price, false returns were requested for stolen items to get cash and products were consumed in the store to avoid payment.

It was a 'huge problem' to say the least.

Packages and cartons of cigarettes were the 'number one' item stolen in the stores and it had much to do with their price and location in the store. For many years, we merchandised them just like other items and that allowed for them to be taken from the shelf and carried through the store like other commodities. This 'access' to the cigarettes is how the thieves generally stole them. They simply worked them into pockets, bags, pants and purses as they went through the store... and then just 'walked out the door' with them.

I had made a decision that a program of 'anti-Shoplifting' was a long-term project. I believed it was necessary to 'catch and prosecute' as many as we could and that prosecution would, in-turn, start deterring others. We had also implemented a policy that everyone found to be Shoplifting would be prosecuted too.

The only exceptions to this rule of ours were young children and they would go downtown with the Moline Police to be picked up at the Police Station by a parent. If they were caught at the store and their parent was shopping, we would allow them to go home with their

parents. Otherwise, everyone went down to the Police Station and the adults (16 and over) had charges filed against them. I would appear in court against them and they would be 'banned' from the store in addition to any fine the Court imposed. It reduced our problem 'substantially' over time.

Lawsuits for False Arrest were a large worry and every retailer knew that there had to be certain facts that could be proven in order to avoid being sued for False Arrest. We had lots of Store Meetings and actually trained our Crew on how to 'successfully arrest' a Shoplifter.

Nancy and Cathy were our best at spotting and catching the thieves. They seemed to have a 'sixth sense' of what was happening and they had the courage to act on their own. Many of our Shoplifters were apprehended because of their diligence. They were GOOD!

One of our most 'infamous' Shoplifters was apprehended by Nancy and it is one of our more 'famous cases'.

Nancy called me on the store's Private Phone and told me she was following an "Older woman in a wheelchair". The 'kicker' was that the older woman was pulling an oxygen tank on wheels and our Customer had a plastic tube running from the tank to her nose for breathing purposes.

Now, Nancy was convinced she saw the woman put some cigarettes in a large purse she was carrying on her lap. Nancy was always right on these things so I asked the usual "Are you sure?" and she confirmed her observation so I went to the front of the store to be in on the apprehension.

As the woman began her exit from the store, I calmly stopped her and asked her if she had put cigarettes in her purse that she had failed to pay for. She acknowledged that she had, so I told her she'd have to wait for the Moline Police to arrive for paperwork and processing. With her condition, I was not able to take her to the Office for a picture, so I got the camera and took her picture in a secluded area of the Front-end of the store.

When the Police Officer arrived, I covered the 'usual' facts with him and then asked if he would search her purse to officially obtain the evidence. He did.

As the Officer took her purse, the woman sat there in her wheelchair and breathed heavily through her oxygen tube. She was very 'nonchalant' about her predicament.

'Lo and Behold', there were 57 packages of cigarettes in the purse. It was even a worse theft than we knew about. It was huge dollars in 'potential loss' and took her theft from simple Shoplifting to a more serious charge of Larceny.

As the Officer was loading her, her wheelchair and her oxygen tank into the Police Squad Car, I leaned over and

jokingly said to him "If you get a half a chance, pinch that tube off on your way to the Station."

Just for an instant, it caught him 'off-guard' and his head swung around like it was on a 'pivot'. When he saw my grin, he broke out in a big laugh.

It was always necessary to keep some humor in everything we did.

It kept the routines from 'Being Routine'...

It is the story of

'The Great Getaway In A Wheelchair'

“Our Store Managers are the true Entrepreneurs of the business.”

Ronald D. Pearson

President, CEO and

Chairman of the Board

(Retired)

“Okay, Which One Of You Was It...??”

From Hy-Vee’s inception as a partnership in 1930, the Founders of Hy-Vee, Charles Hyde and David Vredenburg, believed in communication. In the small communities of Southern Iowa and Northern Missouri where Hy-Vee got its start, there were small ‘austere’ newspapers and very simple radio stations. The Founders believed it necessary to always keep strong relations with their Customers through the use of these ‘news mediums’... They used both.

As the decade of the 1930’s rolled along, it became very obvious that Advertising was one of the ‘key elements’ in getting the Customers to come to ‘The Hyde and Vredenburg Supply Stores’ for their needs. The Founders felt strongly that an Ad should be an ‘invitation’ for the Customers to come in and when they arrived, another important ‘key element’ would be to treat them with respect and to show them how much their business was appreciated. They firmly believed that their Customers “Will go where they were invited and they will return to where they feel welcome.”

Hy-Vee has successfully used that belief for almost 90 years now.

By 1938, the number of the small ‘Hyde and Vredenburg Supply Stores’ grew to fifteen. In that number of stores, each Store Manager ran their own store and there were some ‘definite differences’ in

how the stores were managed. Some of the Store Managers were strong in areas the others were not and vice versa. It was this reason, they decided they needed 'idea sharing' on a regular schedule to keep the stores operating 'close' to the same in each town. It was sort of like 'keeping a buggy between the ditches' while going down a road...All over the road perhaps, but not in the ditch.

So, in search of the 'best communication' they could achieve, several of the Store Managers in these small stores would gather in one of the Stores on an informal basis to discuss strategy for getting Sales and Customers. As I have discussed previously, the Store Managers would gather in a Backroom and they'd drink 'gallons' of coffee and smoke cigarettes 'incessantly' as they talked about 'buying opportunities' and 'newspaper Ad items' and 'Customer ideas'. They'd pile up some full cases of Wheaties or Post Toasties for a table and they'd draw up Newspaper Ads on 'white butcher paper' for each to take back to 'their town' and use as a 'guide' for their local newspaper to print for their weekly Ad.

It was a strategy that worked well and the 'idea sharing' allowed the stores to grow and prosper by using the 'Best of the Best' ideas for their guides. The Store Managers had learned a lot from each other and their ability to buy items in bigger quantities became paramount to the stores' image of 'Low Prices' and so, they continued the 'meetings'.

As the 1930's ended and the 1940's started, these 'meetings' were more important than ever and they became 'Informal-Regular' Managers Meetings. Hy-Vee's 1945 purchase of the Chariton Wholesale Grocery in Chariton, IA gave way to a Central Headquarters facility that would serve as a 'center of everything'.

The formal 'Managers Meetings' began around this time. It was decided that mandatory 'Managers Meetings' would be held 'every other' Wednesday and then a third week of each month was the 'Monthly Inventory' for the complete Accounting of Sales and Profits. One week each month was left 'open' so that the Store Managers were able to be at their stores that Wednesday. These regular 'Managers Meetings' continue today.

It is one of Hy-Vee's most 'successful' decisions ever.

In now over 70 years of these Meetings, some great stories have come out of the 'trips to Managers Meetings' and the 'carpooling' that was done by the Store Managers from the areas with multiple stores.

One trip I made to Chariton, IA for a Managers Meeting is a trip I will remember forever. It was funny then and it's even funnier today.

It happened in 1991 and this is what happened.

I was the Store Manager at the Moline, IL Hy-Vee from 1987-1998 and my 'counter-part' in a close-by

Hy-Vee Store in Rock Island, IL was a great guy named Gene. We rode in to our Weekly Managers Meetings together along with another Store Manager, Chris, from the Milan, IL Store. We got to know each other very well over the years and over 'all the miles' we travelled together, we grew together like "The Three Musketeers". We were always together.

Now, Gene's Dad and Mother (Junior and Hazel) lived in the small Iowa town of Knoxville, IA and it was about 26 miles from their house to Hy-Vee's Headquarters in Chariton. Junior was the retired Store Manager at the Knoxville Hy-Vee and they were perfectly located so we could stop at their house in Knoxville after our Wednesday meeting. Each week, we'd stop and have coffee or a snack before driving the remaining 160 miles back to our towns in Illinois. We all enjoyed our weekly stops at Junior and Hazel's house.

As we talked over coffee one afternoon, Junior, commented that "There was one thing he'd always wanted for their house there in Knoxville." and it was a rather 'peculiar item' to wish for.

Junior wanted a Black Squirrel...

Yes, a 'real-life living and breathing' Black Squirrel for the trees around his house there in Knoxville. He said he'd be "The only guy in town with a Black Squirrel".

Well, it just so happens, the Mississippi River seems to divide the colors of the Squirrels just like it does the States of Iowa and Illinois. Iowa has Red and Gray Squirrels and Illinois has Black and Gray Squirrels. Illinois has almost no Red Squirrels and Iowa has almost no Black Squirrels.

That's where this story starts out...

Quite unexpectedly, the 'opportunity' for Junior to get his Black Squirrel presented itself several weeks after his comments about wanting one. As I was driving to Gene's store in Rock Island, IL one morning about 3:00 AM to get Gene for our trip to Chariton, I came across an injured Black Squirrel in the street. He'd been hit by a car. I stopped and picked him up out of the gutter. He was not really hurt, but he was really 'dazed' and I thought he'd probably survive, but he'd need some 'TLC' in the meantime.

So, upon my arrival at Gene's store, I found a cardboard box with a sturdy lid and I put some newspapers in the bottom of it and I laid the 'dazed' Black Squirrel in the box and I closed the lid. We loaded the box into the trunk of Gene's Cadillac Eldorado and we took off for Chariton, IA...185 miles away.

As we drove, we decided it would be best to stop at Junior and Hazel's house before the Managers Meeting and drop-off the injured 'critter'. We could then stop after the Managers Meeting on our way back to Illinois and check-in on it and make sure he

was doing well. So, that's what we did. We stopped and dropped him off on our way through Knoxville.

After our Managers Meeting was over, we piled in the Cadillac Eldorado and headed up the road 26 miles from Chariton to Knoxville. Like usual, we stopped for coffee and also checked on our 'Little Buddy' the Black Squirrel. He was still pretty 'wobbly' and pretty much 'dazed' and it was then that Junior said "I Think you Boys better take that Squirrel back to Illinois with you. I don't think he's going to make it."

I tried to talk him into keeping it and I told him I thought he'd would be fine, but in the end, we loaded the Black Squirrel back into the cardboard box and 'once again' we put the cardboard box with the Black Squirrel in it into the trunk of the Cadillac and headed out...Now headed 'back' to Illinois with the Black Squirrel now riding the 160 miles 'back' to Illinois with us.

We got home and I put the cardboard box in my car and took it home to my house. I put the injured Black Squirrel in a small cage we had there at the house and I 'nursed him back to health' over the next two or three weeks. At the end of those weeks, he was pretty well-healed and I turned him loose in our trees there in our yard and ultimately in our neighborhood.

He took off like a 'rocket' to the top of an Oak tree in our yard.

Where he went from there, I have no idea. He was 'free' and 'ready to run'. We told the story to 'everyone'. Most people just thought we were 'nuts', but Company President Ron Pearson jokingly said "I've heard some crazy Store Manager stories...Are you sure you and Gene weren't 'hitting' the Black Bottle?" It was funny for sure...

For many years after that day, I'd look at all the Black Squirrels running in the big Oak trees there in our neighborhood and I'd wonder to myself...

"Which One... Yes, 'Which One' of those little 'Illinois Devils' had been to Knoxville, Iowa in the trunk of a Cadillac?" ...

“We’re in the People Business, we just sell groceries on the side.”

K. Donald Canfield

Store Manager

(Retired)

“One Size Fits All” ...

‘Frugality’ is a ‘cornerstone’ of Hy-Vee and that ‘frugality’ grew out of the mere fact that the Company started in 1930 and operated throughout ‘The Great Depression of the 1930’s’. That ‘frugality’ continued on into ‘The War Years’ of the 1940’s when the economy in the United States could not have been more demanding on a fledgling small company from Southern Iowa. Charles Hyde and David Vredenburg were two men whose ‘vision’ of what ‘could be’ included every aspect of being ‘frugal’.

When Dave and Kate Vredenburg’s son, Dwight Vredenburg, was elected to be the first President in 1938, he came in with the ‘Tide of Frugality’ and during his 54 years with Hy-Vee, nothing changed. Every decision that was made to make the Company larger or fancier got ‘scrutinized’ from every conceivable angle and when it was decided that the Company could afford it or it would ‘pay its own way’, it was done... not until.

Some glaring examples of this ‘frugal’ spirit being so scrutinized were Dwight’s purchase of mirrors to put above the Produce Rack to show off the Produce while Dwight was Store Manager at the Centerville, IA store in the late 1930’s and into the mid-1940’s. The purchase of these mirrors by Dwight so infuriated his Father, David, that Dave wanted to ‘fire’ Dwight over it. It was a very ‘sore subject’ and it took lots and lots of ‘smoothing’ by Dwight (along with the

numbers to show it had improved Produce Sales) to win Dave over on it. It eventually did prove out. Produce Sales went up.

Another example was the request in the mid 1960's by Knoxville, IA Store Manager, Junior Briggs, to purchase an electric meat saw to make the Meat Shop more productive. All carcass meats were being 'cut-up' by hand and that included the cutting through bones with a hand saw. All of this took lots of time. Junior had requested that he be allowed to buy a saw and when he was told "No, we can't afford it.", he wasn't going to take the decision as the 'final answer'.

So, after meeting with Dwight and Senior Vice President, and Treasurer, Marion Coons, Junior was told that he could buy the meat saw 'personally' and he would then be reimbursed for it at a later date "After he could show on paper that it had, in fact, saved time and money." they said.

So, Junior borrowed the money from the local bank and bought the saw. He was reimbursed later because it really did 'pay its way' and he was able to show Dwight and Marion 'on paper' that it had. Obviously, Hy-Vee was growing to a point where the investments in some things were pricey, but they were great ways to offset the 'labor and time' on processing. The saw proved to be very valuable in the Meat Shops.

With these and other examples like these over the decades, we were always 'schooled' and 'indoctrinated' to the belief that being 'frugal' was the 'backbone' of Expense Control. You know, the old "Watch the Pennies and Nickels and the Dollars will fall into place" theory as Dwight put it. That theory is still very much 'alive and well' in Hy-Vee now in the 21st Century.

Only 'Buy what we need...No more'.

As the years rolled along in the late 1960's and later, it became a common practice for the Executives of Hy-Vee to hold a Store Meeting with the entire Crew of every new store so they could talk about Hy-Vee's philosophies, customer service and 'frugality'. In doing so, the stores got off to a great start with everyone going the same direction. A two-hour meeting on Monday the day before the Grand-Opening (which is always on a Tuesday), the doors were locked, the phone was put on 'hold' and nothing.... 'absolutely nothing'... got in the way of the Grand-Opening Meeting. These meetings were a great way to let every new employee hear 'straight from Dwight's mouth' that Hy-Vee's philosophies were real.

As it has been said many times, "Old Habits Die Hard" and when the first Galesburg, IL store opened in 1985, the threat of a 'big snowstorm' coming wasn't enough to keep Dwight and the other Hy-Vee Executives from flying over in the company plane for

the 'Big' Grand-Opening Meeting on the Monday afternoon ahead of the Tuesday Opening. The Meeting was scheduled to 'go forth' in spite of the inclement weather that was rolling in.

Flying from Hy-Vee's Headquarters at Chariton, IA to Galesburg, IL was no problem...so it seemed. What had not been anticipated for by 'The Executives' was the amount of snowfall in Illinois versus what the forecast was for Chariton, IA. When they arrived in Galesburg for the meeting, snow was coming down at a pretty good rate and the two-hour meeting was just long enough for the Company Pilot to decide it was 'not safe' to fly home to Chariton that night. So, the decision was to get some rooms and just stay the night in Galesburg.... Rooms that they could 'double-up on' and save the expense of everyone having his own room. There were 4 or 5 of them and that meant three rooms 'not 4 or 5' and old 'Mr. Frugality' started to come 'out of hiding'.

Here's 'The Rest of the Story' as it went around the Company...

Now, 'high-powered' adult men all know what they each want in the way of Grooming Supplies', but 'it was decided' (by Somebody) that for 'one day', everyone could just 'Buck-Up' and share the same types of HBC items. So, as the story has been told, 'multi-packs' could be purchased to save some money on the ordeal. A razor multi-pack, one can of shave cream, a single tube of toothpaste, a multi-

pack of toothbrushes and one can of spray deodorant seemed to be what the group needed...All of that could work, but then came the 'BIGGEST DECISION'.

After the decision was made that they could share all of the aforementioned items, the subject of 'clothing' came up. They could all wear their suits home the next day, but the flaw in the clothing part was...'underwear'...and nobody wanted to wear theirs for two straight days. So, staying totally with the 'frugal part', Dwight convinced the guys that they could get one 'six-pack' of underwear and they'd be set. Yes, they would buy 'six' pairs of undershorts and six undershirts'. Everyone would have 'clean undies'.

It was at that point, that the 'final' and 'most obvious' question came up...Just 'what size' underwear multi-pack should be bought to 'accommodate the group'?

It was Dwight's 'persuasive side' that convinced them that with him being the most 'rounded' person of the group, that the 6-pack of underwear should be 'his size' and you can 'guess' where that left everyone else... With most of the guys being considerably 'less round' than Dwight, it meant their pair of underwear was 'gonna be big'... And they were big...Remember, all six pair of underwear were one size... 'Extra Large'...

In the end, it all worked out just fine, but it came down to 'frugality over comfort' and as it had for over 50 Years, 'frugality won-out'.

The story 'flashed' around Hy-Vee for weeks...It was always told with a lot of laughter and the 'hint of frugality' that it grew out of...

It was the day that it wasn't 'Filling the Boss' Shoes' that mattered, but rather it was a case of

'Filling The Boss' Pants'...

"OOOPS! ...I Forgot That Part !" ...

Way back into the 1930's, it became obvious that the only way the tiny company called 'The Supply Stores' was going to 'survive and grow' included 'training' and 'teaching' those people in the organization that had the 'ability' and 'desire' to move to the top.

In every one of Hy-Vee's nearly nine decades, it has used 'The Cream Will Rise to The Top' theory that is an old Midwest slang saying. It's simple. A Company cannot grow without the people to fill the positions created by that growth.

Everyone must learn 'all they can'.

So, the job of any Manager is to 'teach' the people that he or she has working alongside of them the things they might need to know when they move 'through the ranks' and they are 'then' a Manager too. The things taught are generally the way things are done for the Company's uniformity and sometimes they are done to save money on a repair or a 'fix it'. job. You know... Our old friend... 'frugality'.

In the stores, minor electrical work was done changing light ballasts and simple wall switches and those types of repair. Occasionally, a screw or a nail was needed to put something back together so it would last longer and then there were the little plumbing jobs that could sometimes save money for a store. All the Full-timers knew that 'saving money' paid them more in the 'monthly' and then later 'quarterly' Bonus Checks that came along with a successful Hy-Vee Store. It is almost a 'way of life' to try to conserve so there will be more for everyone to share.

In those 'early years, Charles Hyde and David Vredenburg were paying the Store Managers a salary of $50 per month. In 1932 or 1933, Dave came up with the idea that the profits could be 'split' with the Store Managers and that incentive for them to work 'harder and smarter' would make the 'total left for the company' even larger than before the 'commission arrangement'.

So, that's what was done. The decision to go 50/50 with the Store Managers was 'born'. After a couple of months on the 'new arrangement', one of the Store Managers worked hard and his store produced a lot more profit than before. The Store Manager's commission was $125 for that month as opposed to what it would have been at $50.

When it was discussed at home by Dave Vredenburg, his wife, Kate, she said "Dave, we can't afford to pay those guys that kind of money." It was Dave's reply back that has lived for nearly 90 years. He said "Kate, we can't afford not to because when they're making it for themselves, they're making it for the Company."

It was 'Sheer Genius'...

I was the Store Manager at the Moline, IL Hy-Vee from 1987-1998. It was a very busy and high-volume store located on a very busy street and it was surrounded by 'lots and lots' of Business and Residential Customers. We took care of 'tens of thousands' of Customers each week.

We kept a s mall toolbox at our store in Moline and in 1996, a 'routine repair' got clear out of hand and it sort of backfired on the Assistant Store Manager, Matt, as he went into repair mode.

Here's how it went down... 'Dripping' all the way down...

All of the toilets and urinals used by Hy-Vee in the Restrooms used a 'flush valve kit' that consisted of a rubber diaphragm and a 't-handle piece'. The operation was simple. When the handle on the toilet or urinal was pulled downward, the 't-handle piece' lifted and it let the water flow through the flush valve. As the water flowed, under huge pressure, the rubber diaphragm started to close and by the time it was fully closed, the toilet or urinal was 'flushed clean' and the water shut itself off. It was a 'simple', but 'smart' system of flushing a toilet.

Over the years, I had learned to change those kits when they failed and it took a repair cost from about $125 for the plumber's bill to about $12 for the cost of the flush valve kit and with us doing the 'replacement' ourselves. It was a good 'money-saver'.

Some of these valves needed done several times a year due to the amount of times the toilets and urinals were flushed. I always made sure we had a few extra kits on hand and I would quickly repair one or a member of our Crew, who had learned how, would do it in my absence.

It worked great and saved 'a considerable amount' of money for the store.

So, one day, I was sitting at my desk in the Office that was located in the Basement of the Moline Store. I was busy, but I noticed a drop of water fall on the corner of my desk and then another and then more...I looked into the Bookkeeper's Office next to my Office and I saw some similar water falling...There was also more water beginning to drip in the area just outside my Office where the timeclock was, so I thought I better investigate.... 'AND FAST'.

At this point, I got paged to answer the private Store Phone and as I picked it up, I heard Lynn from The Courtesy Counter sort of scream... "Rick, get up here...We're flooded up here!" so, I hung up the phone and I 'bounded' up the stairs to the Main Floor. As I reached the top of the stairs, I could see water moving in a 'big sheet' across the Backroom Floor and nearing the Basement stairs. I pushed open the door to the Sales Floor and water was on the floor... 'EVERYWHERE'.

It was then that Lynn, from the Courtesy Counter, opened her door and said… "I think it's coming from the Men's Restroom." So, I raced down the short hallway that was now filled with water and I pushed open the door.

Good Lord! There was water just 'gushing' upward about 4 feet high out of one of the urinals and Matt and two others were standing there 'soaking wet' and looking 'very cold' and 'very helpless'. I said "What the Hell happened?" and with that, I got a reply that told the story of the 'Great Flood of '96'.

Over the 'roar' of the gushing water, Matt said "I thought I'd change the flush valve kit in this one so you wouldn't have to do it. I've watched you do it and I thought I knew how."

So, the next question came out of my mouth and I said, "Why didn't you shut the water off before you took the top off?" Then came Matt's answer and it will stick with me forever when I think back about it…

Matt's answer was "PRICELESS" ….

He simply said "OOOPS…I forgot that part."

I reached over and picked up a flat-tip screwdriver from the toolbox and I inserted it into the 'water-turn-off slot' on the valve and I shut the 'geyser' down… All of a sudden, it seemed so quiet…Four of us standing there soaking wet, standing in an inch or two of cold water and looking at each other. I quickly

replaced the flush valve kit put the lid back on the valve and then we ran for the mops.

The next three hours were spent mopping the floors and soaking up the 'absolute deluge of water in the Men's Restroom, the Hallway, the Courtesy Counter, the Seafood Department, the Backroom and even the Basement areas where the water had seeped down to.

What a mess!

As the days rolled along afterward, we started laughing about it and it became known forever as 'The Great Flood of '96'.

We learned our lesson and we never

'Forgot That Part' Again...

“Say What ??” ...

Customers stealing things in Grocery Stores is not a new occurrence. Since all those years ago in Southern Iowa and Northern Missouri in ‘The Hyde and Vredenburg Supply Stores’ of the 1930’s, lots of people have thought of almost every imaginable way to ‘walk into a store with empty pockets’ and ‘walk out of that store with full pockets’. It’s plain and simple ‘thievery’, but that’s not the name that society has given it. It has been called ‘Shoplifting’ for many decades and it is a ‘multi-Billion Dollar loss’ to Retail Stores all over the Country.

Those early Supply Stores were almost ‘protected’ from Shoplifting because the items in those stores were on shelves behind the counters and the Customers would walk along and point at items and the Clerk would then get the products down and it was included in the Customer’s order. All of the individual items were recorded on a ‘Sales Pad’ with carbon paper and then the totals were ‘hand-added’ for a ‘Grand-total’. The carbon paper left a copy for the store and a copy for the customer.

It was very simple accounting, but ‘it worked’.

Our ‘Roots’ and Our ‘Heritage’ are in some innocent settings and as the 1940’s and 1950’s progressed, the move Hy-Vee was making into the larger towns was proving to be ‘expensive’. As these decades moved along, the ‘self-serve’ aspects of modern

Grocery Stores started to be seen in different ways in the Midwest of America. At first, it was a struggle to get the Hy-Vee Customers to 'shop' and pick up their own items off the shelves of the aisles.

When Grocery Carts came along at the Centerville, IA Store around 1940 in the Stores, the Customers 'balked' at using them. Many of those Customers refused them said "I Won't Push Those Baby Buggies". So, a candy bar or a package of gum was put in each cart as an incentive to use them and 'little by little' they were won over.

It was an interesting change for the Customers though. There more changes coming in the years ahead. Many more.

Hy-Vee's Philosophy of 'Speaking to Every Customer' and making those Customers feel like 'The Hy-Vee Crew Was Right There to Help' was a huge deterrent to Shoplifting. The feeling of someone paying close attention, to a Customer made the 'potential thief' more reluctant to take something without paying for it. In spite of that, however, 'Shoplifting' in the stores continued to grow over the years and it was beginning to be apparent by the late 1950's and into the 1960's that 'Huge Losses' were going to result if it were not controlled better. So, elaborate 'shelf layouts' were designed to keep Customer 'traffic' flowing only in one direction through the store to keep the Customer headed toward the Check-out area. Even later, 'undercover personnel' were paid to

roam some stores dressed like and acting like ordinary shoppers to actually 'catch 'em in the act' of concealing and stealing merchandise. Many fancy ways of concealment were devised and Hy-Vee got educated as to 'The Criminal Element' of the World.

It's definitely out there... 'Everywhere'.

In 1973, Hy-Vee created an entire Department called 'Safety and Security' and a 'seasoned pro' named Joe Smith came onboard as its Director. Joe would be instrumental in Safety and Security's success to help the stores with losses of all kinds including Shoplifting.

There are literally 'thousands' of Shoplifting stories that have gone around Hy-Vee over the decades and they range from 'vicious and ruthless' to 'borderline sweet and innocent'. Most are in between those two somewhere. However, it is 'theft' just the same and it must be dealt with.

One Shoplifting story happened in a store I was in and it turned out to be 'funny" and lots of people still laugh about it today.

It's told like this.

In 1992, I was the Store Manager in the Moline, IL #1 Hy-Vee Store and my Assistant Store Manager was a great guy named Tom. Tom was outstanding in every aspect of the position he had there and we had a great working relationship as well as being great friends. Tom was aggressive and we had been working very hard to curb Shoplifting in our store.

We had a Public Housing Complex named Springbrook Courts about 10 blocks from our store and we kept seeing a real pattern of many of our Shoplifters living at 'The Courts'. We devised a 'two-part plan' that proved to be a good one. It was effective for the people from 'The Courts' and also from other surrounding neighborhoods.

The 'first part' of our plan was that when we apprehended a Shoplifter, we prosecuted every one of them if they were above legal age. Everyone got to 'Go Downtown' in the Police Squad Car and if the person apprehended was a juvenile, then their parents would have to come and get them from the Police Station. The only exception to that was if they were a juvenile and they were with their parents in the store. Then, they could go home with their parents.

The 'second part' of our plan was to officially 'Ban' the offender from our store. In doing that, they were then forced to go to Eagle Foods which was our big competitor across the street. We figured that if they stole from us, they'd steal from Eagles. If so, we wouldn't have the losses and Eagles would.

So, one day, Tom apprehended a young girl for stealing an item and he brought her to the Office for paperwork and to wait on the Moline Police to come and get her. It was obvious she had a serious 'speech

impediment' and the whole conversation was tough for Tom to get the information we wanted and be able to understand it as she spoke.

Tom kept asking her questions and then she'd answer, but the whole thing went pretty much 'nowhere' for about 10 minutes. He was repeatedly asking her what her name was. Her answer each time was a very slurred and hard sounding 'Nonya'. I have to admit, I was having trouble understanding her and that added to the issues Tom was having because I couldn't help him. So, I saw Tom write down 'Nonya' in the box on our forms for her 'First Name'.

Then came the chore of getting her to say her 'Last Name' so that we could understand it. Over and over, Tom would ask her for her 'Last Name' and it was the same thing each time...A slurred and almost inaudible answer. Finally, Tom had heard it enough that he took a guess and I saw him write down 'Bizness' in the box for her 'Last Name' ....

It took a few seconds, but it seemed to hit us both at the same time...She wanted us to know her name was 'Nonya Bizness' or in plain old English, she was saying "None of your Business" and when Tom repeated it, she just laughed. It was sure true that she couldn't talk very well, but her mind sure was capable of keeping us guessing for a while. We looked at each other and acknowledged 'the laugh' she gave us and we both knew we'd have 'the bigger

laugh' when she was on her way to the Moline Police Station.

We didn't go any further with the attempts to get her name that day. We'd been humiliated enough. So, when the Police Squad Car came and took her off to the Moline Police Department, we just asked the Arresting Officer to call us back with her name and address when they got it at the Station. They called a little while later and gave it to us. I would have loved to have heard her 'story' to the Arresting Officer.

Tom and I sat around for a little while afterward and taunted each other with a 'slurred voice' and we kept saying to each other 'Nonya' and then we'd laugh. Several others in the store got in on it as we told the story and then lots of people were saying 'Nonya' when asked a question. It put lots of fun in things for a few days.

To this day, when I think of Shoplifters in the Moline Hy-Vee, I think of 'Nonya' and I shake my head.

It was the day in Moline when the girl Shoplifter said

"Nonya Idiots Can Get My Name!" ...

"Is She Good-Looking ??" ...

Make no mistake about it...Since the 'beginning' of 'The Supply Stores' in 1930, Charles Hyde and David Vredenburg utilized 'Part-timers' in the Crews. Times when 'more bodies' are needed during the week and for jobs that are in some cases more 'physical and tedious'. Those jobs seemed to bode well for the store to have lots of Part-timers on the Work Schedules.

The largest segment of a Grocery Store's Crew is Part-time and those Part-timers are sometimes as much as 75% of the Crew in a store. The reason for so many is a 'combination' of things... Now, as it was then, almost 90 years later, it is still the plan of the stores to have 'lots' of Part-Timers for the 'flexibility' it adds to the schedules. It's a 'cost saver' too.

The biggest reasons for 'lots' of Part-timers in a store include things like scheduling and utilizing the talent of great people who only want a few hours per week due to another job or children at home. Sometimes, people only wanted a few hours to go along with school schedules or sports activities at school. Other "Business Reasons' are that the 'framework' of a store's Labor Cost allows for 'some', but not all, of the Crew to work Full-time because of the 'pay and benefits expense' to the store.

In many ways, it becomes a 'juggling act' to have enough Full-timers to fill the spots of Management

and Skill Levels in a store. It takes a certain number of 'skilled positions like cutting meat, clerking and trimming fresh produce, pharmacists, cake decorators, bookkeepers and the 'skilled ordering' of merchandise in all Departments. These are just a few of the other Full-time positions.

The Part-timers fill in the rest.

Part-Timers can be brought into the store's schedule in large numbers at times when the Sales History has shown that the store will be serving the most Customers and preparing related items the Customers' needs. Things like re-stocking after heavy sales volume, bagging groceries, cashiering and so forth. It is a principle of 'Bring in the Crew as Needed' to handle the crowds and then managing the store otherwise to do the 'detailed stuff' like ordering, hiring, training, meat-cutting etc. Pretty much, it's 'People In' and 'People Out' according to Customer trends.

I will always believe that the Part-time Crew is the 'Single Biggest Factor' that will 'Define A Store' in its popularity with the Customers. Many times, the people seen by the Customers are nearly all Part-timers that are there to serve the Customers at the times they shop. Upon entering the store and then on through to the Cashiering and Loading of the Groceries, Customers will be served by Part-timers. Part-timers with ages of 16 and all the way to some

into their 90's, will be 'the ticket to success or failure' with your Customers.

In my many years of working for Hy-Vee, I was at both ends of the spectrum on my employment. I started at age 15 in the Washington, IA Store in 1966 and I worked into Full-time a few years later. I still feel that being a Part-timer prepared me to be a better Full-timer and eventually a better Store Manager because I had 'empathy' for their position and the problems they were dealing with at school, at home or even with a 'guy or girl issue'. Whatever it took to keep the Part-timers enthused was going to be the effort that would keep the overall 'happiness and satisfaction level' up in the store.

In the effort to try and be 'tuned-in' with the Part-timers, I stayed in good touch with them by having short conversations at the Timeclock with groups coming in or in the Breakroom with the Part-timers on a short 'rest stop' to 'recharge' for a few minutes. I got to know them better and I believe they worked harder because they believed I cared...and I did care.

A great example of the 'trust' I had developed with the Part-timers was evidenced in something that happened in 1992 at the Moline, IL Store. I was Store Manager at Moline for many years. It involved a very nice young man named, 'Bob'.

Bob's story happened like this.

Our 'policy' of a Part-timer needing time-off was pretty flexible at the Moline Hy-Vee... as long as a 'request note' was in the 'Time-off Request Box' before the schedules were written, they were honored. It allowed the requests by individuals to be noted as 'Off' on the written schedule before the hours were penciled in for everyone else. We did write our schedules two weeks in advance and that would occasionally cause a wrinkle too on 'last minute' things that would come up for people. In that instance, we would approve of a 'trade of hours' with someone who had a 'skill level' that was close to the person who needed the time-off. For example, a Cashier would have to trade with someone who also had Cashier training, so the schedule didn't get out of balance. The 'trades' usually worked well and we usually approved them when needed.

So, one evening around 5:00 PM, I was working at my desk when Bob stuck his head into the Office and he said "Hey Rick, do you have a minute?" I laid down my pencil as I always did when someone needed something and I said "Sure Bob, come on in and sit down." When he sat down, I asked a few questions about school and how it was going and then I said "So, what's up?" Bob hesitated for a moment and then he said very softly "I have a problem and I don't know what to do." I said to him "Well, let's talk about it and maybe I can help you with it." So, I got up and I closed the door to make sure the conversation was private and then I said "What do you need help with?"

Bob thought for a minute and then he said "Well, I have been chasing this girl for a couple of months trying to get her to go out with me and she finally said 'Yes', but the problem is that she only wants to go Friday and I am scheduled to work." In a sympathetic reply, I said "Oh, that 'is' a problem. Is she good-looking?" Bob nodded his head and he quickly answered "Yeah, she sure is."

So, I said "Have you asked about somebody trading with you?" and the answer from Bob was a quick "Yes, but nobody will trade. I guess they all have plans."

Now, I knew that Bob was a trained Cashier/Stocker and that he'd be doing one or the other on his Friday Shift, so I asked the next question of "What hours are you scheduled on Friday?" Bob replied that he was on the '4-9 PM shift' on Friday.

I said "Hmmm...Let me think for a minute." As I sat there for a few seconds thinking, it dawned on me that I never went home on Fridays until about 7 PM and I knew how to Cashier, Stock Shelves and Bag Groceries, so I quickly said "I have the answer... I'll work for you". My answer must have 'really' caught Bob off-guard because he didn't reply right away. It was the last thing he expected to hear come from my mouth. Then, I went on to say "Yes, that's going to work fine for me. You can have the night off and I'll cover for you." "But" ...

Bob smiled, but he was keeping quiet until he heard the "But" part. Then I continued on and said "Two things have to happen. 'One'...Your Girlfriend needs to know that we write schedules in advance and that you two have to plan ahead to get the time-off you need so we can write the schedules properly. And 'Two'...You're going to 'Owe Me One'...The next time I call you to come in extra when we're short-handed, you have to help me out... DEAL?"

Bob's face broke out into a 'Big Smile' and he quickly said "Deal". We finished with some small talk about what they were going to do and then he was off... 'Free and Clear' to go with his girl on Friday.

So, on Friday, I got all my stuff 'wrapped-up' in the Office, put on my apron and at 4PM on the nose, I reported to the Front-End Manager and I told him "I am working for Bob tonight". The look I got in return was 'PRICELESS' and his answer back was great too... "So, how did he pull that off?" I laughed and said I'd tell him later, but that I was to Cashier, Bag, Stock Shelves or whatever else Bob would be doing until 9PM.

I had a great time that evening and it created a 'real stir' in the Crew that night. We had everything done on time and we had 'lots of fun' doing it. It kept me right in line with the 'communication' I always loved having with the Part-timers.

For many years after Bob graduated from Moline High School, left for College and then went on into his

'working years', Bob would stop in occasionally and see me.

We'd catch up on what we'd each been up to and we'd reminisce about stuff from 'days gone-by' and it never failed that we'd always 'chuckle' about the time...

'Bob Traded Hours With The Boss' ...

“Let your employees help plan and run the Ship.”

Ronald D. Pearson

President, CEO and

Chairman of the Board

(Retired)

"So... Were They Frozen ?"

Nearly ninety years of 'Operations' since those early years of the 1930's 'Supply Stores' has shown our beloved Company called Hy-Vee, Inc. many things that are (and should be) held close to our Hearts. You know...For the sake of 'quality' and the rigid standards that have to be protected for the 'long-haul reputation' of our Company.

Some things in Hy-Vee are just plain essential for the overall success of the Company. Things that fall into this category are things that can easily be changed by 'human effort' and in the haste to get the job done at a higher profit level, the things that are 'twisted' just a little, can send quality 'right down the tube'.

So, when a Store Manager or a Department Manager thinks it's to their advantage to use an inferior quality ingredient, it generally does show up in the end product. If a Customer buys that item and then dislikes it, they probably won't buy it again. It's really pretty 'basic'.

Some examples of Hy-Vee's philosophy are the fact that the Floral Departments don't sell 'stale' or 'close to done' flowers at a discount. Hy-Vee knows that when a bouquet of flowers is given, the person receiving those Flowers will want to look at them for 'many days'. If they 'wilt and turn brown' in a day or so, it is perceived that the quality is poor and that Hy-Vee's flowers are 'not good'. Then, the Customer will

not call on Hy-Vee again to send that 'Special Arrangement' to a loved one. This philosophy holds true with 'day old' Bakery Goods and 'Dark Meats' too...Both will lead to a perception of 'poor quality'. It's best to get them off the shelf and take the loss. You will hear it often in Hy-Vee that "The first loss is the least loss".

That is so true.

Now, for many years, the recipes in the Deli/Kitchens were in a Recipe Book and it was fairly well understood that they would be prepared the same way with the same ingredients in each store so that a Customer buying an item from one Hy-Vee Kitchen would find the same thing in another if they changed stores later. Sometimes this would happen in towns with more than one Hy-Vee Store and a Customer shopped back and forth for convenience reasons. The store with the perceived 'poor quality' would lose-out over time and then Sales and Profits could start into a 'downward trend'.

Because items move up and down in their cost to the stores, it is possible for a store or a department to 'buy ahead' a little on those items that are 'shelf stable' and will last for a long period. These items might be mayonnaise, canned items, ketchup, mustard, dry noodles and items of this nature. They just plain don't spoil quickly. There are items, however, that should not be purchased ahead and those items are the ones that will not stay 'shelf

stable'. Lettuce, cabbage, potatoes, eggs, dairy products and meats are in this category. Some 'meats products', can be frozen and the quality will not be compromised, but overall that's just not the case. Hy-Vee wants it all 'fresh'...

One item that Hy-Vee has always been 'very particular' about is 'Fresh Chickens' for the use in the Kitchens as 'fried chicken'. Fresh Chickens produce the highest quality of taste and that quality can be compromised greatly when they are 'frozen' or held too long in a 'fresh' state. That is why the conversation to the stores was always "Don't freeze Chickens for later use". This was constantly talked about in Kitchen Meetings at Hy-Vee's weekly Managers Meetings and it was always discussed as 'company guidance' because the basic philosophy of Hy-Vee was to let each Store Manager 'run his or her own store' and make the decisions for the 'long-term success of their store'. The hope was that the issue of 'Frozen Chickens' would be avoided with lots of 'Persuasion from the Podium'.

The philosophy of 'local store autonomy' has served Hy-Vee well for nearly 90 years, but it continues to need discussion occasionally on some subjects. It certainly does 'still' help to keep things moving along the Company's 'desired path'.

Now, having said all of that, 'Temptation Is Around Every Corner' in life and a person who is paid on a Commission basis will look for ways to make things

more profitable whenever they can. It's just inherent in a Capitalistic Society and it is said often in Hy-Vee "If your store or department does better, you will do better". And 'for sure', that's the way it needs to be to keep everyone scratching for more Sales and Profits.

Something happened in 1993 that 'turned a lot of heads' the day it happened and it still 'turns those heads' today.

We are still laughing about it almost 25 years later.

This is 'The way it all happened'...

The prices of Fresh Chickens had been fluctuating up and down for a period of time. The price differences were enough to think about 'buying ahead' on those 'sacred' Chickens and hope to 'buy 'em, freeze 'em, thaw 'em and fry 'em'... All of course, with a quick sale in mind.

The Kitchen Manager of Hy-Vee's Rock Island Store had made the decision to do a little 'buying ahead' on the Fresh Chickens he felt they needed for a 'Big Catering' that was coming up soon and his 'buy' was also coupled with a 'Big Sale' just ahead too. It was, he thought, a 'quick buck' for his store and his Kitchen Department. He also knew the time in the Freezer would be 'minimal'. So, he 'gambled' and well...Let's just say 'He had no idea' how his Boss would have to answer for that decision.

Within a few days, all of us Store Managers were in Headquarters for 'Inventory Meetings' to have the Hy-Vee Accountants 'do the numbers' on our stores for the 'month-ended'. That accounting would determine the profits and paychecks of those involved. During those 'Inventory Meetings' at Headquarters, a direct 'one on one' was always necessary with Ron, the President of Hy-Vee, so he could have some time with each of Hy-Vee's nearly 200 Store Managers at the time. Granted, it wasn't a long time with Ron, but it kept him 'in the know' about each store and it gave him some personal input with each Store Manager. In turn, each Store Manager then had a chance to talk to Ron if they needed to. It worked great.

When the 'day and the time' came for us to report to Headquarters, our 'results' were printed and we met with Hy-Vee's 'Upper Management' in groups. 'In Groups'...That means, you get 'praised' in front of a group, but it also means you can sometimes 'take your lumps' in front of others and it could be 'painful'.

It could also be 'funny', but that depended on many factors which were usually going to happen in the 'group setting' also. Most times, it was something someone said that got everything 'stirred up' immediately. Other times, it was 'fodder' for future laughs.

So, there we were in our Group Meeting and Ron asked the Rock Island Store Manager, Gene, why his 'Ending Inventory' was so high in his Kitchen

Department. An 'Up Inventory' means you have more unsold product in your store and thus more to sell to 'free up' the money tied up in it. The goal was to operate on a 'lower inventory'. You know, 'buy it and sell it quickly'

It was Gene's comment that pretty well printed itself in the Hy-Vee History Books of stores when he said "Well, my Kitchen Manager said we bought ahead on Chickens." And just like he had 'Radar Antennas', Ron's eyes and ears were focused 'instantly' on that comment.

"What do you mean you bought ahead on Chickens? You didn't freeze them did you?" Ron said and then he sat there waiting for a response from Gene. After absorbing Ron's question and realizing that he had put himself right in 'The Crosshairs', Gene said "No, we didn't Freeze them."

Ron knew Gene was 'edgy' about it, so then he said "Well, just how do you get them to hold up so they don't spoil?" Ron, knew full-well that there were about 15 or 20 other Store Managers 'hanging on' to every word as he kept looking directly at Gene for an answer.

And Gene's answer was coming...

Oh Boy, was it coming...

It was at this point that the 'Iconic Statement' of the year was made by Gene when he said "We don't

freeze them, we just put them in the freezer and 'frost 'em' a little bit."

HOLY COW !... 'FROST 'EM' ??

Every Store Manager in the room was laughing hard deep down inside as they heard that statement by Gene. I am not even sure how Ron ever kept a 'straight face' on that one because it was not what he expected to hear. He'd heard everything over the years, but not 'Frosted Chickens'.

So, for the nearly 200-mile ride back to our stores, our carload of guys 'laughed so hard' we thought we were going to be sick....

We'd been 'witness' to one of the 'best comebacks ever spoken'...Gene had just shown us the 'Genius' of his quick thinking. Not even Ron had a comeback for Gene's 'Frosted Chickens'.

Almost 25 years later, it 'still' comes up in lots of conversations about

'Crying Fowl Over

The 'Frosted Chickens'...

“Our goal is to have over 50% of our stores ‘New’ or ‘Newly Remodeled’ within the last five years. It’s always our target for keeping our stores modern.”

Ronald D. Pearson

President, CEO and

Chairman of the Board

(Retired)

“We’ll See About That” ...

Competition is actually a ‘Good Thing’ in some cases and it will make ‘A Better Operator’ out of almost everyone. Now, having said that, ‘Too Much Competition’ can really destroy a Market and it will only benefit the Customers that the stores serve. You see, stores have to ‘prosper’ and they have to be strong enough to ‘be competitive’ but also ‘healthy enough’ to be around a long time to really benefit the Customers.

There is an ‘Old Story’ about a man who owned a Grocery Store. He would always have signs in his windows saying “We’re the cheapest in town” and he honestly believed that people shopped with him ‘only’ for that one reason. He had forgotten all about the ‘other reasons’ people do shop at a store and it is really a ‘myriad of reasons’. As time went along, he reduced his Crew due to his ‘low profit margins’ and then he kept letting the cleanliness of his store ‘slide downward’ along with ‘cutting-back his advertising’ to save money. Later, when he had no business left, he closed his doors and then there was ‘no store at all’.

He’d ‘low-priced’ himself right out of business. After he’d closed, he put a sign in his window that said “We were the cheapest in town” ...

Now, as Hy-Vee’s History has shown, ‘new competitors come’ and sometimes, they ‘fall by the

wayside' due to the philosophies of the story just told. Those competitors failed to realize that it is 'all of the Fundamentals of Operation' that keep stores in the 'Success Column'. Clean, well-stocked stores, with friendly Crews, a great location and prices that are 'low enough to be inviting, but high enough to get a 'Fair Profit' in return are the Basic Fundamentals.

Hy-Vee's First President and CEO, Dwight Vredenburg (active from 1935-1989), used to tell us "There is no one key to success. It is instead, a whole ring of keys. There are keys on that ring for each of the Fundamentals of Operation. The Store Managers that use the most of those keys will be the most successful".

Profound words to 'live by' in Management.

One Story that happened to me in happened in 1990 while I was the Store Manager at the Moline, IL Hy-Vee is a story that all of our Crew, who were there, still talk about and 'chuckle over' to this very day.

It played out like this.

We'd been open for about three years and we had enjoyed a 'very strong' three years in our store's success. We had grown rapidly and we'd been very profitable doing it. We had a large Eagle Food Center immediately across the street from us and they were 'going downhill' due to our 'good operation' and 'friendly crew'.

There was also a large empty building in a shopping center in town and it was vacant because a Grocery Store had closed there before we opened. It was a much larger building than ours and one day, we heard 'through the grapevine' and then read in the local newspaper, that a new 'Econo Foods' would take the building and open to compete in Moline. Obviously, we'd have chosen to 'not' have them open, but it was out of our control so, we did a lot of deep self-evaluation and 'tightened our belts' and we got ready for them to open.

During the weeks they were busy preparing their store for opening, they selected a Crew for their new store and they put the Crew's pictures in the newspaper and 'highlighted' the 'experience' of their Crew too. They let everyone in Moline know that their 'Grand Opening' was getting close.

Now, 'ego' coupled with a 'big mouth' can be very dangerous and soon, the Store Manager who was going to Manage the new Econo Foods started coming into our store and 'taunting' our Crew working out on the Sales Floor. He would roam our store and make remarks about the store and how 'theirs would be better than ours'. Our Staff took him for what he appeared to be...'A Big Mouth' and they learned to laugh about it.

When the comments turned to 'our store's Management' (Me), our Crew started to 'draw the line' and they did what 'loyal people do' and they defended

the Management of our store back to him. On one visit into the store, the Econo Foods Store Manager really put his foot in his mouth. He made the statement to one of our Crew that "He was going to give me a lesson in how to run' a Grocery Store".

Of course, he laughed after he said it.

The person to whom he said it repeated it to me and I simply laughed and said "We'll see about that."

Later that week, we had a 'Staff Management Meeting' and the topic of the Econo Foods Manager's comments got brought up. We all laughed about it and I made the statement "Well, the day they close that store, I'll take you all out for lunch and 'treat you' to Chinese Food and afterward, we'll drive by and we'll 'line-up' and spit on their door."

We all Laughed and I could see that there was beginning to be a feeling in our Management Crew of 'Who's going to show who'. It was nearly a 'rallying cry' at that point.

So, the 'new competitor' opened for business and as the months wore along, it was beginning to look like the Econo Foods Store Manager might be the one 'getting the lesson'. Things were not going well for them and they had not even come close to the level they wanted to be at. We were hearing 'rumors' that Econo Foods was closing.

At the end of about 18 months or so, they announced they'd be 'closing their doors'. Our Management

Crew had really 'Risen to the challenge and had 'excelled' in all the areas of 'Dwight's Key Ring' Hy-Vee's people had really accomplished something big.

We were proud.

At our weekly 'Staff Management Meeting', during the week they announced the closing, one of our Department Managers said "Hey, Rick...Are we still going to go for Chinese Food and then spit on the door?" Everyone got quiet.... Would we really do it?

Then, all eyes turned to me and I said "You bet we are...You earned it."

So, the week they closed their doors, I treated about 25 of our people to lunch at the Chinese Restaurant near the shopping center. And then afterward, we drove our 'several carloads' of Crew over to the 'now closed' Econo Foods where we all lined up and simultaneously 'spat' on the door. It was a bit 'crass' and perhaps not one of my 'classier moves', but I have to admit that it was really fun. We all laughed...

Our Crew 'had gotten their revenge'. I could not have been prouder of them...

We were able to hire three of Econo Foods' Crew...They turned out to be three of 'The Best Ever' Hy-Vee Associates I got to work with over all my years. They were an 'asset' to us from 'Day One'...

One of them even went on to be awarded Hy-Vee's coveted 'Legendary Service Award'. I have always been proud of them.

When I think of it all, I shake my head and laugh. It was the time

Econo Foods 'Came to Town' and

'Opened A 'Bad Fortune' Cookie'

“What Color Was It ??” ...

The Deli/Kitchen Departments in the stores of Hy-Vee’s ‘Modern Era’ are a really great source of extra Sales and Profits. These Deli’s came about with the first one being in Des Moines in the mid-late 1960’s and ‘one-by-one’, the Deli/Kitchen Department has been added to nearly every store in Hy-Vee.

As time went along, ‘Catering’ large meals at someone’s house or ‘on location’ at a designated place for a Wedding or a Funeral Luncheon, became a big part of the business too. Hy-Vee’s Deli’s learned to do it all.

Today, in 2017, there are fancy Restaurants, Italian Kitchens, Chinese Food Departments and a ‘whole host’ of foods being prepared for the Customers to enjoy either at the store or to take home for a meal there. Nearly every kind of food you might want is there.

As I have already written about, ‘timeless stories’ for a store’s History sometimes happen when you least expect it and the ‘circumstances’ make you wonder “How in the World could that have happened?”.

In the area called ‘The Quad Cities’, there are actually ‘seven towns’ that make up the area. Davenport, IA, Bettendorf, IA, Milan, IL, Rock Island, IL, Moline, IL, East Moline, IL and Silvis, IL are all nestled together with a combined population of around 400,000 people. They have an illustrious

history going back to around 1830. The Mississippi River 'splits' the towns 'right down the middle' separating Iowa and Illinois.

This story involves the Rock Island, IL Hy-Vee Deli/Kitchen and them 'catering' a 'Special Event' they prepared food for and then took out 'on location' to serve to their Customers in 1990.

Here's how it all 'Served Up'...

The Quad Cities has a beautiful 'civic center' type arena located in downtown Moline, IL. It was opened in the late 1980's. At the time it opened, it was called "The Mark". Now, The Mark will hold about 12,500 people for concerts and it has many rooms that can be rented for meetings and events. Ice Hockey is played there and The Mark is a very popular spot that is used a lot for functions of all kinds in the Quad Cities. It is always the center of 'something happening' in the Quad Cities.

The Rock Island Hy-Vee Deli/Kitchen had been contracted to be part of a 'big Saturday event' at The Mark in 1990 and it meant taking their Deli Delivery Van and Barbecue Roaster trailer over and setting up in front of The Mark. They were to be barbecuing steaks on their Roaster and the meal would include all the 'trimmings' of Baked Potatoes and Salad, Desserts etc. Hundreds of people were going to be there and not only would it be a great Sale for the store, but it was also going to give Hy-Vee some well-

deserved 'exposure and 'KUDOS' for what they could do to 'Cater' parties.

It was going to be 'Great'.

So, the Rock Island Store and their Deli/Kitchen both spent a lot of time and effort getting ready for the 'Big Event' and all of us in the six other Quad City Hy-Vee Stores knew it was happening and we were glad Hy-Vee had gotten the Business Opportunity that it did. We each wished we would have secured the party for our store.

Now, when the Saturday of the 'Big Event' came, we all went about our daily routines and 'running our stores' for the weekend. As the day went by, we all figured that things had gone well for the Rock Island Store and that their day had been a 'Big Success' at The Mark....

Little did we know...

My day finished that Saturday and I went home and ate supper and then we watched television the remainder of the evening. It wasn't until the 10:00 News came on that we heard 'The Rest of the Story'.

It was the 'lead-in story' that the News opened with... "The Close Call at The Mark". As the TV Reporter 'outlined the story', they showed the 'awful pictures' on the television of what took place.

As planned, the Rock Island Hy-Vee Deli/Kitchen had taken their Van and Barbecue Roaster to The Mark

and they had gotten everything set-up on the sidewalk in the area just in front of The Mark. The fire was lit and the Steaks were on the grill for the great meal they had prepared to serve the hundreds of people in attendance. That's when 'it happened' and 'it' changed the course of the whole event.

Grease started dripping down from the Steaks that were on the grill onto the fire below and also onto the tires of the Barbecue Roaster. A large fire soon 'erupted' and it engulfed both the tires and moved frontward to the LP Gas tanks on the grill and in a short time they burst into flames and consumed the Barbecue Roaster. As the fire spread, the Deli Van itself became engulfed in flames and the fire 'roared' through it igniting the gasoline tank on the van too. As the whole thing went from 'bad to worse' in hurry, the tree that the Van and Barbecue Roaster were under and next to caught fire and the tree 'erupted' into flames too. The tree was left as a 'burnt stem' after it was over.

According to the television report, the Moline Fire Department was called immediately and they showed up to douse the flames and calm things down. It was too late to save anything though, the food was ruined, the truck was ruined, the Barbecue Roaster was ruined and even the tree was destroyed as a result of it all. All things considered, it was pretty much a 'Spectacle'.

By the end of the 10:00 News Report, I was just dumbfounded about it all. Nobody would have guessed that would happen at the 'Big Event'. It was late on Saturday night, so I waited until the next day to call the Rock Island Store Manager, Gene, at his home to talk to him. The next morning, I called and we covered 'the happenings' of it all and then I hung up.

The 'Best Part' was yet to come, however.

All day Sunday, the News Media continued to 'Show and Tell' the story from The Mark on Saturday. By Monday morning, everyone in the Quad Cities must have known about it and the humor was starting to come out of it. All of us local Quad Cities Store Managers began 'poking fun' at the whole thing and poor Gene had to endure our 'twisted minds' in the wake of it all. We made comments like "Are you getting a new van?" "I bet it's going to be Charcoal Gray" or other comments about getting a "Burnt Orange colored van".

Then, there were comments about it being an "Expensive way to advertise". We teased him about 'new slogans' that were created like "Let Hy-Vee Cater your next party and burn your house down at the same time" and "The Steaks at Hy-Vee are 'Well-Done'!" .... There was so much poking fun at it.

Poor Gene...

We all 'hooted and hollered' about it and the 'wild comments' were lots of fun. Gene sure took it well. He knew if it had been one of us, he'd have made 'wisecracks' too and this one just happened to be his turn for the 'fickle finger of fate' to get him.

The 'Real Insult' and perhaps the funniest part, however, came to Gene two weeks later in the U.S. Mail. In the mail, he got a letter from The Mark and a 'Bill' for "The cost of the replacement tree and its installation." I think it was just like 'rubbing salt in the wound' as all of the 'wise-cracks' started again. For years, we'd ask "Now which tree is yours there at The Mark?"

It was known with great fondness as

"The Barbecue At The Mark" ...

“Where Did You Guys Go?” ...

In nearly 90 years of operation and now over 240 Stores, Hy-Vee has seen ‘Hundreds of Thousands’...If not ‘Millions’ of ‘Happenings’ take place that you’d swear couldn’t have really happened, but they did!

It’s really amazing sometimes to see those things unfold in a direction that you would have never guessed that it could go. Even ‘fiction writing’ cannot be scripted like it and with one little ‘twist’, the entire outcome can be changed... ‘Just like that’.

One such event happened in 1993 and it happened like this.

We had opened the Moline, IL #1 Hy-Vee in the Summer of 1987 and I was the Store Manager selected to run it. The dense population of 26,000 people in a one-mile radius of our store brought us lots of ‘daily customers’ and Shoplifting had become a problem in the Moline Store. With a Public Housing project about 10 blocks away, we seemed to ‘inherit’ the residents from there and it added a real ‘rough dimension’ to the ‘equation’ of running a Grocery Store.

There was never a dull moment...

The now ‘defunct’ Eagle Food Store across the street from us had an equal problem, so I decided that if we prosecuted all Shoplifters, we could then ‘Ban’ them permanently from our store and they’d migrate over

to Eagles to do their 'lifting' and we'd solve two problems. 1. Slow down our Shoplifters and ...2. send those losses to our competitor for them to stand the losses. It worked really well, but it had its 'trials and tribulations' along the way.

We had several people on our Crew that were real 'Bloodhounds' when it came to 'spotting and catching' Shoplifters. Once they caught the scent of a Shoplifter, I was alerted or our Assistant Store Manager, Tom, was alerted and we usually apprehended the culprit.

Several of the Crew in our store were 'pretty large guys'. At least five were at 6' 3" and over 240 pounds and they were all pretty 'well rounded' and could handle themselves. Now, me, at 5' 8" tall and 155 pounds was always 'pushed around' because the guy Shoplifters thought they could 'intimidate' me with the 'physical shoving' and so forth.

Boy, were they wrong.

The 'big guys' in our Crew were always willing to help chase them down or be 'the muscle' in case things got out of hand. I was usually pretty safe... Well, 'safe' as long as those guys were around anyway.

So, one day in 1993, a young man was in our store and I was alerted that he'd put a package of cigarettes in his pocket. As he went out the Front Door of the store, I was right behind him and Tom and our Bakery Manager, Dave, were right behind me. I

felt safe because they were both 'big guys' and I would be okay with them to back me up.

Just outside the front door, I called for him to "Stop and come back inside". The young kid took off on a 'dead run' across the parking lot. I was in 'hot pursuit' and I was only 6 or 8 feet behind him as we ran 'full speed' across the lot and around the parked cars. So, when we got to 'busy 23rd Avenue' in front of the store, we both bolted across in between the cars like you see in the TV chase movies.

It was great.

Once we crossed 'busy 23rd Avenue', I could see I was gaining on him and by then, I was only about 4 or 5 feet from grabbing him. I was pretty sure I was in better shape than he was and that I would eventually catch up to him. Having Dave and Tom behind me (So I thought) was going to be a big help because I knew I'd be pretty 'winded' and I didn't know what to expect from him in 'taking him' when I caught him.

Well, about three blocks on the other side of 'busy 23rd Avenue', the 'unexpected' happened and the young kid ran into a garage and slammed the side door behind him to slow me down. He grabbed a bicycle in the garage and was out the other end on the bike 'in a flash'.

I had just lost the race. He was gone.

So, I sat down for a minute and caught my breath and then I started back to the store. As I crossed back

over 'busy 23rd Avenue', I saw Dave and Tom standing by a car in the parking lot where the Crew parked their cars. It was very near 'busy 23rd Avenue'. It was a car I had not seen before.

As I got closer to them, I could see that they couldn't contain their laughter any more...I said "Where in the 'Hell' did you guys go?" and that's when I found out how the 'Twist of Fate' had changed the whole thing.

As we had raced through the parking lot in 'Hot Pursuit' of this young Shoplifter, Tom and Dave made a 'last second decision' to jump into Dave's brand-new car and chase him in the car across 'busy 23rd Avenue'. They were convinced I'd stay 'even' with him and they could 'circle around him' and we could apprehend him by trapping him...

Seemed like a good plan... So, they thought.

But 'not so fast'.

It seems that when they got into Dave's new car, they raced across 'busy 23rd Avenue' through the stoplight intersection and then pulled into the neighborhood where I had chased the young kid to, but when they went to get out of the car, the 'Child Locks' on Dave's new car had 'locked them in' and they didn't know how to unlock to doors to get out. It took them so long to get the doors unlocked that the whole thing had 'flashed by' as they 'helplessly' sat there trying to get out of the car to do something.

For years, the 'Child Locks Story' was alive in the Moline Store. It got laughs every time it was ever brought up and it was usually part of a joke pointed at Tom or Dave.

It Was the Day the Child Locks

'Kept The Big Kids In The Car'...

"Let the Company Buyers be the Buyers. You be Sellers at the store level."

Marion M. Coons

Senior Vice-President

and CFO

(Deceased)

"Would The Owner Of

The Mercedes Benz ?" ...

As far back as 1930, in those primitive 'Supply Stores' of Charles Hyde and David Vredenburg's, one thing was certain about the Grocery Business. That 'Certainty' is that you can count on the 'Unexpected Things' to happen at very 'Unexpected Times'. Even in those early days, they never knew exactly what to expect or exactly what time something would happen, but they knew that when they 'least' expected it, 'something' would happen that would change the whole day. The 'hard part' was guessing 'what' was going to happen and the 'fun part' was looking back and laughing later. On a hot Summer afternoon in 1992 in the Moline Store, one such event happened that is still talked about today.

Here is 'The Blazing Story'...

I was the Store Manager at the Moline, IL Store for many years beginning in 1987. It was a great store and sat on one of Moline's busiest streets. Its location in front of the Moline High School with 2500 students and next to Roosevelt Elementary School with 600 students lent itself to many thousands of people coming to them and 'us' each day.

One Friday evening, I was busy working at my desk in the basement Office at the store. It was about 5:30 PM in the afternoon and I was looking forward to

finishing my work and going home. I was paged to take a call on the private Store Phone. When I picked up the phone, a voice on the other end said "Rick, you need to get up here right away. There's a car on fire...Or at least I think it's on fire."

So, I rushed to the front of the store and 'gazed' out the window at a car in the parking lot that everyone was pointing to. There was a 'wisp' of white smoke or steam coming from under the hood of a nearly new Mercedes Benz. It was a beautiful black car. A very expensive car.

So, I calmly walked to the private Store Phone and made an announcement over the loudspeaker to all of our Customers... I said "Attention Shoppers, would the owner of a black Mercedes-Benz with Illinois license plates please come to the front of the store."

So, with that announcement, I figured someone would come to the front and identify themselves as the owner of the Mercedes Benz and we could then go out and 'unlock the car' and investigate the smoke. I waited about 3 minutes and when no one showed up to identify themselves as the owner, I promptly announced 'again' to the Customers that we needed their "Full Attention", and I gave the 'same announcement' as before. Again, no one showed up to claim ownership of the Mercedes Benz.

By now, darker smoke was beginning to come out from under the hood and in front of the grill of the Mercedes Benz. It was looking bad and we knew that

‘indeed’ there was a fire under the hood that was growing and getting out of control. So, I quickly instructed one of our staff to call 911 and “Get the Fire Trucks on the way”. The Moline Fire Department was just down the street and I knew it wouldn’t take long for them to get there. So, we waited on them to arrive...Feeling helpless.

As we waited, I ‘once again’ announced on the loudspeaker “Shoppers, we need your full attention. We have a car in the parking lot that is on fire. It is a black Mercedes-Benz and we need the owner to come to the front of the store immediately.”

Now, I thought this last announcement would surely bring someone to the front of the store. When again, no one showed up, I announced ‘one final time’ over the loudspeaker “Shoppers, please stop what you’re doing and listen to this announcement. There is a car in our parking lot that is on fire. It is a black Mercedes Benz. If this is your car, please come to the front of the store immediately.” Amazingly, ‘still’, nobody showed up. By now, a total of about 6 or 8 minutes had elapsed.

As the Moline Fire Truck rolled onto the parking lot, several of us went out to be of help. By this time, the fire was raging. The fire quickly burned through the engine compartment and was burning into the interior of the Mercedes Benz. The fire then quickly burned the rest of the way through the interior and into the trunk

area. As the fire raged, the heat 'scorched' the cars on each side of the Mercedes Benz. It was a huge 'fireball' for sure. At least 100 people were now gathered to watch the 'show'.

The Fire Department 'turned their 'big water hoses' on it and quickly started putting-out the fire. As the cold water hit the glass in the windows, they all shattered and steam started rolling into the air above the cars that were involved. The Fire Department quickly got the fire under control and then shut-off their 'Big Hoses'.

All that was left was a smoldering 'hunk of junk'.

The once beautiful black Mercedes Benz was now just a 'scorched shell of a car' with wire seats and no windows and it 'smoldered' as we all stood there looking at it. It was nearly unrecognizable as a former 'Luxury Car'. No color was left on it, except the color of 'burned metal' and the heat had melted the tires. All the glass windows had been shattered and the 'crystals' of glass now lay all over the 8' or 10' area around the car.

What a mess...

As we stood there talking to the Firemen and others who had gathered, a very 'unsuspecting

woman' entered the location pushing a grocery cart. As she approached the Mercedes Benz, a look of 'complete terror' came onto her face. She said in a very rapid high-pitched voice "What happened?" I replied "Is this your car?" She said in a rapid voice "Well, it was!"

So, I said to her "We called several times over the loudspeaker for the owner to come to the front of the store and nobody showed up." It was then that she said to me "I never listen to what they say on that loudspeaker."

Now, almost in tears, the woman said "My husband's going to kill me. He loves this car!" So, I asked her if it would help if I called her husband. She said it would and I copied down his phone number. She asked me to also call her Insurance Agent. Her Insurance Agent happened to be my Insurance Agent also and I knew Mike would come over too. His Office was close-by.

So, I went back into the store and phoned her husband. I told him that his wife was fine, but that his car was ruined and that he should come to Hy-Vee and help her. I then called our State Farm agent and I told Mike that that his client needed his help. He said he would come right

over and he did. His Office was less than a block from our store.

As I walked back to the 'steaming car' and large crowd, a very elderly woman was busy 'walking and gawking' at the entire spectacle. As she pushed her grocery cart across the parking lot, the wheel of her grocery cart caught in a storm drain and the entire cart tipped over spilling her groceries all over the lot and the cart landed on her. She called for help and I rushed to help her. She did not appear to be hurt. I helped her get her groceries together and we replaced a few items that had broken. I helped her get the groceries into her car and she left.

The husband of the lady with the Mercedes Benz and the State Farm agent got together to work out the details of the incident for insurance purposes.

There were now two 'severely damaged' cars and one 'totally ruined' car. It looked very costly. There were no problems with the reporting, so I walked back into the store. As I walked in, a tow-truck was arriving to load the Mercedes Benz (or what was left of it) on to the 'flatbed' of the truck. The crowd had started to 'break-up' and go back to what they were doing before the incident occurred.

It was a 'story' that would be discussed by hundreds of people over the next several weeks.

About six weeks later, we received a 'Registered Letter' from an attorney in town. He was representing the elderly woman whose grocery cart spilled and landed on her. She was asking for $25,000 for the 'Pain and Suffering' that she said happened to her as a result of the mishap. We ended up defending ourselves in court and even though we prevailed in court, we had to spend time and money defending our position. Her fall and grocery cart mess were all because of her 'Gawking and Rubber-necking' at the blaze of the Mercedes Benz. It was one day we'll never forget.

It was the day we found out just

"How 'Hot' Those

Mercedes Benz' Really Are !"

“Pay and Benefits are important, but in my opinion, they are not as important as your people knowing you care about them.”

Ronald D. Pearson

President, CEO and

Chairman of the Board

(Retired)

“Would You Hand Me The Soap ?” ...

Almost 90 years ago, Charles Hyde and David Vredenburg started their partnership in ‘The Supply Stores’ of Southern Iowa and Northern Missouri. Their ‘first store’ was in the tiny town of Beaconsfield in Southern Iowa’s Ringold County. The building still stands today and it has been kept in good shape by the town and some help from Hy-Vee over the years. Today, there are 15 people living in Beaconsfield, IA. In the 2000 Census, it had the ‘distinction’ of being Iowa’s “Smallest Incorporated City”.

Those early stores were small and 1200 square feet was fairly normal. The ‘Customer Numbers’ going through them would have been a ‘Couple of Hundred’ per week... ‘Maybe’.

In comparison, the numbers of Customers going through a Grocery Store today is a ‘staggering’ number. At an average of 30,000-40,000 Customers per week in today’s larger stores, that multiplies out to about around ‘2 Million Customers’ per year and that’s ‘year in and year out’ in a Hy-Vee Store. You’ll see every age group and ‘Statistical Group’ you want to name and you’ll see them often.

With those ‘numbers of people’ coming in to the stores, it’s no wonder that so many things happen over the years... Just because of the huge ‘Numbers of People’ and the ‘Mathematical Probability’ that ‘Something’ will happen. Most times, you just shake

your head' and tell yourself that "Now, I've seen everything", but again, you haven't. There will be 'yet another thing' come along to make you say it 'again and again and again'.

While I was Store Manager at the Moline Hy-Vee in the late 1980's and throughout the 1990's, something happened that made me say "Now, I've seen it all.", but again, I still hadn't.

The story goes like this.

Public Restrooms are a part of a Retail Store's 'Busiest Areas'. It's important to keep the Restroom clean and 'well-stocked' with the 'normal items' like liquid soap for the dispenser, paper towels for the towel holder and 'Lots and Lots' of toilet paper. Another important item in those Restrooms is 'emptying' the waste can often.

Now, as a Store Manager, I was really 'picky' about the condition of the Restrooms, so I assigned the 'gals' who worked at the Courtesy Counter the task of overseeing the Ladies Room that was very close to the Courtesy Counter. In turn, I took charge of the Men's Restroom. In my absence, one of my Assistant Store Mangers was to take my 'Restroom Duty' and make sure it got done.

We made sure our 'respective restrooms' were checked and attended to several times each day. The whole arrangement worked very well.

Well, one day, I had made the usual 'rounds' of Restroom Duty several times during the day and it was time to go through again. As I walked down the short hallway to the Men's Room and pushed to door open, I got the 'surprise of the month'.

I won't forget it if I live to be 500 years-old.

Standing there 'naked' from the waist down was an elderly man about 85 years-old. He was standing at the lavatory doing something in the sink. The 'smell' in the room was heavy with the smell of 'human waste'. It seemed to startle him as I came in, so he turned to look at me. I could quickly tell he was washing his pants and undershorts in the sink because he'd had an 'accident' in his pants.

I said "Whoa, are you okay?" He looked up and said "Yeah, I'll be done here in a minute and then I can clean the sink. I'll just let 'em 'hang dry' for a few minutes while I wait and then I'll be out of here."

I quickly 'assessed in my mind' that he was alone at the store and probably wouldn't be able to get home for a while if he worked his plan to "let 'em 'hang dry' for a while", so I said "I think I have a better plan. I'll be right back."

So, I went to the Bakery and I got a 'clean outfit' of the clothing worn by our Bakers. We called the clothes 'Baker's Whites'. I grabbed a pair of pants and a clean medium size jacket. I picked up a medium garbage bag at the Courtesy Counter on my

way by and I returned to the Men's Room. After I entered, I said to my 'new friend' "Why don't you slip your soiled pants into this bag and we'll tie it shut. Then you can put these pants on." I asked him if he'd driven to the store and he said "No, I walked over." so I said we'd take him home. It seemed to please him.

The man asked about returning the 'Baker's Whites' pants and coat to us and I told him to return them in the next week or two and we weren't in a hurry for them. I then asked one of my Assistant Managers to pull his car around back and we'd take him out the back door and drive him home. We made sure he had his two bags of groceries with him...Along with the bag carrying the soiled pants and undershorts. We got him home safely and discreetly.

Nobody knew any different and he was spared the embarrassment of it all.

Now, with the man cleaned-up and his clothing situation taken care of and with him also having been 'delivered' to his house, I was left with the task of cleaning the Restroom from the 'ordeal' it had just been through. So, I put on my 'usual' rubber gloves and wiped down the sink area with 'cleaner' and 'bleach' and then I got the wet mop and 'scrubbed' every inch of the Restroom floor. I used 'bleach-water', so it gave the room a 'fresh look' and a 'sanitary smell'. After it all dried, it was as 'Good as New'.

Within a few days, the man brought the 'Baker's Whites' pants and coat back and he asked for me. I went to the Courtesy Counter where he was and he told me "Thank-you" for the help and the "Loaner Pants" as he called them. It all worked out well.

In the years afterward, I often wondered whatever became of him. Occasionally, I'd see him, but not very many times. When I did, I always thought about what a nice old man he was and about Hy-Vee's 'Heritage of Humility'.

And I remembered fondly about

The Day the 'Stuff' Hit The Sink,

Not The Fan...

“While working at Hy-Vee, you’ll never work harder or love it more doing it”

Dwight C. Vredenburg

President, CEO and

Chairman of the Board

(Deceased)

"You Sure Had A Good Month" ...

In the very first years of Hy-Vee in the early 1930's, the Store Managers were paid $50 per month to 'Manage the Stores'. It was in the first years of the 'Great Depression of the 1930's' and that was a fair wage. For that salary of $50, the Men 'Managing' those stores would have lots of 'unpaid help' from their spouses. The 'help' from those spouses was sort of an 'Unspoken Benefit' to the store and it was understood that their work 'Came Along with The Deal'...

During a discussion of 'How things were going', the Founders of Hy-Vee, Charles Hyde and David Vredenburg decided that "A manager would work harder if he got a piece of the success", so they decided that it would be fair to change the pay structure. They decided they would split the profits of the stores 50/50 with the Store Managers. Yes, they believed that the investment of the Company's Money was 'equally' worth the investment of the Man's Time and so, the 'Split Arrangement' was born. It has worked well and it has been a big reason for Hy-Vee's success.

Later, it was decided that the Full-time Employees of Hy-Vee would work harder if they 'Got A Piece of the Success' too, so a formula was agreed upon and they too, got a piece of the profits and it's called 'The Bonus Check'. The Bonus Checks are calculated '100% on the success of their individual store'. The

'better their store does', the 'better they do' on their Bonus Check. It is a 'Huge Incentive' for everyone to work hard for the 'best results'.

Since those very first days of 'The Supply Stores' in those small Southern Iowa and Northern Missouri Stores, a 'firm handle' on the progress of the stores has been embedded in each Store Manager's life. It's called 'Inventory'. It is a complete accounting of the store for a period of time. Inventory is now a 'Quarterly Counting', but for over 60 years, it was a 'Monthly Counting' and it is very 'intense' and it produces lots of 'nervous people'. Those results are how the Store Manager was (is) paid and Bonus Checks calculated.

It is tedious and 'Very Stressful'.

If something is not included in the equation, then the numbers are 'skewed' and it will reflect 'up or down' the following Inventory Month/Quarter. You see, everything must be accounted for to be correct and it is complex.

Each Store Manager will have his or her own story of 'Inventory' because it is an individual store event and no Store Manager is left out. Every Store Manager can remember when something didn't get accounted for and it changed the numbers... Dramatically.

There is one story of 'Inventory' that happened in early 1990's and it is remembered and laughed about

to this day...I was there when it happened and it 'Truly was Funny'.

Here's how it happened.

The Store Manager in the Milan, IL Hy-Vee Store was a man named Chris. My store in Moline, was 'geographically close' to Milan and therefore, Chris and I 'Carpooled' along with Gene from The Rock Island, IL Hy-Vee Store. Each week, we'd all three carpool in to Headquarters together in Chariton, IA and then later to West Des Moines, IA. We were all great friends and sort of like 'The Three Musketeers' as we always 'rode together' and 'stuck together' pretty well on Ads and philosophy as well as 'Day to Day Operations' of our stores.

Now, Hy-Vee is in the business of 'Sales and Profits' and Inventory is 'huge' in those numbers. Hy-Vee wants those numbers to be accurate and 'in-line' with all the other stores. It is so important, that Hy-Vee's President and CEO devotes 'four days' of his schedule each 'Inventory' to meet individually with each Store Manager for a 'review' of that Store Manager's progress for the Quarter (formerly Monthly). Each of the meetings with the President and CEO and the Store Managers may only be 15 or 20 minutes for each store, but it is a time when the two people can talk 'one on one' and each can get 'input' from the other. That part is a strong function of the Inventory process.

'Miscounts' in the amount of merchandise remaining in the store, forgetting to account for an invoice that needed to be paid, failing to add in a 'bill' for an expense and other things that happen through 'human error' can make the Inventory numbers look 'good or bad' one month and then opposite 'good or bad the next month as a result of that mistake in the accounting. It does occasionally happen 'accidentally', but it should 'never' happen 'intentionally'.

That is 'Taboo' in Hy-Vee. Accuracy is the Policy.

Now, over the years, every Store Manager figured out that some of their months were naturally better than others...There are many reasons such as 'time of year', 'weather' and so forth. Those variations have been going on for nearly 90 years of Hy-Vee's History.

They don't change.

So, in order to protect themselves against the 'Up and Down Spikes' in the results, 'sand-bagging' on the Numbers a bit has been known to happen... Not in ways to 'falsify' the numbers, but more to 'level-out the Numbers'. You know, in case the numbers looked 'too good' for what was expected.

In the attempts to 'level-out' the 'too good' Month results from one month to the next, a 'Too Good month would find the Store Manager 'not counting' a little of the leftover merchandise on hand. It would reduce the current month's profit. When it was then

'counted' the next month, it would affect that month by making it look better. Sort of saving a little for a 'Rainy Day'...Like a little 'Reserve' or 'Kitty' to have when they had a 'tough month' and they 'needed it'.

Good or Bad, the 'Numbers are the Numbers' and they should not be changed and to do it was 'highly frowned' on at Headquarters. It was discouraged 'at all times'. In fact, it would draw a lot of 'scrutiny and reprimand' if discovered.

So, one day, Chris and Gene and I were at Headquarters reviewing our 'Monthly Results' with the Accountants and with Ron, Hy-Vee's President and CEO. All of these short meetings were held with other Store Managers waiting around you for their turn to talk to Ron. It was a nervous time, but you 'Took Your Lumps' or 'Took Your Praises' right in front of the others and it could be awkward and 'sometimes', funny too. Mostly awkward though. Nobody wanted to be 'called out' in front of the others.

As Chris from Milan began his conversation with Ron, it was obvious by the comments, that Milan Hy-Vee had just finished a 'Banner Month' and the Numbers were 'GREAT'...Chris had 'Big Profits'...

All through the conversation, Ron's comments were 'glowing' and it must have given Chris a 'false sense of security' because when Ron soon said "Chris, why do you think your Month was so good?" Without

missing a beat, Chris replied "Well, Ron, it is because we counted everything."

'Whaaaaaaaat?' ... None of the rest of us in the room could believe our ears. Immediately, every other Store Manager in the room 'swung their heads around' to look at Chris and Ron. They all knew what Chris had meant, but it certainly wasn't something you just 'casually' tell the President of Hy-Vee.

What Chris had just said was like 'putting a Bullseye target on his back for Inventory'...Chris had "Counted Everything?" Gene and I wanted to laugh out loud, but it certainly wasn't the time to do that...We just kept our laughter to ourselves and saved it for the 200-mile ride back home...We'd get our 'laughs' in with Chris on that long ride.

For now, we just wanted to see how he'd get out of it...So, as Chris stood perfectly still and waiting for Ron's reply, we could see Ron calculating Chris' remark back to him and finally, Ron said "What do you mean you 'Counted Everything'? I thought you are supposed to count everything every month?"

It was at this point, Chris knew he had 'put his foot in his mouth' in a 'BIG WAY' and so, he didn't say a word...He just giggled...There was 'nothing' he could say now. It was best to keep his mouth shut and 'take his lumps'...And that's what happened. Along with Chris, all of the rest of us got told 'Pretty Plainly' by Ron that Inventory meant "Counting Everything and Not Messing with The Numbers...Period."

So, for 200 miles, we 'chided' Chris about 'Counting Everything' and then we'd all 'laugh at the top of our lungs'...It was a 'HOOT' for sure.

It has never been forgotten and over 20 years later, we still tease Chris about 'Counting Everything'...and then we 'Laugh' and then we 'Laugh Some More'...

It was the month Chris

Ran the Numbers... 'All Of Them' !

“We think in terms of how low we can sell and not how much we can get from an item.”

Ronald D. Pearson

President, CEO and

Chairman of the Board

(Retired)

“Yes, That’s Right...Go Home !” ...

From its inception in 1930 in the little town of Beaconsfield in Ringold County, IA, the early ‘Hyde and Vredenburg Supply Stores’ of the era believed in treating people like they were ‘valuable’ to the Operation and it is ‘well-rooted’ in the philosophy of the now almost 90-year-old Grocery Chain. The Employees and Associates of Hy-Vee are the Biggest Asset the Company has and the ‘Upper Management’ will always be quick to tell anyone that ‘The Crew has made this Company’. Of course, it has taken ‘Millions’ of Customers too, but the ‘Loyal and Dedicated Crews’ in the stores have done their jobs to ‘Keep the Customers Coming Back’...

Week after Week and Year after Year...

Now, Hy-Vee is a ‘non-union’ Company and when Hy-Vee entered the Quad Cities Market in early 1985 and opened the Rock Island Store, the other competitors in the market were staffed by employees that were members of the labor union representing Grocery Workers. Hy-Vee’s Retail Employees had only been Union Members in one small Department in one store for about a year back in the very early 1970’s. Otherwise, the Hy-Vee Employees had always felt that they were treated so well that they did not need the union to represent them.

As the other stores came on board for Hy-Vee in the Quad Cities, it was obvious that Hy-Vee was doing

some 'Major Damage' to Eagle Food Stores and to Jewel Foods. With the openings of Hy-Vee Stores in Rock Island, Milan, Bettendorf, Davenport and then Moline, the 'mood' in the Union Stores was pretty 'dismal'. The employees of the Eagle and Jewel Stores had begun doing what most union Store Employees do and they started giving very poor service and they also 'displayed bad attitudes' to the Customers.

It was 'just the opposite' of what they should have done.

This 'mood' was a noticeable difference from the Hy-Vee Employees and their 'Customer Comes First' attitudes and when the 'impact of it all' started showing in the Competitors' stores, their Employees' 'hours' were cut back and the Service got even worse. The whole thing became a 'hotbed' of unrest for the Eagle and Jewel Stores with their Employees. It was not good for them.

A lot of this 'unrest' happened at the Eagle Food Store across the street from Hy-Vee in Moline. I was the Store Manager that 'opened' that store for Hy-Vee in 1987. As the first couple of years rolled along, we could hear 'rumblings' that the Employees of those competing stores were really 'upset and very discouraged'. Eventually, they began to form groups to 'picket' a few of the Hy-Vee Stores.

So, in early Spring of 1990, they began 'picketing' our store in Moline. They were positioned on the

sidewalk along a very busy street in front of Hy-Vee called '23rd Avenue'. They were not on our parking lot, but rather they lined the sidewalk on the edge our parking lot and they walked back and forth with their derogatory signs.

Now, you can imagine the 'aggravation' I felt as I drove in and out of our parking lot for about 'five or six days' in a row and saw people carrying signs that were very 'rude and disrespectful' to Hy-Vee and the to the fact that the Hy-Vee Stores were 'non-union'.

During those days with the Picketers, we did what we did best at Hy-Vee and we stayed focused on the Customers and we treated them with great respect and kindness throughout the ordeal. We did not talk badly of the Picketers and we made no comments as to our 'opinions' of the union they were part of. We figured that the Customers would have their own opinions about the situation and we'd stay out of it.

As the days rolled along with the Picketers in front of the Moline Hy-Vee, it was obvious that the Picketers were bringing their friends and families to 'walk' with them carrying their signs and we saw children as young as 4 or 5 years-old out there by the busy 23rd Avenue 'walking' with their Mother or Father and carrying small signs about the 'bad guys' at Hy-Vee. As Hy-Vee's Customer's 'Crossed the Line', it all became a 'spectacle' for sure.

As more days went along with the Picketers in front of the Moline Store, even the Part-time Crew at Hy-

Vee was getting rather upset about the signs and the 'name calling' as people entered our parking lot and it was starting 'to get personal' with our Crew...Little did I now at the time, just 'how personal' it was going to get...But, it was going to...

This is how it all came 'Across the Line'...

After a long day of routine activities combined with the tension of the Picketers, I got home for supper one evening about 6:30 PM and as I entered the house, there was a bit of a 'congregation' of my family in the kitchen waiting for me to arrive home. My wife and 'All Three' of our children were there and I knew 'something was up'... I didn't know that we needed a 'Family Meeting', but that's what was about to 'unfold' and it centered around the Picketers at our Hy-Vee.

After I got settled for a few minutes, I took off my 'Store Manager Hat' and I put on my 'Dad Hat'. It was then, that I found out that there was a 'feud' going on between our son and our daughter. Our son, Brandon, was in high school and worked Part-time at our Hy-Vee.

At this point, I looked around the table at everyone and then I asked "Okay, what's up? Why are you two arguing?" ... And the 'answer' made me 'Proud' as a Dad... I had some explaining to do to our eleven-year-old daughter, Kristin, but I was still 'Proud as a Dad'.

It seems that when our 16year-old son, Brandon, had gotten home from school, he walked in to our house to find his sister entertaining a 'Grade-School Friend' for a few hours after school... Under 'normal circumstances', this would have been great and he would have been very nice to his 'Little Sister's Friend', but when Brandon recognized the 'Little Visitor' as a young girl who'd been 'walking the Picket Line' with her Dad and carrying a 'derogatory sign', he 'kicked her out of our house' and told her to "Go Home!" He had even 'escorted' her to the door with no hint of being nice at all.

And 'that's' when the fight started.

Now, on one side of the argument and from a Dad's point of view, I could see why our daughter, Kristin, was so upset. She had 'no idea' that her friend was with her Dad on the Picket Line the day before and she was just angry at her brother. From the 'other side of the argument' and from a Store Manager's point of view, Brandon, the 'Big Brother', was going to be loyal to the family and make sure the little girl knew that she had caused herself a 'problem', so he took charge...

And she was 'Outta' There'!

After about an 'hour of conversation' over supper, things were pretty smooth and everyone was 'friendly' with each other again. It calmed down a lot... But in the end, I was sure proud of Brandon for 'sticking-up' for his family and Hy-Vee... He knew

'Which Side His Bread Was Buttered On'. He was on his way to 'Big Things' at Hy-Vee.

It became the 'Day of Reckoning' for

The Little Girl Who

'Crossed The Line'...

The End...

Well, not really...There'll never be an end to the things going on behind the scenes at Hy-Vee. The Fun, the Laughs, the Hard Work and the Dedication will all continue 'on and on and on'...And yes, there'll be more stories come along that happened ...

'As The Timeclock Turned' ...

I sincerely hope you have enjoyed this look into 'The Wonderful Company' named "Hy-Vee".

Oh, gotta' go... They just called me 'up front' to bag groceries...

Customers come first at Hy-Vee...

Rick